Στον αγαπητον Κωστάκη, (c/o PARIKIAKI)
εκ μέρους του Γιωργαγτ
Φιλικά Ανετά
Λονδίνο
18/11/8

IN TURKEY'S IMAGE

PUBLISHED UNDER THE AUSPICES OF THE
SPEROS BASIL VRYONIS CENTER FOR THE STUDY OF HELLENISM
AS THE FOURTH TITLE IN THE SERIES
Subsidia Balcanica, Islamica & Turcica

IN TURKEY'S IMAGE

The Transformation of Occupied Cyprus
into a Turkish Province

Christos P. Ioannides

Published in New Rochelle, New York, by
Aristide D. Caratzas

In Turkey's Image: The Transformation of Occupied Cyprus into a Turkish Province

Copyright © 1991 by Aristide D. Caratzas, Publisher

Aristide D. Caratzas, Publisher
30 Church Street, P.O. Box 210
New Rochelle, N.Y. 10802

Library of Congress Cataloguing-in-Publication Data
Ioannides, Christos P., 1946–
In Turkey's image: The transformation of occupied Cyprus into a Turkish province /
Christos P. Ioannides.
266 pages -- (Subsidia Balcanica, Islamica & Turcica: 4th)
Includes bibliographical references and index.
1. Cyprus -- History.
I. Title. II. Series.
DS54.95.N67I55 1991
956.4504

ISBN: 0–89241–509–6

Printed in the United States of America

To my mother Ioanna,
in memoriam

Contents

Preface

Throughout history, the eastern Mediterranean and the Middle East have been a world stage where great civilizations have emerged and empires have clashed. It was in this region that the three monotheistic religions—Judaism, Christianity and Islam were born. Nowhere else in the world have so many civilizations, cultures, and religious and ethnic groups coexisted and fought with one another over the centuries. The great achievements that have come out of this part of the world have been matched by endless conflict.

In the midst of this cosmogonic region lies the island of Cyprus. It is located in the eastern Mediterranean just 140 miles from Damascus, 210 miles from Jerusalem, and 240 miles from Alexandria and the Suez Canal. The rich history of Cyprus has been interwoven with its Hellenic and Byzantine cultural heritage. This heritage is evident in the island's ancient Hellenic monuments and ruins, as well as in its Byzantine churches. The Graeco-Byzantine heritage of Cyprus is also reflected in contemporary Cypriot culture. Over 80 percent of the population speaks the Greek language. The Greeks of Cyprus are Christian Orthodox by faith, and they have preserved many of the Graeco-Byzantine customs and traditions of their ancestors. Less than 15 percent of the Cypriot population speaks the Turkish language and follows Turkish Muslim traditions.

Since Cyprus is in a strategic location, serving as a stepping stone to the Near East, it has been invaded and conquered repeatedly over time. For instance, Richard Coeur de Lion, King of England, became master of Cyprus in 1191 when he defeated its Byzantine ruler, Isaac Komnenos. The king was on his way to the Holy Land during the Third Crusade. About four centuries later, in 1571, the Ottoman

Turks defeated the Venetians and conquered the island. At the time of the Ottoman conquest, the population of Cyprus was overwhelmingly Greek and Christian Orthodox. About 1600, following the introduction of Muslim settlers from Anatolia in the aftermath of the Ottoman conquest, the Cypriot population was 85 percent Greek Orthodox and 15 percent Ottoman Muslim.

Ottoman rule over Cyprus lasted until 1878 when Britain became the colonial master of the island. When the British took over, the Cypriot population was 74 percent Greek Christian and 24 percent Turkish Muslim. When British colonial rule ended in 1960 and Cyprus became an independent republic, the population was 77 percent Greek Christian and 18 percent Turkish Muslim. The Greek majority and the Turkish minority were unable to forge a political modus vivendi in the new state. By the end of 1963, they found themselves in a bloody conflict. As a consequence, relations between two NATO allies—Greece and Turkey—have suffered gravely and have been marked by repeated crises.

Following the overthrow of the president of Cyprus, Archbishop Makarios, by the Greek military regime in July 1974, Turkey invaded the island republic. The Turkish army still occupies 38 percent of Cypriot territory. Following the invasion, the government in Ankara began systematically colonizing the occupied zone with massive numbers of Anatolian settlers. At the same time, Turkey embarked upon the Turkification and Islamization of the area. Thus, since 1974, Turkey has succeeded in transforming the occupied part of Cyprus from Greek Christian to Turkish Muslim. The primary agent of this radical transformation of occupied Cyprus has been the Turkish armed forces, the champions of secularism and the professed guardians of Turkey's sociopolitical system. The 1974 Turkish invasion, occupation, colonization and Turkification of part of Cyprus has been a historic event, not only for Cyprus, but for Turkey as well. For the first time since 1938, when the founder of modern Turkey, Kemal Atatürk, died, the Turkish armed forces have conquered a foreign land.

The Turkish conquest of part of Cyprus poses challenging questions to scholars, diplomats and policymakers who wish to acquire a deeper understanding of the underlying causes behind Turkey's actions on the island. Because the Cyprus conflict has been taking place in a strategic region, a great deal of scholarly attention has been given to the role played by Cold War diplomacy, NATO, the United States and the

Soviet Union in this dispute and in Graeco-Turkish relations in general. This study adopts a different approach as it focuses on the *domestic* determinants of Turkey's policy toward Cyprus. This approach requires an analysis of the ideological and political dynamics that have guided Turkish behavior on the Cyprus issue over the last four decades. Particular emphasis is placed on the ideology of Pan-Turkism, or Turkish irredentist nationalism, as it pertains to Cyprus. In pursuing its objectives in Cyprus, Turkey has also made use of Islam, a subject that is examined in this study.

Turkey's policies toward its western neighbors—Greece and Cyprus—have acquired special significance since the Iraqi invasion of Kuwait in August 1990. The humiliating defeat of Iraqi leader Saddam Hussein's army by a U.S.-led military coalition has eliminated Iraq as a major regional power and has resulted in the reshaping of the existing power balances in the area. This development raises serious questions concerning the role Turkey will play in the region. It is doubtful, however, that Ankara will adopt a new posture toward Cyprus and Greece.

In researching this book, I have visited Cyprus on several occasions over the last three years. There, I have been assisted by many individuals, too many in fact to be mentioned by name. I would like to express my most sincere thanks to them for the valuable assistance they have given me. I would also like to thank all the people in Greece who have helped me with my research.

An early draft of the manuscript was read by Professor Stanley Kyriakides. I owe my gratitude to him, not only for his critique of my work, but also for the insights he has shared with me on the Cyprus issue over the years. I would also like to thank my publisher, Aristide D. Caratzas, who kept encouraging me to pursue this study. Many thanks to Theodora R. Bauguess for typing the manuscript. Finally, I am greatly indebted to Susan M. Spencer who worked so hard and so diligently in editing the manuscript. I express to her my deepest thanks for the superb job she has done. Needless to say, of course, any errors of omission or commission are mine alone.

CHRISTOS P. IOANNIDES
SACRAMENTO
APRIL 1991

1
Researching the Settler Issue

Turkey invaded Cyprus on 20 July 1974, five days after the military junta then ruling Greece staged a coup against the president of Cyprus, Archbishop Makarios. By the third week of August, the Turkish army had occupied 38 percent of Cypriot territory and effected the de facto partition of the island republic. Since then, Turkey has been carrying out a policy of colonization in the country by sending substantial numbers of Turks from Anatolia to the occupied zone for permanent settlement. Thus, for the first time since the Ottoman conquest of Cyprus in 1571, a period of more than four centuries, a foreign element—the Anatolian settler—is being brought onto the island in massive numbers with profound ethnodemographic and political consequences.

On 15 November 1983, under the umbrella of the Turkish army, the Turkish-Cypriot "Legislative Assembly" announced the Unilateral Declaration of Independence (UDI). The UDI proclaimed that the occupied area would be an independent "state" called the "Turkish Republic of Northern Cyprus" (TRNC) with Rauf Denktash as its "president." The TRNC replaced the "Turkish Federated State of Cyprus" (TFSC) which had been proclaimed by the Turkish Cypriots on 13 February 1975. Denktash had also been the "president" of the TFSC. Because the TRNC is an illegal entity as far as international law is concerned, it is not recognized by the Cypriot government, the United Nations or the international community at large, with the exception of Turkey. In turn, Turkey and the TRNC do not recognize the universally acknowledged government of the Republic of Cyprus.

The occupied part of Cyprus covers 1,350 square miles—an area about the size of Rhode Island—and is, therefore, easily controlled by the Turkish army. The Turkish occupation army consists of approximately 35,000 Turkish troops, according to the Cypriot government estimate.[1] It has extended its hegemony over a Turkish-Cypriot population estimated to be about 98,000. In other words, there are about 26 Turkish soldiers per square mile of occupied territory, and the ratio between Turkish-Cypriot civilians and Turkish soldiers is about three to one. By any standard, this represents an extraordinary military presence per square mile, as well as per civilian inhabitant.[2] The preponderance of Turkish armed forces in the TRNC is not without political implication and, overall, the TRNC maintains a militaristic character. There are also 5,000 Turkish-Cypriot army personnel in the occupied zone who come under the command of the Turkish army.

This study aims at analyzing the colonization of occupied Cyprus and its transformation into a Turkish province by discussing the following issues: population and immigration patterns, the number of settlers and their social origins, the legal incorporation of the settlers into the TRNC, the settlers' role in politics, and Turkey's absorption of the TRNC. These developments are discussed in conjunction with Turkey's political dynamics, particularly the ideology of Turkish irredentist nationalism, or Pan-Turkism, which dates back to the end of the nineteenth century and has decisively influenced Turkey's policy toward Cyprus since the 1950s.

Several factors pose serious methodological problems for researchers attempting to carry out a systematic study of the Turkish colonization of occupied Cyprus:

First, the state of mutual nonrecognition between the TRNC and the Cypriot government has resulted in severe restrictions on the entry of academics and journalists into the occupied zone, making it extremely difficult to conduct field research.

Second, the movements of the academics and journalists who are admitted to the TRNC are severely restricted. Not only are most visitors assigned an official guide, but many areas of the TRNC have been designated "military zones," making them off-limits to everyone except the Turkish forces.

Third, and most importantly, both the Turkish government and the Denktash regime have consistently denied that Turkish nationals have been settling en masse in occupied Cyprus. These denials have been official and categorical.

A report in *The Guardian* on 13 October 1975 and other news reports on the colonization of Cyprus by Anatolian settlers prompted the British government, acting as a guarantor power, to ask the Turkish government to clarify the matter.[3] On 14 October, the Turkish government denied for the first time that settlers from Turkey were colonizing Cyprus.[4] The "Turkish Federated State of Cyprus" also denied that colonization was taking place through a statement by TFSC "Defense Minister" Osman Örek appearing in the Turkish-Cypriot *Special News Bulletin* on 15 October.[5]

On 20 October 1975, Cypriot Representative to the United Nations Zenon Rossides lodged a formal protest at the UN in which he charged that Turkey was sending Anatolian settlers to colonize Cyprus. On 24 October 1975, the TFSC responded officially to the charges when TFSC "Representative" to the UN Vedat Çelik sent the following letter to UN Secretary-General Kurt Waldheim on the instructions of Rauf Denktash (emphasis added):

I have been instructed by the President of the Turkish Federated State of Cyprus to refer to the letter of Ambassador Rossides, the representative of the Greek-Cypriot Administration, which was circulated as a document of the General Assembly and the Security Council (A/10305-S/11954) on 20 October 1975 and to inform you that the allegations contained therein *are totally unfounded and have been deliberately fabricated by the Greek-Cypriot* Administration as a part of a wider political campaign.

The allegation that there is a massive immigration of Turkish nationals from Turkey to Cyprus with the purpose of changing the demographic character of the island within a pre-planned partition project is not only completely contrary to the truth but also a distortion of the actual facts. All that is taking place is that *skilled technicians and workers* are being imported from Turkey on a temporary basis as *"guest workers"* to meet the immediate needs of the economy.

In order to meet the labor shortage that exists in industry, agriculture and tourism and reactivate the economy, therefore, *skilled labour* is being imported from Turkey on a seasonal basis, but there is *no question of these people acquiring Cypriot citizenship or taking up permanent residence in the island.*

By far the biggest number of people who have come to Cyprus since August 1974 are Turkish Cypriots who had emigrated to Turkey, Great Britain and other Commonwealth countries in the past years under political, administrative, social and economic pressures by the Greek-Cypriot Administration and are now being given the opportunity to return to their homeland and lead a normal life under conditions of security, in accordance with the Constitution and the relevant citizenship laws of the Republic of Cyprus.

It would be useful to note that there are more than *300,000 Turks of Cypriot origin in Turkey alone* who are entitled to come and settle in Cyprus under Annex "D" of the Treaty of Establishment (1960) not to mention the thousands of Turkish Cypriots in other countries. There are more Turkish Cypriots presently living abroad who are willing and ready to return to Cyprus, now that conditions of security have been restored, than we can possibly house on the island.

There is, therefore, no need for the Turkish-Cypriot authorities to draw on Turkish nationals in order to change the population ratio on the island as alleged by the Greek side.[6]

On 12 November 1975, Vedat Çelik also presented a statement on the issue of the settlers to the UN Special Political Committee (emphasis added):

The allegation that Cyprus is being colonized by Turkey is again most unjust, most unfair and *most unfounded. . . . I assure all the members of this august body that there is no colonization of Cyprus.* In my official letter to the Secretary-General which has been circulated as an official document of the General Assembly and the Security Council, document A/10310 and document S/11859 respectively of 24 October 1975, contains our official reply to these unfounded allegations.[7]

On 27 November 1975, Rauf Denktash himself dealt with the question of the settlers while he was in New York to attend the UN General Assembly deliberations (emphasis added):

The EOKA movement during the 1954-59 period *caused nearly 30,000 Turks to leave the island.* They settled in the United Kingdom, Australia, Canada and other places, including Turkey. It is their right to come back and so far about 10,000 have returned. . . . We need seasonal workers and when we feel a shortage of labor we import them from Turkey. *So a change in the demographic situation is a false alarm.* I repeat that the Turks of Cyprus who were made to leave the island because of economic or administrative discrimination at the hand of the Greeks can now come back to a secure life in the north of Cyprus, and, indeed, it is their national duty to do so.[8]

On 13 December 1975, Vedat Çelik presented a statement to the UN Security Council on the settler issue:

Another allegation this afternoon is that there is a massive immigration of population from Turkey. This is what we have been hearing for the past year from the Greek side. This allegation is completely baseless. It is unfounded. The people who are returning to Cyprus are Turkish Cypriots who have been forced to leave the island under the threat of EOKA and under economic, political and military pressure by the Greek-Cypriot administration during the past 20 years. These people are Turkish Cypriots and it is their natural right to return to Cyprus now that relative security of life and property has been restored in the north of the island.[9]

It is important to present, in some detail, the responses of the Turkish government and the Turkish-Cypriot regime in late 1975 to reports of settlers in occupied Cyprus. Massive colonization of the occupied zone was already well under way when these responses began in October of that year. In fact, a minimum of 22,000 settlers arrived in Cyprus in 1975, the highest number recorded in any year since colonization started in the aftermath of the July 1974 invasion (see table 4).

Up until today, the Turkish government and the Denktash regime have essentially maintained the position advanced in Vedat Çelik's letter to Kurt Waldheim on 24 October 1975. They continue to deny that a systematic and massive colonization of occupied Cyprus has ever taken place. Rauf Denktash stated the following in February 1986 regarding the arrival of settlers from Turkey:

It has occurred at a time that seasonal workers have come and gone. A number among them have settled. Most of them are of Cypriot origin. The number of those who are not of Cypriot origin is very small.[10]

The official Turkish and Turkish-Cypriot position on the colonization issue is also reflected in the statistics appearing in the *TRNC Statistical Yearbook, 1987,* the most recent official publication giving demographic figures and other statistical data regarding the occupied zone. The publication does not include crucial information concerning immigration and makes no mention of Anatolian settlers. All Turkish nationals arriving in the TRNC are accounted for as "tourists." But while the *Statistical Yearbook* provides detailed data on "tourists" *arriving* from Turkey, it fails to provide any data for *departing* Turkish "tourists," and no explanation is given for this omission.[11] The data provided by the *Statistical Yearbook* should be treated with great caution as they are not independently verifiable.

In this study, in the absence of field research and official statistical information from the TRNC on the colonization issue, other sources have provided conclusive evidence to support the thesis that massive colonization has occurred in occupied Cyprus since 1974. These sources include accounts given by settlers who have deserted the occupied zone for the government-controlled part of the island, reports appearing almost daily in the Turkish-Cypriot and Turkish press which include statistics on the number of settlers, and statistical data on population, immigration and refugees in the official publications of the Cypriot government. These Cypriot government data are considered accurate and are verifiable by international organizations and independent observers. The author has also relied on documents of the U.S. State Department and the British government, and reports in the American and British press. Given the circumstances inhibiting direct observation of the colonization process, however, it should be kept in mind that the figures quoted on the number of settlers in this study represent estimates.

Turkey's systematic policy of colonizing occupied Cyprus has received very little international attention. It appears that this has been the case because the colonization process has been surreptitiously implemented under the guise of what the Turkish government and the Denktash regime refer to as the movement of "tourists," "seasonal and skilled workers," and "Turkish-Cypriot immigrants returning home from Turkey."[12]

NOTES

[1]The Turkish occupation army is deployed offensively. According to estimates provided by the Cypriot government, this army consists of two infantry divisions supported by 290 battle tanks, 200 APCs, 120 pieces of artillery, 200 heavy mortars, 550 anti-tank guns, 5,000 administrative and general-use vehicles, eight reconnaissance aircraft and 12 helicopter gunships. It also has air support from the Turkish air force in Turkey. Turkish fighter planes can reach Cyprus in under five minutes. The estimates of the International Institute of Strategic Studies (IISS) and the Cypriot government regarding the occupation army's supply of equipment are quite similar. See *Military Balance: 1989-1990* (London: International Institute of Strategic Studies, 1989), 78. In contrast, there are 10,000 troops in the Greek-Cypriot National Guard which is defensively deployed. It has 24 tanks, about 150 APCs and a variety of anti-tank weapons, but it has no air cover because Cyprus has no air force.

[2]The comparable figures in the case of Afghanistan while it was occupied from late 1979 to early 1989 by 100,000 Soviet troops were as follows: 2.5 Soviet soldiers per square mile and one Soviet soldier per 160 Afghanis.

[3]In one of the first reports on the subject of colonizing Cyprus, the British newspaper *The Guardian* wrote that "the operation is taking place in considerable secrecy." See "Unwanted Minority 'Dumped' in Cyprus," *The Guardian*, London, 13 October 1975.

[4]*BBC World News*, 18 hours GMT, 14 October 1975.

[5]Turkish-Cypriot *Special News Bulletin*, Nicosia (15 October 1975).

[6]See text of UN Document A10310, S/11859, 24 October 1975 reprinted in *Foreign Policy of Turkey at the United Nations*, vol. 3, *Cyprus Question*, ed. and comp. Ambassador Yüksel Söylemez, Turkish Ministry of Foreign Affairs, Department of International Organizations (Ankara, 1983), 476-477.

[7]Söylemez, *Foreign Policy of Turkey at the United Nations*, 486.

[8]Ibid., 502.

[9]Ibid., 514.

[10]Denktash's statement was reported by *Ankara Radio*, 2 February 1986.

[11]*TRNC Statistical Yearbook, 1987*, "Turkish Republic of Northern Cyprus," TRNC "Prime Ministry," "State" Planning Organization, Statistics and Research Department (Nicosia, December 1988), 197.

[12]See note 3.

2

The Ethnodemography of Cyprus in Perspective

In order to place the ongoing colonization of Cyprus by settlers from Turkey in perspective, a short historical background on the ethnodemography of the island is in order. About 1600, some 30 years after the Ottoman conquest of Cyprus in 1571, approximately 135,000 *rayas*, the Greek Orthodox subjects of the Sultan, lived in Cyprus. The Greek Orthodox inhabitants, who were indigenous to the island, made up about 85 percent of the total population. The Ottoman Muslim population was about 23,000, or roughly 15 percent of the population.[1] These Muslims, who were the first Turkish settlers in Cyprus, consisted of two groups: (1) members of the Turkish garrison (and their families) who remained on the island following the Ottoman conquest, and (2) colonizers from Anatolia who were sent to Cyprus by the Sultan to establish the first Muslim community on the island.

As in all conquered Ottoman territories, land in Cyprus was divided into *timars* (military fiefs) in accordance with the Sultan's *firman* (imperial edict). Usually, the best land was given to the *sipahis* (feudal cavalry men), who were part of the Turkish garrison on Cyprus, and to other officers of the Ottoman army.[2] The Greek Orthodox Church of Cyprus was allowed to retain ownership of ecclesiastical land under the *millet* system.

Throughout the Ottoman rule of Cyprus which lasted 307 years (1571-1878), the ratio between Christians and Muslims fluctuated. The trend in the seventeenth century was toward a decrease in Christians and an increase in Muslims. This trend became more pronounced in the eighteenth century. While there are no accurate demographic data for the three centuries of Ottoman rule, it is generally agreed that the overall population of Cyprus decreased in the eighteenth century, falling below 100,000, while the percentage of Muslims increased substantially.[3] The decrease in the Christian population can be attributed to a combination of factors. First, the process of converting Christians to Islam was accelerated. Second, an increasing number of Christians emigrated in order to escape Ottoman oppression, intolerable taxation and poverty. Indeed, at that time, Cyprus was one of the most maladministered and neglected *vilayets* (provinces) of the empire, as local pashas ruled at whim. Prolonged droughts and epidemics only made poverty worse.[4]

The trend toward a decreasing number of Greek inhabitants was reversed in the nineteenth century as the Ottoman Empire entered the *Tanzimat* era, a period of reforms which contributed to the relative amelioration of the inferior social condition of the *rayas*.[5] By the time Ottoman rule came to an end in 1878, the Greeks of Cyprus once again constituted the great majority of the population—about 74 percent.

In 1881, three years after the beginning of British rule, the Colonial Office completed its first census. The British census, reflecting the demographic structure of Cyprus at the end of three centuries of Ottoman rule, was the first reliable census to be carried out in Cyprus. Therefore, it acquires special significance. According to this census, the total population of Cyprus was 185,630 in 1881. The 137,631 Greek Orthodox inhabitants accounted for 73.9 percent of the total population, while the 45,458 Muslim Turks made up 24.4 percent of the population. The 174 Armenians, 830 Maronites, 1,275 Roman Catholics, 173 Protestants, 68 Jews, five Copts and 16 gypsies accounted for a little over one percent of the population (see table 1).[6]

Cyprus became an independent republic in 1960, following 82 years of British rule, and that year the Cypriot government carried out a census. It was conducted jointly by Greek- and Turkish-Cypriot civil servants following British guidelines. According to the 1960 census, the total population of Cyprus was 572,707, of which 441,568 (77.1 percent) were Greeks and 103,822 (18.1 percent) were Turks. The remaining 4.8 percent were other Christians—Maronites, Armenians and Roman Catholics (see table 1).

TABLE 1: DISTRIBUTION OF POPULATION BY ETHNIC GROUP, 1881–1988*

YEAR	TOTAL	GREEKS		TURKS		ARMENIANS		MARONITES		OTHERS	
		No.	%	No.	%	No.	%	No.	%	No.	%
1881	185.630	137,631	73.9	45,458	24.4	174	0.1	830	0.4	1,537	0.8
1931	347.959	276,573	79.5	64,238	18.4	3,337	1.0	1,704	0.5	2,068	0.6
1946	450.114	361,199	80.2	80,548	17.9	3,686	0.8	2,083	0.4	2,598	0.6
1960	572.707	441,568	77.1	103,822	18.1	3,627†	0.6	2,706†	0.5	20,984	3.7
1973	631.778	498,511	78.9	116,000	18.4					17,267	2.7
1983	653.400	523,100	80.1	121,900‡						8,400	1.3
1988	687.500	550,400	80.1	128,200‡						8,900	1.3

SOURCES: Great Britain, *Cyprus Annual Reports* (under varying titles) (Colonial Office, 1879-1959); Great Britain, *Census Reports* (Colonial Office, 1881, 1946, 1960); Republic of Cyprus, *Demographic Reports* (under varying titles) (Nicosia: Department of Statistics and Research, 1960-1988).

* All the figures and percentages in this chart are reported as they appear in the original sources.

† In accordance with the 1960 Cypriot constitution, the small Armenian and Maronite communities opted to belong to the Greek-Cypriot community. In this chart, the figures for the Armenian and Maronite populations are included in the population figures for the Greeks in 1973, 1983 and 1988. In 1973, the combined Armenian and Maronite populations made up about 1.5 percent of the population.

‡ The figures for the Turkish-Cypriot population for 1983 and 1988 represent Cypriot government estimates based on earlier demographic trends in the Turkish-Cypriot community. They do not take emigration into account.

Since the 1963 constitutional breakdown, the Cypriot government has been unable to collect demographic data in the Turkish-controlled areas. Still, the government's estimates of the Turkish-Cypriot population since that year, which have been projections based on earlier demographic trends in the Turkish-Cypriot community, have generally been considered accurate. Its estimate of 116,000 Turkish-Cypriot inhabitants, released in December 1973, is of particular importance since it can be assumed that the number of Turkish Cypriots was approximately the same at the time of the July 1974 invasion. Without a reliable estimate of this population just prior to the invasion and *before* the influx of Turkish settlers which started early in 1975, it would have been even more complicated than it is now to estimate how many settlers have moved into occupied Cyprus since 1974. According to an official report by the Turkish-Cypriot "Ministry of Justice and Interior" dated 20 October 1974, Turkish-Cypriot population at the time was 115,758.[7] Since the Turkish-Cypriot population figure released in December 1973 by the Cypriot government is comparable to that released in October 1974 by the Turkish-Cypriot administration, it can be assumed that a reliable estimate of the number of Turkish Cypriots living in Cyprus in 1974 is about 116,000.

After 20 October 1974, Turkish-Cypriot population figures compiled by the Turkish-Cypriot administration are substantially higher than those released by the Cypriot government. The reason for this discrepancy is apparently the fact that subsequent figures produced by the Denktash regime make no distinction between the two major components of the population in the Turkish-controlled area—the Turkish Cypriots and the settlers—and, therefore, group them together as "Turkish-Cypriots." This is the only logical and credible explanation for the phenomenal population growth recorded in the Turkish-occupied zone as indicated in the *TRNC Statistical Yearbook, 1987*.[8] For example, the official Denktash regime figure for the Turkish-Cypriot population in 1978 is 146,740. In other words, between 1974 and 1978, there was an increase of 30,982 Turkish Cypriots (146,740 minus 115,758), according to the Denktash administration figures. This represents a 26.8 percent population increase in four years, or an average annual growth of 6.7 percent during this period. Such annual population growth is inconceivable. Turkey itself, considered to be a country of high population growth, experienced a 2.2 and 1.8 percent average annual population growth in 1975 and 1980, respectively.[9]

The Cypriot government estimated the Turkish-Cypriot population in 1983 to be 121,900, while official U.S. estimates placed it at about

120,000 that year.[10] The fact that these figures are comparable is further confirmation of the reliability of the Cypriot government figures on Turkish-Cypriot population trends.

The Cypriot government estimate of the Turkish-Cypriot population for 1988 was 128,200 (see table 1). It is estimated that from 1974 through the end of 1987, about 30,000 Turkish Cypriots left the TRNC (see table 3). This means that the actual Turkish-Cypriot population by 1988 was around 98,000.[11] In other words, the Turkish-Cypriots, as a percentage of the total population of Cyprus, declined from 18.4 percent in 1974 to 14.2 percent in 1988. The Turkish-Cypriot population figure released by the TRNC for 1987 had been 165,035.[12] The apparent incorporation of the settlers from Turkey into this figure artificially raised the Turkish-Cypriot percentage of the overall population that year to about 25 percent.

Although no official estimates on the size of the Turkish-Cypriot population have been released by the TRNC since 1987, an October 1990 Turkish-Cypriot press report quoted the TRNC administration as saying that the overall population figure in the TRNC for 1989 was 169,272. *Goode's World Atlas* places it at 172,000 for 1990.[13] If one allows for emigration (discussed below), the actual population of Turkish Cypriots by 1990 should be about 98,000.

EMIGRATION

There can be no accurate statistics on Cypriot population if emigration is not taken into account for the periods both preceding and following 1974. More importantly, this factor is central to the debate over Anatolian settlers. Turkish officials, officials of Denktash's administration and Denktash himself have advanced estimates of the number of Turkish Cypriots emigrating to Turkey from Cyprus between 1878 and 1974 which range from 250,000 to 500,000. This period covers the years of British rule, from 1878 to 1960, and the years of intercommunal unrest from independence in 1960 to the Turkish invasion. Among those who emigrated, according to the Turkish side, were tens of thousands of Turkish Cypriots whom it claimed had been forced to leave Cyprus in the 1950s and 1960s due to "Greek pressure and intimidation." During the initial phase of the massive introduction of settlers into Cyprus (1974-1977), the Turkish side presented the issue of inhabitants of Turkey moving to the island as one revolving around the return of Turkish-Cypriot immigrants to what it called a "liberated Turkish Cyprus" following the invasion.

Different figures on Turkish-Cypriot emigration have been given at various times by Turkish officials and the Turkish-Cypriot administration. For example, on 14 November 1954, in an address to the First Committee of the UN General Assembly, Turkey's Representative to the UN Selim Sarper referred to the "more than 300,000 Turks who have left Cyprus for various reasons" and are living in Turkey, England and other countries.[14] Engaging in elaborate arguments as to why the Greek-Cypriot majority in Cyprus was not entitled to the right of self-determination, Sarper referred to the Greek-Cypriot demand for a plebiscite on the issue and argued that any discussion of such a plebiscite should address the matter of these Turkish Cypriots living outside Cyprus. Sarper cited a provision of Article 88 of the peace treaty signed at the end of the First World War as justification for the Turkish government's view that these 300,000 Turkish-Cypriot immigrants should be allowed to return to the island to vote on plebiscites. This provision gave individuals who were born in Silesia, but later emigrated, the right to vote on a plebiscite held in Silesia. Specifically, Sarper stated (emphasis added):

This portion of the treaty provides that, irrespective of sex, every person over the age of twenty *who was born in the area where the plebiscite was to be held* and everybody else found to have been resident there, starting from a date fixed by the Plebiscite Commission [1904], would be entitled to vote.

On the day of the plebiscite, *350,000 Germans who were born in this area but had later emigrated from it* arrived at the locality where the plebiscite was being held and cast their vote.[15]

It is important to emphasize the fact that Sarper was calling on *300,000* Turkish Cypriots who were *born* in Cyprus, but were living abroad at the time, to return to the island to vote on the plebiscite proposed by the Greek Cypriots. If such a large number of Turkish Cypriots had left Cyprus and most of them were still alive, it is logical that the overwhelming majority would have been born on the island after the implementation of British rule, that is after 1878, and not under the Ottoman rule that preceded it. Therefore, they would have been included in Colonial Office population records. In addition, they would have left Cyprus during British rule and would have been included in Colonial Office records on emigration.

However, Colonial Office records indicate that very few Turkish Cypriots had emigrated to countries other than England by 1954, and no more than 70,000 Cypriots (Greek and Turkish Cypriots combined) lived in England by that year. While there are no statistics on the ethnic breakdown of Cypriot immigrants in Britain at the time, it is reasonable to estimate, on the basis of emigration data after 1955 (see table 2), that the ratio between Greeks and Turks emigrating to Britain from Cyprus was four to one in 1954. Even if one allows a ratio of three Greeks to one Turk, the number of Turkish Cypriots in Britain could not have exceeded 23,000 that year.[16]

In August 1955, eight months after Sarper's speech at the UN, the Turkish government circulated an official memorandum presenting the Turkish position on the Cyprus issue. Referring to Sarper's argument about Turkish Cypriots living abroad, the memorandum stated the following:

... more than 250,000 Cypriot Turks have their home in Turkey and most of them still have a few members of their families living on the island [Cyprus].[17]

If the relatives of these Turkish-Cypriot immigrants were still alive in Cyprus in 1955, it would be another indication that the overwhelming majority of these immigrants were born on the island after the beginning of British rule and would have been included in Colonial Office population and emigration records. The fact that they were not included in these records is further evidence that such a large number of Turkish Cypriots could not possibly have emigrated to Turkey by the mid-1950s.

In his statement to the London Tripartite Conference on Cyprus in 1955, Acting Turkish Foreign Minister Fatin Rüstü Zorlu said 300,000 Turkish Cypriots had emigrated to Turkey.[18] On 24 October 1975, Vedat Çelik also placed the figure at 300,000 and said that a number of them had started returning to Cyprus.[19] On 2 July 1956, Turkish Prime Minister Adnan Menderes put the number at 500,000.[20] On 23 July 1986, Rauf Denktash stated that there were 250,000 Turkish Cypriots in Turkey.[21] On 3 October 1974, he had argued that nearly 30,000 Turkish Cypriots "were forced by the Greeks to leave Cyprus" between 1954 and 1960 alone, while thousands of others left after 1960.[22]

According to the Turkish and Turkish-Cypriot figures on emigration, an extraordinarily high percentage of the Turkish-Cypriot population has left Cyprus for Turkey, and the number of Turkish Cypriots living in Turkey is from 2.5 to five times larger than the number living in Cyprus. The high degree of uncertainty among Turkish and Turkish-Cypriot officials as to how many Turkish Cypriots have actually emigrated to Turkey is reflected in the wide variation in the estimates they have given for the number of these emigrants—250,000 to 500,000. It raises serious questions as to the credibility of the figures put forward by the Turkish side.

Turkish-Cypriot leaders have also asserted that there has been massive emigration of settlers from Greece to Cyprus. In February 1986, Rauf Denktash stated that the whole issue of Turkish settlers in the TRNC was fabricated by the Greek Cypriots in order to hide the fact that tens of thousands of settlers from Greece were colonizing the government-controlled part of Cyprus.[23] In May 1989, TRNC "Foreign Minister" Kenan Atakol said he had ascertained that "120,000 Greeks were living in southern Cyprus with false papers." He said that "the Greek Cypriots and Greeks aimed at changing the demographic structure of the island."[24] There is absolutely no evidence to support the claim by Denktash and Atakol concerning the migration of settlers from Greece to Cyprus. The government-controlled part of Cyprus covers only 2,220 square miles and is an open society. It would be virtually impossible to hide 120,000 settlers moving into the area from Greece. United Nations officials, foreign diplomats and journalists who move around freely throughout this part of Cyprus have not reported seeing or hearing anything about "settlers from Greece" in the region.

There is also no evidence whatsoever to support the Turkish claim that there was mass Turkish-Cypriot emigration to Turkey during the British colonial administration (1878-1960) of the magnitude suggested by Turkish and Turkish-Cypriot officials. The demographic data collected by the Colonial Office up through 1959 document emigration for both Greek Cypriots and Turkish Cypriots. Overall, under British rule, emigration patterns tended to follow the Greek-Turkish population ratio. For every 4.3 Greeks leaving Cyprus, one Turk emigrated from the island. This emigration ratio continued from the time of independence up through 1970. From 1971 to 1973, the ratio changed, mainly because of economic reasons. As Cyprus experienced an economic boom, Greek-Cypriot emigration declined. On the other hand, Turkish-Cypriot emigration remained steady (see table 2). The Greek- and Turkish-Cypriot economies, by that time, had moved in different directions. Most Turkish Cypriots lived in enclaves and had very limited economic interaction with the prospering Greek-Cypriot side.

Although emigration data are much more detailed after the Second World War, British authorities did observe and record any mass emigration by Greek or Turkish Cypriots that took place before the war. The only case of extraordinary Turkish-Cypriot emigration before the war occurred between 1924 and 1927. Under the Treaty of Lausanne in 1923, Turkish Cypriots living under British colonial rule in Cyprus could become Turkish citizens if they chose to emigrate to the newly established Turkish state. As a result, about 5,000 Turkish Cypriots left for Turkey between 1924 and 1927. By 1928, however, the Colonial Office reported that many of the Turkish Cypriots who had left under the terms of the treaty had since returned to Cyprus because they were disappointed with living conditions in Turkey. There is documentation to indicate that the Turkish Cypriots who emigrated to Turkey between 1924 and 1927 were neither pressured nor forced to leave Cyprus.

The Turkish view is and always has been that Turks who left Cyprus during colonial rule were "forced" to do so either by the Greeks or by the British authorities. The fact that the only case of substantial Turkish-Cypriot emigration to Turkey during British rule occurred between 1924 and 1927 demonstrates otherwise. A documented study on the subject by Greek-Cypriot author Dr. George Georgallides reaches three important conclusions. First, for a number of reasons, mainly the availability of large tracts of land in the newly established Turkish republic, the Turkish government encouraged Turkish Cypriots to emigrate to Turkey. Second, British authorities in Cyprus discouraged such emigration. Third, the Greek Cypriots generally played no role in the matter, but a few expressed sympathy for the Turkish-Cypriot emigrants who had changed their minds and returned to Cyprus after a brief stay in Turkey.[25]

More relevant for the purposes of this study are the statistics for the years of ethnic tension between 1955 and 1959, and 1963 and 1973. These are the years the Turkish-Cypriot administration has claimed that tens of thousands of Turkish Cypriots were forced to emigrate—many to Turkey—due to what it described as "Greek pressure." According to British colonial data and Cypriot government statistics, the number of Turkish Cypriots emigrating between 1955 and 1973 totalled 16,519, an annual average of about 900 Turkish Cypriots. The respective figure for the Greek Cypriots is 71,036 emigrants, an annual average of about 3,740 (see table 2). About 92 percent of the Turkish Cypriots emigrating between 1955 and 1973 went to Britain, Australia, and Canada. About eight percent emigrated to a variety of other countries, including the United States. Of this eight percent, only two percent went to Turkey. In other words, between 1955 and 1973 about 300 Turkish Cypriots left Cyprus and settled

permanently in Turkey, according to combined British colonial and
Cypriot government data (see table 2). British demographer L.T. St.
John-Jones estimates that 280 Turkish Cypriots emigrated to Turkey
between 1955 and 1973, a figure which represents 0.3 percent of total
Cypriot emigration during this period.[26] This figure is consistent with
British colonial and Cypriot government data.

TABLE 2: EMIGRATION BY ETHNIC GROUP
AND TURKISH-CYPRIOT EMIGRATION TO TURKEY, 1955-1973

YEARS	GREEK CYPRIOTS	TURKISH CYPRIOTS	TURKISH CYPRIOTS EMIGRATING TO TURKEY
1955	4,817	862	n.a
1956	3,621	893	5
1957	3,534	928	13
1958	3,897	608	16
1959	4,211	1,248	7
1960	11,764	2,220	12
1961	10,726	2,543	1
1962	5,056	870	4
1963	2,305	453	n.a.
1964	3,995	992	47
1965	2,380	566	36
1966	2,855	538	21
1967	2,540	900	15
1968	2,169	503	30
1969	2,027	337	12
1970	1,741	567	14
1971	1,649	612	35
1972	868	449	19
1973	881	430	3
TOTAL	71,036	16,519	290

SOURCE: Great Britain, *Cyprus Annual Reports* (Colonial Office, 1955-1959); Republic
of Cyprus, *Statistical Abstracts*, 1965 and 1973 (Nicosia: Department of Statistics and
Research).
NOTE: A total of 93,622 people emigrated from Cyprus between 1955 and 1973. Of
these, 71,036, or 75.9 percent, were Greek Cypriots and 16,519, or 17.6 percent,
were Turkish Cypriots. The remaining 6,067 were primarily British and Armenians.
The figures on Turkish-Cypriot emigration (middle column) represent total Turkish-
Cypriot emigration on a yearly basis. The figures on Turkish-Cypriot emigration to
Turkey (right column) are part of total Turkish-Cypriot emigration and are, therefore,
included in the middle column.

One could still argue, however, that the emergency situation between
1955 and 1959, and 1963 and 1973, might have caused government
authorities to underestimate Turkish-Cypriot emigration to Turkey,
and, therefore, their figures for these periods could be disputed. From
1955 to 1959, however, British colonial authorities kept accurate emi-

gration data that are beyond dispute. Emigration statistics compiled between 1960 and 1963 are also considered accurate because Turkish-Cypriot officials served in the immigration agencies of the Cypriot government and produced these statistics jointly with the Greek Cypriots. In the final analysis, emigration data from the years of British rule (1878 through 1959) and the first four years of independence (1960 through 1963) cannot be disputed.[27] The only Cypriot government emigration statistics that can conceivably be challenged are those between 1963 and 1973.

After December 1963, the Cypriot government remained in control of the airport and all ports and coastal areas from which Turkish Cypriots might leave legally for Turkey. The total area under Turkish-Cypriot control did not exceed four percent of Cyprus. The only coastal regions controlled by Turkish Cypriots were five tiny enclaves in Limnitis, Kokkina, Galinoporne, Zygi and Larnaca. Access to them was controlled by the Cypriot government and monitored by the United Nations Peacekeeping Force (UNFICYP). Conceivably, a small number of Turkish Cypriots could have left for Turkey illegally through these coastal enclaves, but the number could not have been more than a few hundred who had been transported into these isolated areas from other Turkish-Cypriot enclaves scattered throughout Cyprus. Such a possibility would have been unlikely, however, considering that UNFICYP detected no such movement into these areas.

One has to consider that the Turkish-Cypriot side discouraged the Turkish Cypriots from leaving Cyprus between 1963 and 1973. Any mass exodus during this period of national emergency would have undermined morale among Turkish Cypriots. It was a period when a siege mentality prevailed in the Turkish-Cypriot enclaves. This mentality was a reflection of the conflict dynamics in Cyprus at the time, the dynamics that are often inherent in a majority-minority conflict. Under these conditions, it was considered "unpatriotic" to emigrate. In addition, the Turkish-Cypriot side considered the government of Archbishop Makarios to be illegal and urged the Turkish Cypriots to avoid acting in a way that might imply recognition of the Cypriot government. This included applying for a passport from the government, which issued one to any Turkish Cypriot who wanted to leave the island. The government's willingness to issue passports to the Turkish Cypriots was perceived by the Turkish-Cypriot leaders as an attempt to undermine their community's will to resist the temptation to emigrate. According to Professor Kemal Karpat, who is sympathetic to the Turkish-Cypriot side, "very few Cypriot Turks decided to leave their homes despite constant efforts by the Greek-Cypriot government to encourage their emigration."[28]

Furthermore, the Turkish-Cypriot emigration policy was strictly regulated by the leadership in the Turkish sector of Nicosia. Departure from Cyprus was allowed only after a special permit had been issued by the district military commander. As an additional disincentive to emigrate, the central Turkish military command in Nicosia issued orders providing for the confiscation of the property of Turkish Cypriots departing "illegally" or violating the terms of their travel permits.

In the final analysis, between 1963 and 1973, the Cypriot government was in a position to control the flow of Turkish-Cypriot emigration efficiently and it kept accurate emigration records. These records show that a total of 6,347 Turkish Cypriots—a yearly average of 577—left Cyprus during this period. Very few of them, 232, went to Turkey. The fact that the Cypriot government records contain no evidence of any substantial emigration to Turkey during these years, coupled with the fact that the Turkish-Cypriot side discouraged the Turkish Cypriots from leaving Cyprus, would indicate that the Denktash regime's claim of a mass exodus of Turkish Cypriots to Turkey between 1960 and 1973 is totally unfounded.

Since 1974, the Turkish-Cypriot side has not revealed the number of Turkish Cypriots leaving Cyprus to settle abroad.[29] There are strong indications, however, that Turkish-Cypriot emigration has accelerated since the Turkish invasion. It is estimated that the exodus of Turkish Cypriots from the TRNC between 1974 and 1987 was 2.5 times greater than it was between 1960 and 1973. Thus, 30,379 Turkish Cypriots are estimated to have left the TRNC between 1974 and 1987 (see table 3), as opposed to 11,980 between 1960 and 1973 (see table 2). The fact that Turkish Cypriots continued emigrating after 1974 when they lived in their own "state" and were not faced with what Turkish authorities claimed was "Greek pressure and intimidation" indicates that they left Cyprus primarily, though not exclusively, for economic reasons, just as the Greek Cypriots did. It is also likely that the Turkish-Cypriot exodus after 1974 was precipitated by the massive influx of Anatolian settlers.

TABLE 3: TURKISH-CYPRIOT EMIGRATION, 1974-1987

YEAR	ARRIVALS OF TRNC "NATIONALS"	DEPARTURES OF TRNC "NATIONALS"	DIFFERENCE (EMIGRANTS)
1974	5,098	6,093	-995
1975	13,635	29,842	-16,207
1976	30,764	31,454	-690
1977	33,570	35,540	-1,970
1978	35,549	36,410	-861
1979	47,839	46,858	+981
1980	51,204	53,245	-2,041
1981	53,233	52,371	+862
1982	49,870	51,764	-1,894
1983	58,918	60,660	-1,742
1984	57,123	56,472	+651
1985	53,860	54,599	-739
1986	55,076	58,788	-3,712
1987	59,297	61,319	-2,022
TOTAL	605,036	635,415	30,379

SOURCE: This table has been compiled by the author from two official TRNC sources: the *Yearly Action Report* (YAR) (Nicosia: Police General Directorate of the TRNC) and the *TRNC Statistical Yearbook, 1987*, TRNC "Prime Ministry," "State" Planning Organization, Statistics and Research Department (Nicosia, December 1988). The YAR provides data for the years 1974 to 1986, while the *Statistical Yearbook* covers 1980 to 1987. The data for 1980 to 1986 in the two sources are all but identical. (The minor discrepancies between numbers are statistically insignificant.) The difference between arrivals and departures each year logically represents emigration. For the years 1974 to 1986, the total difference between arrivals and departures is 25,367. This figure has generally been considered by several Turkish-Cypriot newspapers to represent emigration for that period.

NOTE: The *Yearly Action Report* (YAR) was published in the Turkish-Cypriot newspaper *Yenidüzen* on 15 February 1989. The Turkish-Cypriot newspaper *Ortam*, 18 May 1989, put the number of Turkish-Cypriot emigrants leaving Cyprus from 1974 to 1989 at 30,000 and said they emigrated mainly to Britain, Canada and Australia. The same figure has also been reported in *Yenidüzen*, 2 February 1990.

The trend in Turkish-Cypriot emigration from 1963 to 1973 is consistent with the trend from 1959 to 1962, a period of relatively peaceful conditions and increasing cooperation between Greek and Turkish Cypriots. From 1959 to 1962, 6,881 Turkish Cypriots left Cyprus, while 6,347 emigrated between 1963 and 1973, the period of ethnic conflict (see table 2). A similar pattern of emigration during these two periods also applies to Greek Cypriots. From 1959 to 1962, a total of 31,757 Greek Cypriots emigrated, while 23,410 left the country between 1963 and 1973 (see table 2).

It should be noted that emigration was especially high for both Greek and Turkish Cypriots in 1959 and 1960, the transitional period from colonial rule to independence. Both groups took advantage of being able to enter Britain as British subjects up until August 1960. Thus, in 1959 and 1960, 15,975 Greek Cypriots and 3,468 Turkish Cypriots left Cyprus primarily to emigrate to Britain (see table 2).

These emigration data demonstrate the following beyond a reasonable doubt: First, Greek- and Turkish-Cypriot emigration patterns have paralleled the population ratio between the two communities. Second, both Greek and Turkish Cypriots have emigrated primarily for economic reasons. Third, there has been no mass Turkish-Cypriot emigration to Turkey and, therefore, there could not have been any massive Turkish-Cypriot return from Turkey after 1974. The Turkish claim that from 250,000 to 500,000 Turkish Cypriots, who were presumably born in Cyprus, emigrated to Turkey during British colonial rule is undoubtedly contrived.

Reliable demographic and emigration data from British authorities during the 82 years of British rule and from Cypriot government authorities during the first 14 years of independence (up until 1974) indicate that there was no significant change in the 4.3 to one ratio between the Greek- and Turkish-Cypriot populations over that 96-year period. However, the Turkish-Cypriot population declined after the Turkish invasion, and, by 1988, the population ratio was 5.6 Greek Cypriots (550,000) to one Turkish Cypriot (98,000). It is quite paradoxical that one of the side-effects of the Turkish occupation was the altering of the population ratio between Greek and Turkish Cypriots in the Greeks' favor by 1988. But the massive introduction of Turkish settlers since 1974 has illegally and artificially altered the overall demographic structure of Cyprus at the expense of the Greeks. There are strong indications that, by 1988, the actual Turkish-Cypriot population, as a percentage of the island's total population, had dropped to 14.2 percent. The introduction of settlers, however, had artificially raised the TRNC population to about 25 percent of the country's total population by that time.

NOTES

[1]There are no precise population figures for the period of the Ottoman conquest and thereafter. The figures quoted on the Greek Orthodox and Muslim populations toward the end of the sixteenth century represent estimates which are derived from a combination of sources found in the work of Theodore Papadopoullos, *Social and Historical Data on Population: 1570-*

1881 (Nicosia: Cyprus Research Center, 1965), 33-34, and L. W. St. John-Jones, *The Population of Cyprus* (London: University of London, Institute of Commonwealth Studies, 1983), 27-28. Papadopoullos cites Ottoman sources as well as Western consular reports on population. For various estimates of the population after the Ottoman conquest, see also Sir George Hill, *A History of Cyprus*, vol. 4 (Cambridge University Press, 1952), 31-36.

[2]Bernard Lewis, *The Emergence of Modern Turkey* (London: Oxford University Press, 1969), 90-91; Papadopoullos, ibid., 27; Hill, ibid., 5.

[3]For the evolution of the population figures in Cyprus between 1700 and 1800 and for demographic accounts of the region for the same period—often confusing or contradictory—see Papadopoullos, ibid., 43-52, and Hill, ibid., 31-36.

[4]Papadopoullos, ibid., 49; St. John-Jones, *The Population of Cyprus*, 32. On the subject of the conversion of Christians to Islam, see Theodore Papadopoullos, "Prosfate Exislamisme Agrotikou Plethysmou en Kypro" (Recent Islamization of the Rural Population in Cyprus), *Kypriakai Spoudai* 29 (1965): 27-48.

[5]For the significance of the *Tanzimat* era, see Lewis, *The Emergence of Modern Turkey*, 76-127, 169-173.

[6]For a detailed analysis of the 1881 Colonial Office census, see Papadopoullos, *Social and Historical Data on Population*, 78-88.

[7]This Turkish-Cypriot report was prepared to reflect the overall number of Turkish Cypriots on the island, both in the "Autonomous Turkish Cypriot zone" and in the government-controlled area, on 19 October 1974. At the time, a considerable number of Turkish Cypriots were still living in the government-controlled part of Cyprus, while several thousand Greek Cypriots still lived in the Turkish-occupied zone. By early 1975, all Turkish Cypriots living in the government-controlled area were transferred to the north. According to the report, "a total of 99,871 people live in the Autonomous Turkish Cypriot Zone: 83,719 Turks, 14,577 Greeks, 1,376 Maronites, and 202 British and foreign nationals. Out of 32,039 Turks who have remained outside the Autonomous Turkish Cypriot zone, about 10,000 Turkish Cypriots are enclaved in the British sovereign bases in the Limassol District and 12,000 in the Paphos District. About 4,200 are enclaved in other villages in the Limassol District and in Limassol itself. About 3,209 are enclaved in the Nicosia District. About 2,630 are enclaved in the Larnaca District. The members of the Turkish Peace Forces, and Turkish citizens who have special duties in the Turkish Cypriot Zone, were not included in this report." The report was submitted by Ahmed Sami, "General Secretary, Ministry of Justice and Interior, Turkish Cypriot Administration," 20 October 1974. The report is found in an official publi-

cation of the Cypriot government entitled *Colonization of Occupied Cyprus,* Republic of Cyprus, Government of Cyprus Public Information Office (Nicosia: December 1979), 18.

[8]For the post-invasion period, the *TRNC Statistical Yearbook, 1987* gives official population figures for the following years: 1978: 146,740; 1980: 149,610; 1982: 153,239; 1985: 160,287; 1986: 162,676; and 1987: 165,035. See *TRNC Statistical Yearbook, 1987,* 11-12.

[9]For the average annual population growth in Turkey, see "Population: Getting More Crowded but Becoming Younger," in *Turkey in the 2000s* (Istanbul: Nezi Demirkent, 1987), 21-23.

[10]U.S. Congress. House. Committee on Foreign Affairs. Subcommittee on Europe and the Middle East, 98th Cong., 1st sess., 13 June 1983. Report prepared by Library of Congress, Congressional Research Service, Foreign Affairs and National Defense Division (Washington, D.C.: U.S. Government Printing Office, 1983), 26.

[11]Turkish-Cypriot opposition leader Alpay Durduran estimated Turkish-Cypriot population to be 99,000 in 1987. See the Turkish-Cypriot newspaper *Yenidüzen,* 15 May 1987. Another member of the Turkish-Cypriot opposition, Hasan Erçakica, placed Turkish-Cypriot population in early 1990 as low as 80,000. See *Yenidüzen,* 23 February 1990.

[12]See *TRNC Statistical Yearbook, 1987,* 12.

[13]For the 1989 population estimate of 169,272 in the TRNC, see the Turkish-Cypriot newspaper *Birlik,* 14 October 1990. For the 1990 population estimate of 172,000 in the TRNC, see *Goode's World Atlas,* 18th ed. (New York: Rand McNally, 1990), 24. Considering that, according to TRNC population figures, the average annual population growth between 1980 and 1987 was 2,200, the TRNC population figure for 1990 should be about 172,000. See *TRNC Statistical Yearbook, 1987,* 11-12.

[14]See the speech by Selim Sarper at the UN on 14 November 1954 reprinted in *Turkey and Cyprus: A Survey of the Cyprus Question with Official Statements of the Turkish Viewpoint,* Turkey, Ministry of Foreign Affairs (London: Embassy of Turkey, 1956), 43-44.

[15]Ibid.

[16]For Cypriot emigration to England in the 1950s and thereafter, see St. John-Jones, *The Population of Cyprus,* 99-104.

[17]See *Turkey and Cyprus: A Survey of the Cyprus Question,* 23, for text of memorandum.

[18]Ibid., 53-54.

[19]For UN document containing Çelik's statement, see note 6, chapter 1, and

Foreign Policy of Turkey at the United Nations, 477.

[20]See interview with Menderes, "Turkish Warning on Cyprus," *Daily Telegraph*, London, 2 July 1956. Reprinted in *Turkey and Cyprus: A Survey of the Cyprus Question*, 70.

[21]See *Birlik*, 23 July 1986.

[22]Turkish-Cypriot *Special News Bulletin*, 4 October 1975.

[23]*Newspot* (in English), published by the Directorate General of Press and Information of the Turkish government, Ankara, 14 February 1986.

[24]"Over 120,000 Greeks from Greece Became Greek-Cypriot Nationals and Settled in Cyprus," *Newspot*, 11 May 1989.

[25]See George Georgallides, *A Political and Administrative History of Cyprus: 1918-1926* (Nicosia: Cyprus Research Center, 1979), 410-420. See also the reports of the Colonial Office in *Colonial Reports*, Annual No. 1366, Cyprus Report for 1926, 43; *Colonial Reports*, Annual No. 1406, Cyprus Report for 1927, 40; and *Colonial Reports*, Annual No. 1471, Cyprus Report for 1928, 36.

[26]St. John-Jones, *The Population of Cyprus*, 99-100.

[27]The British author H.D. Purcell, who is not unsympathetic to the Turkish Cypriots, discussed the Turkish claim of mass emigration of Turkish Cypriots to Turkey as follows: "The Turkish claim that there are 300,000 persons of Cyprus origin now in Turkey would seem to be considerably exaggerated, especially since the Turkish proportion of the Cyprus population does not seem to have dropped more than seven percent during the British period. In 1881, the number of Muslims was 46,389 (as opposed to 136,629 Greeks and 3,066 others), that is to say 24.9 percent. At the census of 1911, there were 56,428 Muslims, 214,480 Greek Orthodox and 3,016 others, so that the Muslim percentage of the population was 20.1 percent as opposed to the Greek Orthodox percentage of 78.8 percent. At the 1951 census, there were 81,000 Muslims (17.9 percent), 362,000 Greek Orthodox (80.2 percent) and 8,300 others (1.9 percent). In 1960, the percentage of the Turks was 18.1 percent, of Greeks 78.3 percent." See H.D. Purcell, *Cyprus* (New York: Frederick Praeger, 1969), 241.

[28]Kemal H. Karpat, "War on Cyprus: The Tragedy of Enosis," in *Turkey's Foreign Policy in Transition: 1950-1974*, ed. Kemal H. Karpat (Leiden: E.J. Brill, 1975), 189-190.

[29]The *TRNC Statistical Yearbook, 1987* does not provide any data on emigration as such. On the other hand, under the title "Tourism," it provides some general data on arrivals and departures. Still, no specific figures are given for departures of Turkish tourists. See *TRNC Statistical Yearbook, 1987*, 193-207.

3

Turkish Colonization of Occupied Cyprus

In his article "Ottoman Methods of Conquest," the Turkish scholar and prominent authority on the Ottoman Empire, Halil Inalcik, refers to the colonization of Cyprus immediately following the Ottoman conquest of the island in 1571:

> In order to make their conquest secure, the Ottomans used an elaborate system of colonization and mass deportation *(sürgün)*. . . . Evidently mass deportation was practiced by the Ottoman state from the earliest time.

> The documents of later periods confirm this old tradition of mass deportation and give interesting details. According to an imperial decree of deportation dated 13 Djumâda I, 980 (24 September 1572), one family out of every ten in the provinces of Anatolia, Rum (Sivas), Karaman and Zulkadriye were to be sent to newly conquered Cyprus. The expressed motives for this particular deportation were the rehabilitation and security of the island. The settlers were to be chosen from every level of the society, peasantry, craftsmen, etc. However, the first people to be sent to the island were peasants with insufficient or unfertile lands, the poor, the idlers and the nomads. These people, equipped with their implements, were to be registered in the *defters* and transferred to the island. These deportees were given a special exemption from taxation in their new homes for a period of two years. As these people did not usually like to abandon their homes, the officials concerned were ordered to carry out these measures with firmness. At a later date, convicted usurers and criminals were sent to Cyprus as a punishment for their crimes.[1]

There are undoubtedly very important differences between the Ottoman conquest and colonization of Cyprus in 1571 and the Turkish invasion, occupation and colonization of Cyprus in 1974. Still, there exists a fundamental similarity between these two periods of conquest. In both cases, the transfer of populations from Anatolia to Cyprus commenced almost immediately after occupation. Moreover, in both cases, the colonization of Cyprus was carried out as a systematic policy of the government.

Since 1974, an estimated 74,000 Turkish settlers have colonized Cyprus. They can be divided into three broad categories: 2,000 civil servants and their families, laborers and tourist industry personnel; 10,000 former Turkish military personnel and their dependents (a group that should be considered separately from the Turkish occupation forces currently serving in Cyprus and their dependents); and 62,000 Anatolian peasants.

The civil servants—mainly administrators and their technical support staff—began arriving in Cyprus in fall 1974. Their mission was to maintain the economic infrastructure and vital public services of the occupied zone, including the communications and transportation networks, and the systems for providing electricity and water. They also kept the industrial plants left behind by the Greek Cypriots operational. These civil servants were granted "citizenship" and they were allowed to bring their families with them to the TFSC. Laborers also started arriving in fall 1974 and immediately began working on military infrastructure projects, such as the expansion of ports and roads, and the construction of an airport. By early October 1974, tourist industry personnel from Turkey had arrived to maintain and operate the hotels and other enterprises related to tourism in the Famagusta and Kyrenia districts.

Also among the first Turks to settle in Cyprus were those who had previously had either a direct or indirect association with the Turkish armed forces. Under the rubric of "military personnel and dependents," one can distinguish three subgroups: families of soldiers killed during the invasion, retired officers and their families, and demobilized soldiers and their families.

On 25 February 1975, the "Council of Ministers" of the self-proclaimed "Turkish Federated State of Cyprus" approved a resolution concerning its "Citizenship Law." According to this "ministerial" decision, "the wives, children, parents and brothers of members of the Turkish armed forces killed during the period between 20 July 1974 and 20 August 1974" were eligible for "citizenship" in the "Turkish Federated State of Cyprus."[2] In other words, the extended families of "soldier martyrs" killed during the invasion could settle in Cyprus and become "citizens" of the TFSC. It is estimated that about 3,000 relatives of these Turkish soldiers took advantage of this offer and settled in Cyprus during the first year after the invasion. This category of settlers was entitled to "immovable property" and was given land and a home.

According to this "Citizenship Law," "members of the Turkish armed forces who have served in Cyprus or persons who have served in the ranks of the Turkish Resistance Organization, *Türk Mukavemet Teşkilâti* (TMT), in Cyprus or in Turkey" also became eligible for TFSC "citizenship."[3] But the provisions of this law are so vague that almost any retired Turkish officer could have applied for "citizenship." Founded in 1957, TMT was controlled by Turkish army officers who came clandestinely to Cyprus. The organization also had members in Turkey. Some of the officers who served in the 650-member contingent of the Turkish army in Cyprus after 1960 (established under the Zurich-London agreements of 1959) were also TMT members. Because TMT was a secret organization, it is all but impossible to determine the names of officers who served in it in Cyprus or in Turkey. It is, therefore, impossible to prove whether a particular Turkish officer retiring in Cyprus was a TMT member.

An estimated 500 to 700 retired officers of the Turkish army, some of whom were leading figures of TMT, have taken advantage of the "Citizenship Law" and settled in Cyprus with their families.[4] The officer corps enjoys a special social status in Turkey and this is reflected in the way retired army officers have benefited from the allocation of property in occupied Cyprus. In the late 1960s and early 1970s, many wealthy, upper class Greek Cypriots built villas in the Kyrenia district, a well-known Mediterranean resort. Following the invasion, many of these villas were given either to Turkish officers serving in Cyprus or to retired Turkish officers. Thus, a considerable number of retired officers and their families, totalling about 2,000 people, reside in the villas of Kyrenia, Bellapais, Agios Georgios, Karavas and Lapithos.

The provision allowing "members of the Turkish armed forces who have served in Cyprus" to become "citizens" was applicable not only to officers, but to soldiers as well. The combined figure of demobilized soldiers and their family members in Cyprus is estimated to be 5,000. They were generally given homes on small parcels of land, usually half an acre in size, in villages.

By far the largest group of Turks settling in Cyprus has been the 62,000 peasants from Anatolia, who have arrived on the island since January 1975. Based on Turkish-Cypriot sources, it is estimated that 22,375 Anatolian peasants settled in Cyprus from January to December 1975, arriving at an average rate of 465 per week (see table 4). They came ostensibly as "seasonal workers," as the Turkish side has labeled them, mainly to harvest citrus fruit in the areas of Famagusta, Morphou, Karavas and Lapithos.[5] However, most of them did not return to Turkey when the citrus fruit season ended in April. On the contrary, thousands of extra "seasonal workers" arrived throughout 1975 and settled in towns and villages all over the occupied area. In the summer of that year, several thousand settled in the Kyrenia district where there were no summer crops requiring harvesting. The summer fruits and vegetables in the Kyrenia region had always been produced in small family gardens in which just enough for local consumption were grown.

In 1976, the number of arrivals dropped significantly to an estimated minimum of 3,093. This drop was primarily due to administrative and absorption problems created by the sudden influx of settlers. Turkish-Cypriot authorities were simply incapable of accommodating such a large number of settlers since they were still preoccupied with administrative, social and legal problems created by the movement of over 40,000 Turkish Cypriots from the south to the north in the aftermath of the invasion. In 1977, the rate of arrivals accelerated again as 10,874 settlers came to Cyprus that year.

TABLE 4: TURKS SETTLING IN OCCUPIED CYPRUS
ARRIVALS AND DEPARTURES OF TURKISH NATIONALS IN AND FROM
THE TRNC, 1974-1989 (TRNC STATISTICS)

YEAR	ARRIVALS	DEPARTURES	DIFFERENCE (SETTLERS)
1974	5,573	4,193	(+)1,380
1975	73,831	51,456	(+)22,375
1976	83,440	80,347	(+)3,093
1977	108,016	97,142	(+)10,874
1978	104,738	103,108	(+)1,630
1979	95,095	92,956	(+)2,139
1980	69,810	68,727	(+)1,083
1981	62,660	64,912	(-)2,252
1982	65,018	66,172	(-)1,154
1983	78,649	76,386	(+)2,263
1984	93,333	90,403	(+)2,930
1985	103,698	102,754	(+)944
1986	105,729	105,492	(+)237
1987	147,965	n.a.	n.a.
1988	173,351	n.a.	n.a.
1989	214,566	209,837	(+)4,729
TOTAL	1,585,472	1,213,885	(+)50,271

SOURCE: This table has been compiled by the author from three official TRNC sources: the *Yearly Action Report* (*YAR*) (Nicosia: Police General Directorate of the TRNC); the *TRNC Statistical Yearbook, 1987*, TRNC "Prime Ministry," "State" Planning Organization, Statistics and Research Department (Nicosia, December, 1988); and the records of the Office of the "Prime Minister" of the TRNC. These sources all refer to arrivals and departures of Turkish nationals. The *YAR* provides data for 1974 to 1986, while the *Statistical Yearbook* covers 1981 to 1987. The records of the Office of the "Prime Minister" cover 1988 and 1989. The data in the *YAR* and the *Statistical Yearbook* are all but identical for the years 1981 to 1986. (The minor discrepancies in numbers are statistically insignificant.) The data on departures are drawn from the *YAR* since the *Statistical Yearbook* provides no data on Turkish nationals leaving the TRNC. The difference between arrivals and departures each year logically represents Turkish nationals who have been settling in the TRNC. The excess in the number of arrivals, indicated by (+), represents the settlers. In 1981 and 1982, more Turkish nationals left Cyprus than arrived. The excess in the number of departures is indicated by (-). It is unclear why these 3,406 Turkish nationals returned to Turkey. A 1976 report in the British press referred to the issue of settlers returning to Turkey and said that most settlers have remained in Cyprus. It said, however, that some of them have sold everything that was given to them when they arrived, have pocketed the money and have gone back to Turkey (see *Sunday Times*, 26 September 1976). The fact that departures exceeded arrivals in some years may indicate that there were Turkish citizens who came to the TRNC, stayed there for a period exceeding one year, and then decided to return to Turkey. It is noteworthy that the rate of arrivals of Turkish nationals in the TRNC dropped by 25 to 40 percent between 1980 and 1983. On the other hand, in 1987, arrivals increased by 42,236, or 40 percent over the 1986 figure.

NOTE: The *Yearly Action Report* (*YAR*) was published in the Turkish-Cypriot newspaper *Yenidüzen* on 15 February 1989. The figure 46,000 has been considered by some Turkish-Cypriot politicians and by some newspapers to represent the overall number of Turkish nationals settling in the TRNC by 1986. Newspapers in Turkey presented higher figures at a much earlier period. In its 16–19 December 1978 issue, the Turkish newspaper *Tercüman* (Istanbul) reported that "it's rumored that there are about 60,000 settlers." On 26 March 1979, the Turkish newspaper *Aydinlik* (Istanbul) wrote that the number of settlers was "around 50,000."

From August 1974 to the end of 1977, a total of 37,713 settlers arrived in Cyprus. For the next nine years (1978 through 1986), the arrival of settlers continued, but at a much slower pace, averaging a minimum of 945 per year. Thus, according to Turkish-Cypriot sources, by the end of 1986 there were about 46,000 settlers in the TRNC. There were about 50,000 by the end of 1989 (see table 4). The U.S. State Department, which considers the issue of the settlers to be marginal, has acknowledged the presence of 30,000 to 35,000 settlers in the TRNC by 1986.[6] It should be noted that the State Department, in openly and persistently criticizing the Jewish settlements in the Israeli-occupied West Bank, has adopted a much clearer position on the establishment of these settlements than it has on the issue of settlers in

occupied Cyprus. It considers the settlements in the West Bank to be
an impediment to peace.

According to TRNC statistics, the 1987 population figure in the
occupied zone was 165,035. Since the Turkish-Cypriot component of
the population did not exceed 100,000 that year, the logical conclusion is that the difference of about 65,000 represented the number of
settlers. (That year, the British government estimated that there were
35,000 settlers in the TRNC.[7]) Taking into account the continued
flow of settlers into Cyprus between 1987 and 1990, the number of
settlers living in the occupied zone in 1990 should have exceeded
65,000 and is estimated to have been about 74,000. This figure is
based on the total population figure for the TRNC in 1990 which is
estimated to be about 172,000.[8] The Turkish-Cypriot component of
the population was expected to be about 98,000 in 1990. Logically,
the difference between 172,000 and 98,000—about 74,000—represents the number of settlers. It is possible that this figure could be even
higher considering that Turkish-Cypriot emigration has been continuing along with the influx of new settlers. Given this trend, it is not
inconceivable to suggest that the number of settlers could be close to
equaling the number of Turkish Cypriots.[9]

The problem of verifying the precise number of settlers persists. The
following can be stated with a reasonable degree of confidence: Since
1974, settlers have been arriving at an uneven pace. By 1990, the
overall number of settlers should have reached 74,000. As the number
of settlers continues to increase and Turkish Cypriots continue to emigrate, the population ratio between settlers and Turkish Cypriots is
shifting to favor the settlers.

If the 35,000 troops in the Turkish occupation army are added to the
74,000 Turkish settlers, the number of Turkish nationals in the TRNC
in 1990 would have been 109,000, compared to about 98,000 Turkish
Cypriots. In the final analysis, if military personnel are included in the
overall population figure, the majority of the residents living in the
TRNC as of 1990 could very well have been Turkish nationals.

ORIGINS AND RECRUITMENT OF ANATOLIAN PEASANTS

The Anatolian peasants who have settled in Cyprus have come primar-
ily from areas around Antalya, Mersin, and Adana in southern Turkey;
Lake Van in eastern Turkey; Konya in central Turkey; and Trabzon
(Trapezous) and Sürmene in the Black Sea region.[10]

Cyprus has a certain relevance for settlers whose relatives were killed during the invasion, and for retired officers and demobilized soldiers who served in Cyprus and later settled there. For the Anatolian peasants, however, Cyprus has no particular meaning. It is quite plausible that a substantial number of them had little or no clear idea of where Cyprus was located before their departure from Turkey. This could be particularly true with regard to peasants coming from central, eastern or northern Turkey.

A typical Anatolian peasant family, usually consisting of a father, mother, and two or three children, represents the most traditional sector of Turkish society. The majority of the family members are illiterate, and they speak Turkish with a variety of accents that differ from the Turkish-Cypriot accent. These Anatolians are used to living in rather primitive conditions and are much more traditional in their outlook and customs than the Turkish Cypriots. They are unfamiliar with the amenities of life they encounter in the Greek-Cypriot villages they colonize. Usually, the men are dressed in baggy pants and the women wear long colorful dresses. The settlers' family life and social life revolve around Islam. Reportedly, some of the men practice polygamy.[11]

There have been signs of discontent among Turkish Cypriots as the number of these settlers has grown. Many of the Turkish Cypriots have criticized the settlers for what they describe as "immoral" and "arrogant" behavior.[12] It is likely that one of the factors pushing Turkish Cypriots to emigrate after 1974 has been the mass influx of settlers. These settlers offer a pool of cheap labor which lowers wages below the level that has been acceptable to Turkish-Cypriot workers. On the other hand, the settlers have complained that they are discriminated against by the Turkish Cypriots.[13].

Turkish-Cypriot discontent over the settlers does not necessarily imply that the Turkish-Cypriot leadership has opposed the settlement policy. On the contrary, Rauf Denktash has been an ardent advocate of this policy since it was first implemented. In fact, he appears to be the champion of further colonization in Cyprus. This was evident in the summer of 1989 when he invited Bulgarian Muslims who had fled to Turkey to come and settle in Cyprus. Simultaneously, his regime banned Bulgarian diplomats from entering the TRNC.[14] Initially, only a few Bulgarian Muslim families were allowed to settle in the TRNC where they were granted "citizenship." In the summer of

1990, however, there were reports that some more Bulgarian families
had started settling in the village of Agia Trias in the Karpasia region.[15]

Entire Anatolian families from villages in central, eastern, northern and
southern Turkey have been transferred in groups to settle in particular
villages in occupied Cyprus. Each family has been given a house and a
piece of land. This pattern of settlement does not represent the normal
emigration process of Turks along the lines, for example, of those emigrating to Germany. It has required a government policy under which
Turkish authorities have planned, organized and implemented the settlement program. A report in the London *Sunday Times* on 26
September 1976 presents the transfer of settlers to occupied Cyprus as
part of a plan by the government in Ankara. According to this report,
"the overwhelming majority of the immigrants are peasants uprooted
from poor villages—mainly on Turkey's Black Sea coast and [in] the
center-south region."

Over the years, the interviews and stories about Turkish settlement in
Cyprus which have appeared in press reports have been supplemented
by the vivid accounts of settlers who have deserted to the Greek-
Cypriot side. Given the secrecy surrounding the colonization policy
and the paucity of data on peasant recruitment, the deserters' stories
have become a valuable source of information concerning the recruitment of settlers and their transfer to occupied Cyprus.

In the aftermath of the July 1974 invasion, centers to recruit settlers for
transfer to Cyprus opened in a number of Turkish cities, including
Ankara, Istanbul (Constantinople), Mersin, Adana and Trabzon. In
Ankara and Istanbul, recruitment was carried out in the "consulates"
of the "Turkish Federated State of Cyprus." The TFSC representative
in Ankara at the time was the founder of TMT, Riza Vuruşkan, who
had retired from the Turkish army. In other cities, the mayor's office
served as the recruitment center. The opening of these centers was
accompanied by announcements in the media telling those who
wished to go to Cyprus as "seasonal workers" to apply at the centers.
Similar announcements were made by *muhtars* (headmen) in villages.[16]
It appears that the Ankara and Istanbul recruitment centers attracted
individuals possessing certain skills, such as hotel management. It is
from this pool of individuals that the hotels of Kyrenia and Famagusta
were manned in 1975. The recruitment offices in Mersin, Adana, and
Trabzon served as regional centers for recruiting peasants from the surrounding areas.

Yusuf Veli Akyüz, a 21-year-old peasant settler who was recruited from the province of Trabzon in the Black Sea region, explained the recruitment process in detail when he escaped from the occupied zone and was given asylum by the Cypriot government in June 1978.[17] Akyüz said that, sometime in early November 1974, the recruitment center in the city of Trabzon sent an official notice to the *muhtar* of Kaliyan Çayirlik, a village of 150 families. Acting on this notice, the *muhtar*, Mahmud Yadirin, announced to the villagers that anyone who wished to go to Cyprus as an immigrant should make his or her wishes known. Subsequently, another notice from Trabzon was sent to the *muhtar*. The notice described what each family that chose to emigrate would be given in Cyprus. Specifically, the *muhtar* told the villagers that the government was promising each family a furnished home, 50 donums of land (5 Cypriot acres), a refrigerator and a television. In addition, the government was offering an allowance of 800 Turkish lira per month ($22) for about a year, until the peasants were fully settled in Cyprus. The government also promised to cover all the expenses involved in moving the villagers to Cyprus.

Seventy of the 150 families living in Kaliyan Çayirlik applied to emigrate to Cyprus, Akyüz said. On 6 January 1975, they left for the Trabzon recruitment center where they were issued passports. On 18 January 1975, they were taken from Trabzon to the port of Mersin. There, they were joined by about 130 other families. On 21 January, 200 families left by boat for Famagusta where they arrived the next day. After spending a few days at a Famagusta school which served as a transit center, they were transferred to the village of Vasilia in the Kyrenia district for permanent settlement. All travel and accommodation expenses from Trabzon to Famagusta were paid by the Turkish government, as promised, Akyüz said.

Other settlers have mentioned the transfer of as many as 2,000 settlers at a time from Turkey to Cyprus by boat. They have also stated that the expenses for travel and accommodations from their place of departure in Turkey to their destination in Cyprus were paid by the Turkish government.[18]

Once in Vasilia, Akyüz said, each family was given a home and an allowance of 800 lira per month for about a year, as promised. They were also provided with supplies of flour, macaroni and rice. Finally, the settlers were given land in proportion to the size of each family. On the average, a family would be given a total of 1.2 acres of land, which included a lemon grove, land with irrigation facilities and fields for the cultivation of grain.

The method of recruitment described revolved around a government promise of property and a better life in Cyprus. The villagers of Kaliyan Çayirlik appeared to have a choice concerning whether or not they wanted to settle in Cyprus. There were other cases, however, where the Turkish government employed a combination of promises and paternalistic persuasion which left the peasants little choice. In this regard, the case of a village in the Adana region is characteristic. Since the 1950s, a group of peasants in the Adana region had carried on a running dispute with the *aghas*—the landowners of the area—who claimed ownership of the land around their village. The case went to court and, after years of bureaucratic wrangling, the peasants learned they had lost the case in 1973.[19] In a report published in the Turkish-Cypriot press, these peasants described what had happened to them:

> The court decision was that the land we have been cultivating for 100 to 150 years belonged to the *aghas*. The government then sent the gendarmes against us. Our homes and our lands were confiscated and the government informed us that we were to be transferred elsewhere. In the meantime, there was the Turkish landing in Cyprus. So the following proposition was made to us [by the government]. You can go to the Amic valley in Hatay [Alexandretta], where there is plenty of land with electricity, water and roads. Or you could go to one of those villages in Cyprus. There, you will be given land, tractors, cars, credit and seed. Make up your mind quickly. Realizing that in either case we had to emigrate, we chose Cyprus.[20]

This account suggests that the settlement of these villagers in Cyprus was the result of Turkish government pressure to relocate. The relocation and forced migration of populations was a common practice in the Ottoman era.[21] This practice was continued, though on a much smaller scale, following the inception of the modern Turkish state in 1923.

Turkey's relocation policies have mainly affected the country's largest ethnic minority, the Kurds. Since 1925, the Turkish government has periodically implemented relocation programs affecting hundreds of thousands of Kurdish peasants in order to quell recurring Kurdish rebellions.[22] These programs have been part of a wider campaign to suppress Kurdish national identity and bring about the forced assimilation of the Kurdish minority into Turkish society. This minority is estimated to be about 10 million people, or 18 percent of the Turkish population.[23] In this campaign of assimilation, the Kurds of Turkey are euphemistically referred to as "mountain Turks"—*Dağ Türkleri*—or "easterners" (*Doğu'lu*).

The Turkish government policy of relocating Kurdish peasants is still continuing. Reportedly, in late October 1989, about 500 Kurdish farmers were forced to leave Dereköy, a village in southeastern Turkey. Turkish authorities have also ordered the evacuation of 10,000 Kurdish peasants from a total of 30 other villages.[24] In April 1990, the Turkish government gave additional powers to the governor of 11 southeastern provinces which are still under marshal law in an effort to step up its military campaign against Kurdish insurgents in these provinces.[25] Under these powers, the governor can order the evacuation of entire Kurdish villages and his decisions are not subject to appeal.[26]

A small number of settlers in occupied Cyprus are Kurds. This is indicated by the fact that nine of the 19 settlers who deserted to the Greek-Cypriot side in spring 1990 were Kurds. Three of them were baptized in the government-controlled area and became Christian Orthodox. None of the Kurdish deserters expressed a desire to return to Turkey as have several of the other settlers who have deserted the TRNC since 1975.[27] In all likelihood, there are 3,000 to 4,000 Kurdish soldiers among the 35,000 troops of the Turkish occupation force in Cyprus.[28] There are, however, no reports of any mass transfers of Kurdish settlers to the island.

Relocation programs have also affected other ethnic groups in Turkey besides the Kurds. In the 1920s, a group of Lazes, a small minority living in the Black Sea region, were relocated to eastern Thrace. Their native language, Laz, is Caucasian, but they now speak Turkish. Lazes also constituted the majority of the 3,000 settlers transferred to the islands of Imbros (Gökçeada) and Tenedos (Bozcaada) in 1964 and 1965 as part of a campaign begun in May 1964 by the Turkish government to Turkify these islands. The transfer was among a series of measures Ankara used to pressure the Greeks living on these islands and in Istanbul into leaving Turkey.[29] Within two decades, most of the Greeks had left both islands. According to a report of a neutral commission in 1934, Imbros and Tenedos had a combined Greek population of 8,100 that year.[30] By 1987, there were only 400 Greeks on Imbros and 150 on Tenedos, most of whom were elderly people. There are now 7,150 Turkish settlers on Imbros and 1,000 on Tenedos. Most of them settled after 1964 and took over the homes and property of the Greeks who had moved away.[31]

The Turkification campaign on Imbros and Tenedos was not unrelated to developments in Cyprus. In fact, it resulted from the rapid deterioration of Greek-Turkish relations following the outbreak of intercommunal violence in Cyprus during the 1963 Christmas holidays. The Turkish objective was not only to force the Greeks to leave Turkey, but also to pressure the Greek government to "restrain," as the Turkish government put it, the Makarios government in Nicosia. In its campaign on Imbros and Tenedos, Ankara was using the Greek minority in Turkey as a pressure point vis-à-vis Greece, as it had in 1955. As was the case in 1955, Greece was unable to provide any effective protection for the Greeks in Turkey who felt more or less abandoned by the government in Athens.

In 1975, in the aftermath of the Turkish invasion, the Turkish government relocated Lazes to Cyprus, a policy that had been so effective in Imbros and Tenedos.[32] They started arriving in Cyprus early in the year and settled in the Karpasia peninsula region. Following their arrival, most of the Greek Cypriots remaining in the area moved away. However, in 1976, 4,095 Greek Cypriots were still living in occupied Karpasia, mainly in the Rizokarpaso area.[33] One of the Greek Cypriots who had remained up to that year described his experiences as follows:

In March 1976, as my wife and three children were about to have dinner, we were paid a visit by two uniformed men. One was a Turkish-Cypriot policeman. The other was a Turk from Turkey. Speaking in Greek, the policeman told me that in one week's time, I would have to leave my home and go to the other [Greek-Cypriot] side. I asked why is it so? He told me that he was sorry, but those were his orders. If we don't leave, he said, the police cannot guarantee our security. We can take our furniture with us, he said, and left. In order to protect my family from the Laz settlers who had filled the area, we left our home for our side a week later.[34]

The total number of Lazes in occupied Cyprus today remains unclear, though it is certain that they represent a minority among the settlers. By 1990, only 593 Greek Cypriots remained in the Karpasia area.[35] The homes and property of the Greek Cypriots who left the area have been taken over by settlers from Turkey.

The examples of settlers in Cyprus from the Trabzon and Adana regions, the presence of Lazes and Kurds among the settlers, and the method of recruiting these settlers lead to the following observations:

First, the transfer of settlers to occupied Cyprus should be seen in the broader historical context of the Turkish policy of relocating populations for reasons of state. A primary objective of this policy has been the consolidation of a homogeneous Turkish nation which is not plagued by minority problems. Indeed, relocation of populations has allowed the Turkish state to initiate a Turkification process in territories where non-Turks constituted the majority. These territories include Alexandretta (Hatay) in the 1930s, Imbros and Tenedos in the 1960s, and occupied Cyprus in the 1970s.

Second, the colonization of Cyprus represents an official policy of the Turkish state. This policy has been planned and implemented by the Turkish government in cooperation with the Denktash regime. The Turkish government has had the power and authority, by virtue of being an occupying power, to promise and give the settlers land, homes, and movable property (such as cars and tractors) in occupied Cyprus that still legally belong to the Greek Cypriots.

Third, the major inducement for the peasants to leave their villages in Turkey and settle in occupied Cyprus has been the promise of a home and land. Without such an official promise by the Turkish government, it would have been problematic for whole families to leave their villages in Turkey in order to settle in Cyprus.

Fourth, the fact that the territory Turkey occupies in Cyprus is the most fertile on the island has made the migration of impoverished, landless peasants from Anatolia to Cyprus an even more attractive proposition than emigrating, for example, to Germany.

Fifth, the spoils of conquest in Cyprus suddenly made territory available for settlement. Turkey has been able to defuse domestic pressures emanating from the antagonisms between landowners and landless peasants, albeit to a very limited degree, by transferring peasants to the empty Greek villages and towns in Cyprus which are surrounded by fertile land.

SPATIAL DISTRIBUTION OF SETTLERS

As Turkey invaded Cyprus, 201,000 Greek-Cypriot refugees were forced to flee southward away from the advancing Turkish army. About 38,000 of them returned to their homes when they discovered that these homes were not in the occupied zone but were just south of the Attila line in the government-controlled area. Immediately following the invasion, 12,289 Greek Cypriots remained enclaved on the Karpasia peninsula. By 1990, about 11,700 of them had left for the free area. Therefore, about 174,700 Greek Cypriots fled from the Kyrenia, Nicosia, and Famagusta districts as a result of the invasion, leaving their empty housing behind them.

These Greek-Cypriot refugees had lived in a total of 142 villages, towns (*komopoleis*), and cities.[36] Ninety-three villages and seven towns had been exclusively Greek, while there had been a mixed population of Greek and Turkish Cypriots in 37 villages, three towns and two cities. In 27 of the villages where both Greek and Turkish Cypriots had lived, and in towns and cities where there had been a mixed population, over 75 percent of the population had been Greek. Fifty villages that became occupied had been inhabited exclusively by Turkish Cypriots before the invasion.

All available information indicates that the colonizers from Turkey settled in 62 villages, seven towns and three cities—72 localities in all. In the Kyrenia district, they settled in 18 villages, two towns and one city. In the Nicosia district, which was only partially occupied, they moved into nine villages, two towns and one city. In the Famagusta district, the colonizers settled in 35 villages, three towns and one city (see table 5).

TABLE 5: DISTRIBUTION OF SETTLERS IN OCCUPIED CYPRUS

DISTRICT	VILLAGES			TOWNS		CITIES
	Localities Settled	Settlers Only	Settlers & Turkish Cypriots	Settlers Only	Settlers & Turkish Cypriots	Settlers & Turkish Cypriots
Kyrenia	21	7	11		2	1
Nicosia	12	2	7		2	1
Famagusta	39	17	18	1	2	1
TOTAL	72	26	36	1	6	3

Given the scarcity of urban space for settlement on one hand and the availability of rural homes and land on the other, it was logical that the great majority of the colonizers would initially move into villages and towns, that is rural and semi-rural areas. In addition, land suitable for cultivation is inherently rural and it was precisely this type of land that the Turkish government wanted to make available to the landless Anatolian peasants. However, as Turkish Cypriots who are living in urban areas emigrate, more urban space is being made available for settlers. It is apparent that the Anatolian peasants have now settled in most areas of the occupied territory.

The city of Varosha in the Famagusta district was the largest urban center to be occupied by Turkish forces, but the downtown area has been excluded from the settlement program and has been a ghost town since August 1974. There have been reports, however, that there are settlers residing in the Varosha suburbs in sections which are separate from those inhabited by Turkish Cypriots. One of the areas is inhabited by immigrants from Antalya and is referred to as the neighborhood of the Antalyans. In Neapolis, a suburb of Nicosia, settlers are also residing separately from the Turkish Cypriots in their own neighborhoods. The Greeks living in Kyrenia up to July 1974—approximately 3,000—fled after the invasion, and their homes were taken over by retired military personnel from Turkey and Turkish Cypriots who were primarily from Limassol and Paphos.

About 60 percent of the settlers, or about 46,000, have settled in the Famagusta district which had a larger number of abandoned Greek villages and towns than the Kyrenia and Nicosia districts. The availability of land and houses in the Famagusta district was, therefore, greater. The remaining 28,000 settlers are living in the Kyrenia and Nicosia districts where they are distributed almost evenly with about 14,000 in each district.

Of the 62 villages where settlers reside, 26 (42 percent) have been settled exclusively by Anatolian peasants, including the town of Rizokarpaso. The remaining 36 villages are inhabited by a mixed population of Anatolian settlers and Turkish Cypriots. The same holds true for six of the seven towns which are occupied and the three occupied cities. (A list of the villages, towns, and cities where settlers reside appears in table 6.)

TABLE 6: RENAMED VILLAGES, TOWNS AND CITIES COLONIZED
BY ANATOLIAN SETTLERS IN OCCUPIED CYPRUS

NAME	OTTOMAN NAME	TURKISH NAME AFTER 1974	POPULATION COMPOSITION
		NICOSIA DISTRICT	
Avlona	Awlona	n.a.	M
Katokopia	Qato Qopya	Zümrütköy	S
Kythrea (town)	Kitrya	Değirmenlik	M
Masari		Sahinler	M
Morphou (town)	Omorfi	Güzelyurt	M
Nicosia (city)	Lefkoşa	Lefkoşa	M
Nikitas	Nikita	Güneşköy	M
Pentagia	Pendaya	Yeşilyurt	S

NAME	OTTOMAN NAME	TURKISH NAME AFTER 1974	POPULATION COMPOSITION
Philia	Filya	Serhadköy	M
Skylloura	Sqilori	Yilmazköy	M
Zodia (Kato)	Qado Zotya	Aş. Bostanci	M
Zodia (Pano)	Pano Zotya	Yu. Bastanci	M

KYRENIA DISTRICT

NAME	OTTOMAN NAME	TURKISH NAME AFTER 1974	POPULATION COMPOSITION
Agios Ambrosios	Aya Weres	Esentepe	S
Agios Georgios	Aya Yorgi	Karaoğlanoğlu	M
Agios Epiktitos		Çatalköy	M
Agios Ermolaos	Aya Rmola	Sirinevler	S
Chartzia	Kharcha	Karaağaç	M
Diorios	Yorgo	Tebebaşi	M
Kalogrea		Bahçeli	M
Kazafani	Qazafani	Ozanköy	M
Kyrenia (city)	Kirine	Gime	M
Klepini	Qlepini	Arapköy	M
Kontemenos	Qondemeno	Kördemen	S
Karavas (town)		Alsancak	M
Kormakitis	Qormakiti	Koruçam	M
Lapithos (town)	Lapita	Lapta	M
Lamakas Lapithou	Lamaqa	Kozan	S
Livera		Sadrazam Köy	S
Orka		Kayalar	S
Panagra		Geçitköy	M
Sychari		Kaynakköy	M
Thermia		Doğanköy	M
Vasilia	Wasilya	Karsiyaka	S

FAMAGUSTA DISTRICT

NAME	OTTOMAN NAME	TURKISH NAME AFTER 1974	POPULATION COMPOSITION
Acheritou		Güversinlik	S
Angastina	Anqastina	Aslanköy	S
Agios Andronikos	Aya Androniqo	Yeşilköy	M
Agios Georgios	Aya Yorgi	Aygün	M
Agios Elias	Ayo Ilya	Yarköy	S
Agios Theodoros	Aya Totoros	Çayirova	M
Agia Trias		Sipahi	S
Akanthou (town)	Aqattu	Tatlisu	M
Davlos	Dawlod	Kaplica	M
Eptakomi	Eftaqomi	Yedikonuk	M
Famagusta (suburbs)		Magosa	M
Flamoudi		Mersinlik	S
Gaidouras	Gaydura	Korkuteli	S
Gastria	Qastrya	Kalecik	S
Gypsou	Ipsoz	Akova	M

NAME	OTTOMAN NAME	TURKISH NAME AFTER 1974	POPULATION COMPOSITION
Koilanemos	Kilanemos	Esenköy	S
Koma Yialou	Qomiyoli	Kumyali	M
Komi Kepir	Qomi Kebir	Büyükkonuk	M
Kontea	Qondeya	Türkmenköy	M
Lapathos	Lapatoz	Boğaziçi	M
Leonarissos	Leonariso	Ziyamet	S
Limnia	Limnya	Mormenekşe	M
Lysi (town)	Lisi	Akdoğan	M
Marathovounos	Maratowuno	Ulukisla	M
Melia	Milya	Yildirim	M
Mousoulita	Musilida	Kurudere	S
Neta		Taslika	S
Patriki	Padriki	Tuzluca	S
Prasteio	Prastyo	Dörtyol	S
Pyrga	Pirga	Pirham	S
Rizokarpaso (town)		Dipkarpaz	S
Spathariko	Ispatriqo	Otüken	M
Stylloi	Istilloz	Mutluyaka	S
Tavrou	Tawri	Pamuklu	M
Trikomo (town)	Triqomo	Iskele	M
Vasili	Wasili	Gelincik	M
Vathylakas	Watilaqa	Derince	S
Vatyli	Wadili	Vadili	M
Voukolida	Woqolida	Bafra	S

KEY: S: Settlers only; M: Mixture of settlers and Turkish Cypriots

NOTE: In table 6, the villages, towns and cities are presented using their historic Greek names (left column); their Ottoman names, which are identical to or are derived from the Greek names (middle column); and the new Turkish names they have had since 1974 (right column). The Ottoman names and most of the Turkish names are found in the study by I. P. Theocharides, *Names of Villages in the Occupied Area of Cyprus According to Ottoman Documents* (Nicosia: Kailas Press, 1980). The Turkish names are also found on the maps of occupied Cyprus published by the Denktash regime after the 1974 invasion. See *Tourist Map of the "Turkish Federated State of Cyprus,"* TFSC "Ministry of Tourism and Information" (Nicosia, 1976).

The fact that such a large number of the settlers from Turkey live separately from the Turkish Cypriots is an additional indication that these settlers could not have been Turkish-Cypriots who emigrated to Turkey and later returned to the villages in Cyprus where they had formerly lived. Turkish-Cypriot society remains, to a large extent, a traditional society. Family ties still form the basis for group loyalty. As in other Muslim societies, the family in Turkish-Cypriot society has a patriarchal structure and the family unit is still an extended one.[37] The official position of the Turkish government has been that most of the 250,000 to 500,000 Turkish-Cypriots it claimed were living in Turkey still had family members living in Cyprus.[38] If this had been the case, it would have been inconceivable for returning Turkish-Cypriot immigrants to settle in villages inhabited exclusively by settlers rather than return to their villages to join their extended families.

NOTES

[1] Halil Inalcik, "Ottoman Methods of Conquest," *Studia Islamica* 2 (1954): 123.

[2] *Official Gazette*, "Turkish Federated State of Cyprus," Nicosia, 25 February 1975.

[3] Ibid.

[4] On the settlement of retired army officers who were leading figures of TMT, see *Sunday Times*, London, 26 September, 1976.

[5] According to Turkish-Cypriot official Osman Örek, the migrants from Turkey were "seasonal workers who arrived for crop-gathering and returned home at the end of their contract." *The Guardian*, 15 October 1975.

[6] See the testimony by Rozanne Ridgway, Assistant Secretary of State for European and Canadian Affairs, before the Subcommittee on Europe and the Middle East of the Committee on Foreign Affairs, House of Representatives, Washington, D.C., 19 June 1986, 51-52. In 1983, the State Department estimated the number of settlers to be around 25,000. See the testimony by Special Cyprus Coordinator Richard M. Haas before the Subcommittee on Europe and the Middle East of the Committee on Foreign Affairs, House of Representatives, Washington, D.C., 2 November 1983, 27.

[7] See *Foreign Affairs Committee Report on Cyprus*, (London: HMSO, May 1987), xvii.

[8] See note 13, chapter 2.

[9] In February 1990, *Yenidüzen* reported that the Denktash administration had not disclosed the results of the census conducted on 14 January 1990 because the figures demonstrated a "striking change in the structure of the population. Of the 160,000 persons who continue to live in the TRNC, 80,000 are Turkish Cypriots and 80,000 are mainland settlers." See *Yenidüzen*, 14 February 1990.

[10] Reported in the Turkish-Cypriot newspaper *Soz*, 18 April 1980. See also *Yenidüzen*, 2 February 1990.

[11] Referring to the settlers in an interview with the Turkish newspaper *Güneş*, Istanbul, 3 March 1990, Turkish-Cypriot opposition leader Özker Özgür said "they are uneducated, they support polygamy and they are

influenced by religion." Concerning the reports that some settlers practice polygamy, see Robert McDonald, *The Problem of Cyprus*, Adelphi Paper No. 234 (London: International Institute of Strategic Studies, Winter 1988/89), 21.

[12]In May 1978, the late Dr. Fazil Küçük, the Turkish-Cypriot leader who died on 22 January 1984, wrote a series of articles critical of the settlers and their "immoral behavior." See the Turkish-Cypriot newspaper *Halkin Sesi*, 24 and 25 May 1978. The well-known Turkish journalist Mehmed Ali Birand wrote an article in the Turkish newspaper *Milliyet*, Istanbul, 13 March 1984, in which he referred to the friction between the settlers and many Turkish Cypriots. He was critical of the settlers' "arrogant behavior." A week earlier, the Turkish newspaper, *Günaydin*, Istanbul, 3 March 1984, also reported that many Turkish Cypriots were dissatisfied with the settlers. See similar reports in the Turkish-Cypriot newspaper *Ortam*, 10 and 26 June 1985, and *Yenidüzen*, 27 January 1986. On the same subject, see Tozun Bahcheli, *Greek-Turkish Relations since 1955* (Boulder, Colo.: Westview Press, 1990), 111-112.

[13]Bahcheli, ibid., 111-112.

[14]Throughout the summer of 1989, the Denktash regime made a concerted effort to mobilize Turkish-Cypriot political, cultural and professional associations in support of the settlement of Bulgarian Muslims in the TRNC. See *Halkin Sesi*, 15 and 22 June 1989; *Birlik*, 24 June 1989; and *Ortam*, 6 June 1989.

[15]See the Turkish-Cypriot newspaper *Kibris*, 24 June 1990.

[16]Several settlers who deserted to the Greek-Cypriot side told authorities that they were informed about the opportunity to settle in Cyprus either through announcements in the media or through announcements by the village *muhtar*. For instance, Sepahetin Serin, a settler from the Selefke region who deserted in 1982, stated that he had heard about the settlement opportunity in an announcement on the radio. Yusuf Veli Akyüz from the Trabzon region, who deserted the TRNC in 1978, said he was told about settling in Cyprus by his village *muhtar*. Information about Sepahetin Serin is based on confidential interviews conducted in Cyprus in May 1990. Information about Yusuf Veli Akyüz has been published in *Colonization of Occupied Cyprus*, 13-15.

[17]Ibid., 13-15. At the time of his defection, Akyüz was serving as a soldier in an army contingent, comprised of settlers and Turkish Cypriots, in the TFSC. His basic reason for defecting was what he called "oppression and barbarism" in the army and the torture he suffered at the hands of the police when he was arrested following a fight at a wedding he was attending. He was also disillusioned by the poor economic conditions prevailing

in the TFSC. In 1981, Akyüz returned to occupied Cyprus. He deserted once more to the Greek-Cypriot side on 5 May 1988. On 7 July 1988, the Cypriot government deported Akyüz to Turkey via Athens.

[18]Sepahetin Serin and Ösgur Kamisioğlu, settlers who deserted to the Greek side, said they boarded the ferryboat "Truva" (Troy) in Mersin in March 1975 along with 2,000 other settlers "without paying a ticket." Kamisioğlu said he made the trip with his father Zahit. This information is based on confidential interviews conducted in Cyprus in May 1990.

[19]This incident should be seen in the wider context of the highly uneven distribution of land ownership in Turkey. In 1973, the landowners with the largest holdings constituted only three percent of all farm owners, but these landowners controlled about 30 percent of all cultivated land and received 33 percent of total agricultural income. Moreover, between 1963 and 1973, there appeared to be a substantial rise in the number of landless peasants and agricultural laborers. See Robert Bianci, *Interest Groups and Political Development in Turkey* (Princeton: Princeton University Press, 1984), 63-64.

[20]See *Soz*, 18 April 1980.

[21]Ömer L. Barkan, "Les Déportations comme Méthode de Peuplement et de Colonisation dans l'Empire Ottoman," *Revue de la Faculté des Sciences Economiques de l'Université d'Istanbul* 2 (1946-1950): 524-569. See also Inalcik, "Ottoman Methods of Conquest," 103-129.

[22]William E. Hazen, "Minorities in Revolt: The Kurds of Iran, Iraq, Syria and Turkey," in *The Political Role of Minority Groups in the Middle East,* ed. R.D. McLaurin (New York: Praeger, 1979), 52.

[23]Regarding the estimates of the Kurdish population in Turkey, see *Wall Street Journal,* New York, 14 September 1988; *Christian Science Monitor,* Boston, 25 August 1989; *New York Times,* New York, 3 November 1989; and *Washington Times,* Washington, D.C., 2 March 1990. In a report from Turkey on 11 April 1990, *The Wall Street Journal* reported that "the Kurds may constitute 20 percent of the country's population." In addition to the 10 million Kurds in Turkey, there are 5.6 million Kurds in Iran and 3.5 million in neighboring Iraq. Iraq has engaged in systematic repression of the Kurds who demand autonomous status. The Iraqi government has reportedly destroyed large numbers of Kurdish villages in order to enforce a relocation program aimed at creating a Kurd-free buffer zone along Iraq's border with Turkey. It is also widely documented that the Iraqi army used chemical weapons against the Kurds on two occasions in 1988. In March 1988, several thousand Kurds died when the city of Halabja was bombed. In September 1988, about 50,000 Iraqi Kurds fled to Turkey in order to escape an Iraqi army assault. The U.S. government has asserted that Iraq

used poison gas against the Kurds during these attacks. See the reports in the *New York Times*, 9 September to 19 September 1988; 31 March 1989; 3 November 1989; and *Christian Science Monitor*, 31 August 1989.

[24]Reported in the *Baltimore Sun*, Baltimore, 10 November 1989.

[25]Clyde Haberman, "On Iraq's Other Front," *New York Times Magazine*, New York, 19 November 1990, 46.

[26]On the latest developments surrounding the suppression of Kurdish national culture in Turkey, the Kurdish insurgency in the eastern provinces, and the campaign by the Turkish military to defeat the Kurdish guerrillas, see *New York Times*, 3 November 1989, 6 February 1990 and 17 June 1990; *Christian Science Monitor*, 15 August 1989 and 27 March 1990; "The Dirty War in Kurdistan: Murder, Torture and Abuse in a Forgotten Place," *Newsweek* (21 May 1990): 20. For a more general account of the history of the suppression of Kurdish culture in Turkey, including proscribing the use of the Kurdish language, see Martin Short and Anthony McDermott, *The Kurds* (London: Minority Rights Group, 1981), 4-7. See also Martin Short and Anthony McDermott, *Destroying Ethnic Identity: The Kurds of Turkey* (New York: Helsinki Watch Report, March 1988).

[27]These nine Kurdish settlers sought and were granted asylum by the Cypriot government. Temur Okal, Süleyman Cian, and Nesmetin Fikret were baptized and given the Christian names Christos Andreou, Nikos Ioannou and Kyriakos Sophokleous, respectively. Hüseyin Donan, Celal Ozpei, Attila Kurt, Fahretin Tip, Ertogan Inik and Yusuf Nurcin were not baptized or given new names. This information is based on confidential interviews conducted in Cyprus in May 1990.

[28]This figure is based on the estimate that about 10 percent of the conscripts in the Turkish army are ethnic Kurds. See Mehmed Ali Birand, *The Generals' Coup in Turkey: An Inside Story of 12 September 1980* (London: Brassey's Defence Publishers, 1987), 39.

[29]On the Greeks of Imbros and Tenedos and the measures adopted by the Turkish government to pressure them to leave these islands, see Alexis Alexandris, "To Meionotiko Zetema, 1954–1987" (The Minority Question, 1954-1987), in *Elleno-Tourkikes Scheseis: 1923-1987* (Greek-Turkish Relations 1923 1987), eds. Alexis Alexandris et al. (Athens: Gnosis Publishers, 1988), 515-523. See also Alexis Alexandris, "Imbros and Tenedos; A Study in Turkish Attitudes toward Two Ethnic Greek Island Communities since 1923," *Journal of the Hellenic Diaspora* 71 (1980): 5-31, and Alexis Alexandris, *The Greek Minority in Istanbul and Greek-Turkish Relations, 1918-1974* (Athens: Center for Asia Minor Studies, 1983), 280-283.

[30]See Alexandris, *The Greek Minority*, 143.

[31]See Alexandris, "To Meionotiko Zetema," 518-519.

[32]The arrival of thousands of settlers in Cyprus in 1975 prompted speculation in the Western media as to their place of origin in Turkey. One of the first reports that Lazes were settling in the Karpasia region was "Unwanted Minority 'Dumped' in Cyprus," *The Guardian*, 13 October 1975. This was also reported in the BBC program "The World Today," 15 October 1975. Both reports said that a large number of the settlers were Lazes. They were described as a "rather mysterious people from a northern Black Sea coast."

[33]This figure represents a Cypriot government estimate which is consistent with the UNFICYP estimate.

[34]Interview by the author with K.G. in Limassol, Cyprus, 18 May 1990. Since he left his home in Karpasia in 1976, K.G. has lived in Limassol and works there as a taxi driver.

[35]See "Report of the UN Secretary-General on the United Nations Operations in Cyprus," S/21340, New York, 31 May 1990.

[36]A *komopolis* (pl. *komopoleis*) is a rural center where the population is primarily engaged in agriculture. The population of a *komopolis* can exceed that of a city. A city, however, is the administrative center of a district. For example, Kyrenia, with a population of slightly more than 3,700, was a city, while Morphou, with a population of 7,000, was a *komopolis*.

[37]On the traditional structure of the Turkish-Cypriot family and the "modified extended family," see Vamik Volkan, *Cyprus—War and Adaptation: A Psychoanalytic History of Two Ethnic Groups in Conflict* (Charlottesville: University of Virginia Press, 1979), 53-60.

[38]See *Turkey and Cyprus: A Survey of the Cyprus Question*, 23.

4

The War Years, EOKA and Pan-Turkism

The mass transfer of Anatolian settlers to occupied Cyprus was bound to have a profound political, economic and social effect on the TRNC. The Turkish government claims that the TRNC is an independent state deserving international recognition, but Ankara's settler policy raises the question of whether the Turkish Cypriots, those claiming to have founded the TRNC, actually have political autonomy as a community. In the 1950s, Turkish irredentism advocated the territorial and political union of Cyprus with Turkey. Turkey seemed willing to accept *taksim*, or the partition of Cyprus, but considered it to be a significant concession. Both union with Turkey and partition involve the integration of the Turkish-Cypriot community with Turkey and its absorption by Turkey, with the Turkish Cypriots simply becoming Turks living in a Turkish province.

The political status of the Turkish-Cypriot community was complex even before the TRNC was established in 1983, and it has become particularly complex since then. Despite the fact that the TRNC is recognized only by Turkey, which was instrumental in its creation to start with, it has created the domestic infrastructure and administrative apparatus that characterize a state, including a constitution; executive, legislative and judicial branches of government; a police force; armed forces; a central bank and a customs authority.

The analysis and interpretation of the political and social status of ethnic and religious groups within a state is a complex exercise filled with pitfalls. This is especially so in the Middle East where an ethnic and religious mosaic involves complicated interrelationships among groups within each society. It is with this in mind that the political ties between the Turkish Cypriots and Turkey are examined. These ties have developed along two dimensions. The first dimension concerns the subordination of the Turkish-Cypriot community to Turkey. The second pertains to the legal and political incorporation of the settlers from Anatolia into the TRNC.

THE ENOSIS MOVEMENT

An examination of Turkish-Cypriot ties with Turkey requires a review of the Turkish-Cypriot community in the 1950s, the period when Turkish Cypriots became politically active. It is also necessary to briefly examine Ankara's position on the Cyprus issue in the periods during and after the Second World War, and in the period preceding the EOKA campaign which began in 1955.

Up until the 1950s, Turkish-Cypriot society lagged behind that of the Greek Cypriots in terms of political mobilization and organization. Historical, social and economic factors accounted for the later development of the Turkish-Cypriot community's nationalist ideology and its more gradual political mobilization.[1] The intense politicization of this community by the mid-1950s occurred under crisis circumstances caused by the anti-colonial campaign of EOKA (*Ethnike Organosis Kyprion Agoniston*, or the National Organization of Cypriot Fighters) and the intercommunal conflict. Since that time, the Turkish-Cypriot body politic and its elite have developed close ties with the Turkish military and have become increasingly dependent on it.

The EOKA military campaign opposing British rule in Cyprus started on 1 April 1955 under the leadership of General George Grivas. He adopted the *nom de guerre* "Digenis," the name of a Byzantine hero who became legendary, and subsequently became known as George Grivas-Digenis. Politically, the Greek Cypriots were led by Archbishop Makarios, the head of the Greek Orthodox Church of Cyprus, who represented them in the capacity of ethnarch. Both EOKA and Archbishop Makarios enjoyed overwhelming popular support. Makarios, who was to become the first president of Cyprus in 1960 when it became a republic, was a charismatic leader who commanded the support and loyalty of the vast majority of Greek Cypriots for 25 years.

The objective of EOKA was to force the British to grant Cyprus the right to self-determination which was bound to lead to *Enosis*, or union, with Greece. In a plebiscite sponsored by the Greek Orthodox Church of Cyprus on 15 January 1950, 95.7 percent of the 244,747 eligible Greek-Cypriot voters cast their ballots in favor of *Enosis.* The *Enosis* movement was a manifestation of the ideology of modern Greek nationalism.[2] Up until 1922, Greek nationalism had revolved around the *Megali Idea* (the Great Idea). The *Megali Idea* was an ideal of Greek irredentist nationalism which aimed at liberating the unredeemed Greeks under Ottoman Turkish rule—including the Greeks of Cyprus—and creating *Megali Ellas* (Great Hellas), a revived Byzantium. The pursuit of the *Megali Idea* and the dream of Great Hellas were buried in 1922 when the Greek forces marching toward Ankara were defeated and destroyed by the army of Kemal Atatürk, the founder of modern Turkey and its first president (1923 to 1938). This monumental Greek defeat, known as the *Mikrasiatike Katastrophe* (the Asia Minor Catastrophe), deprived the *Megali Idea* of its raison d'être which was the redemption of the Greek populations of Asia Minor. As a result of the Greek defeat and the population exchange that followed, about 1.4 million Greeks left Turkey for Greece.

The question of Cyprus remained open, however, because the island had been a British colony since 1878. In 1922, the Greek majority of the island represented 78.8 percent of the population, while the Turks represented 19.7 percent. After 1922, the Greek-Cypriot community began to intensify its nationalist agitation by demanding *Enosis* more vociferously. Led by the Greek Orthodox Church, Greek-Cypriot nationalists staged a rebellion in October 1931 which was put down by the British. The *Enosis* movement was temporarily suppressed.

During the Second World War, the Greeks and the Greek Cypriots had high hopes that the British would facilitate *Enosis* in the event of an allied victory. In the Greek mind, the sacrifices of the Greek nation during the war, in and of themselves, were enough to neutralize any claims Turkey might have had concerning Cyprus. According to Greek logic, Turkey's deliberate decision to stay out of the war and not oppose the Nazis disqualified it from becoming a beneficiary of any post-war settlement. Turkey's calculations were quite different, however, since Cyprus was very much on the Turkish mind as Ankara maneuvered its way very dexterously through the war years.

Turkey's stand during the war has been characterized as one of the "evasive neutral."[3] On 18 June 1941, however, nine weeks after Nazi Germany attacked and occupied Greece, Turkey signed a 10-year non-aggression pact with Germany.[4] Four days later, on 22 June 1941, Germany invaded the Soviet Union. The Turkish government's stand toward Nazi Germany can be described as one of sympathetic ambivalence. This attitude allowed Turkey to behave throughout the war in a way that did not alienate it from the allies, especially Britain. Ankara had a definite interest in not being excluded from the redrawing of the map of territories around Turkey after the war, whatever its outcome might be.

The role of Pan-Turkish irredentism was not an insignificant factor in Turkish diplomatic maneuvering during the war.[5] Pan-Turkish groups in Turkey favored Nazi Germany and hoped that a German victory would allow Turkey to reap territorial benefits from the Dodecanese islands and Cyprus, and from areas where Turkic groups resided—the southern part of the Soviet Union, northwestern Iran and northern Iraq.[6]

The extent to which these Pan-Turkish ambitions dictated the government's policy during the war remains a matter of controversy. The author of *The Evasive Neutral,* Frank Weber, argues that Pan-Turkish (Pan-Turanian) considerations carried considerable weight in Turkish government calculations:

British as well as German sources strongly suggest that Pan-Turanianism [Pan-Turkism] was not simply a mass enthusiasm popularly engendered, but an official program of the Turkish government, continuously though surreptitiously cultivated. Ankara preferred to use subordinate diplomats or non-official spokesmen in order to obscure the origins of the Pan-Turanian movement, but there was little doubt that those origins were in the highest echelons of the Turkish leadership.[7]

With this in mind, one can better evaluate Turkish concern over the future of Cyprus in a post-war settlement.

Pro-Greek feelings were evoked among the allies, especially the British public, by Greece's resistance against fascist Italy and Nazi Germany, and by the fact that the Greek army fought side-by-side with British forces against the Germans in Greece. In addition, Greek-Cypriot volunteers fought along with the British forces in Greece and in North Africa. About 20,000 Greek Cypriots enlisted in the British army and formed the "Cyprus Regiment" which came under the British Middle East Command. About 2,500 of them were killed, wounded or taken prisoner.[8] It was in the context of Graeco-British brotherhood in battle that Greece brought the Cyprus issue to the surface during the war. Greece stated publicly that it expected the allies, Britain in particular, to recognize Greek sacrifices for the common cause, and, as the Greeks put it, "award" Cyprus, a British colony, to Greece.[9] After all,

Greek thinking went, union with Greece was also the wish of the great majority of the Cypriot population—the Greek Cypriots.

These developments alarmed Turkey which had been watching the war from its neutral position. There was great concern in Ankara that Britain might adopt a pro-Greek stand on the Cyprus issue. Consequently, Turkey impressed upon Britain that it would never acquiesce to any British policy which might lead Cyprus into union with Greece in a post-war settlement.[10] Turkey's evasive neutrality allowed the government in Ankara to perform a delicate balancing act with regard to the Cyprus issue, as it managed to maintain rather positive relations with Britain while maintaining its sympathetic ambivalence toward Germany. Turkey believed that Germany would enjoy supremacy in the eastern Mediterranean if it won the war, and this would force Britain to dispose of Cyprus in a fashion favoring Pan-Turkish ambitions. These ambitions were clearly expressed by the renowned Pan-Turkish theoretician Hüseyin Nihal Atziz who admired Hitler and wanted Turkey to become an ally of Nazi Germany. Writing during the war, Atziz said Cyprus would be one of the primary benefits to accrue to Turkey if Ankara were to enter into an alliance with Hitler and the Axis then proved to be victorious. Atziz wrote: "At the end of this war, we can at least conquer Cyprus, Syria, Iraq, Iran and the Russian Azerbaijan...."[11] The Turkish government did not rush to embrace Atziz's extremism. It did, however, keep an eye on Cyprus which had been at the top of Atziz's list of coveted territories.

The British decision to rebuff Greek demands for *Enosis* and hold onto Cyprus following the war did placate Turkey in the war's immediate aftermath. But, as a consequence of Britain's determination to keep its colonial possession, Greek-Cypriot agitation resumed after the war and culminated in the EOKA guerrilla movement of 1955. As the Greek-Cypriot campaign against British rule intensified, British forces in Cyprus were unable to suppress the popular anti-colonial movement and defeat the EOKA guerrillas. Britain, therefore, was eager to see Turkey pressure Greece even more in international fora—especially the United Nations—to stop advocating the right of the Greek Cypriots to self-determination and to cease its support for EOKA.

In an attempt to contain Greece's support for the Greek-Cypriot cause and counter the EOKA campaign more effectively, the British government solicited and received Turkish support for its policy on the

Cyprus issue. In addition to pouring more troops into Cyprus, Britain took a series of calculated measures leading to Anglo-Turkish collaboration against EOKA, a move which precipitated violent conflict between Greek and Turkish Cypriots.[12]

What is most significant is that Turkey has maintained an active interest in Cyprus since the Second World War that has been internally motivated and has only partially been a reaction to the Greek demand for *Enosis*. In other words, Turkish irredentism in the direction of Cyprus has exhibited remarkable continuity since the beginning of the Second World War. This irredentism, driven by Pan-Turkish considerations, became much more forceful in the immediate aftermath of the EOKA campaign. But, certainly, Turkey's interest in Cyprus and its explicit territorial ambitions concerning the island preceded the EOKA campaign by at least 15 years. The Greek-Cypriot decision to resort to armed struggle in 1955 to achieve *Enosis* intensified Graeco-Turkish antagonism over Cyprus, but it was not the causal factor behind Turkey's territorial ambitions on the island.

When the founders of EOKA, including Archbishop Makarios and George Grivas, were making secret preparations for the armed struggle, they perceived the EOKA campaign as being directed exclusively against the British. There was nothing in these preparations to suggest that EOKA's leadership had ill intentions with respect to the Turkish Cypriots or planned any hostile action against them. In fact, the prevailing attitude on the part of the founders of EOKA was that the Turkish Cypriots would remain neutral in the struggle against the British. Therefore, they saw no reason to be concerned about how the Turkish Cypriots would react to the anti-colonial campaign. EOKA founders believed there was no need to prepare any contingency plans to deal with a possible outbreak of Turkish-Cypriot violence.

This attitude was expressed clearly in a historic document of EMAK (*Ethnikon Metopon Apeleutheroseos Kyprou*, or the National Front for the Liberation of Cyprus). Up through January 1955, the secret organization preparing the guerrilla campaign against the British in Cyprus was called EMAK. It was renamed EOKA by Grivas sometime in February 1955. Among the founders and key leaders of EMAK were the Cypriot-born brothers Savvas and Socrates Loizides, lawyers who lived in Athens. On the night of 25 January 1955, Socrates Loizides and other members of EMAK waited on a remote beach in the Paphos district of Cyprus for the arrival of a caique from Greece loaded with arms and ammunition. Somehow, the British were informed of the operation, and they arrested Loizides and captured the caique. In Loizides's briefcase they found a document that described the purpose and objectives of EMAK. It presented the organization's position toward the Turkish Cypriots, the Communist party (AKEL) and other political parties in Cyprus, civil servants, policemen, and anyone else who might betray EMAK. The tone of the document was conciliatory toward the Turkish Cypriots in general. Referring to the Turkish Cypriots, the document stated the following:

The policy of EMAK toward the Turks:

We see the Turks as brothers. We have nothing against them and we shall not do any harm to them. We are asking them not to disturb us, not to stand in our way, not to become instruments of the British and not to aid them against our struggle. They [the Turks] should rest assured that after liberation we are going to live in peace and love, all of us together, as Cypriots, Greeks and Turks alike. Turks and Greeks are compatriots and they have to live freely in peace and brotherhood. The British are foreigners. They are the enemies of all of us as they are attempting to divide us. They have to go.[13]

The document was clearly anti-communist. Its attitude toward the communists and their party, AKEL, was hostile in tone and sounded a warning to them. Unlike the Turkish Cypriots, they were not called "brothers." They were asked not to oppose EMAK or get involved in the liberation struggle. "There should be no doubt that AKEL and its followers ought not to get involved in our revolutionary struggle. Their involvement is both unnecessary and it will harm our struggle. Their non-involvement will constitute their most patriotic act," the document stated.[14]

EOKA's initial policy toward the Turkish Cypriots was similar to the one expressed in the EMAK document. The Turkish-Cypriot community was not harmed and was kept out of the conflict with the British.[15] However, on 30 June 1955, three months after the EOKA campaign began, supporters of Turkish-Cypriot leader Dr. Fazil Küçük circulated leaflets throughout Cyprus calling on the Turkish-Cypriot youth to oppose EOKA. A week later, new Turkish-Cypriot leaflets were urging the Greek Orthodox Church of Cyprus to stop its involvement in politics and were calling on the British to ban the raising of Greek flags in Cyprus. In July 1955, in response to these leaflets, EOKA issued its own leaflet in Turkish which was circulated in the

Turkish sector of Nicosia.[16] It explained that EOKA's struggle was not directed against the Turkish Cypriots but only against British colonialism. EOKA's policy toward the Turkish-Cypriot community was explained in the leaflet as follows:

Our intentions toward the Turkish inhabitants of the island are pure and friendly. We are looking at the Turks as our genuine friends and allies and, as far as we are concerned and to the extent it is in our power, we will not condone any harm whatsoever against their life, dignity, honor and property.[17]

While EOKA followed this policy with respect to the Turkish-Cypriot community in general, the organization found it necessary to take action against a very limited number of individual Turkish Cypriots, not because of their ethnicity, but because they were engaged in specific activities against EOKA. Most of these Turkish Cypriots were policemen serving in the British Special Branch, the police intelligence bureau which made widespread use of torture in interrogating EOKA prisoners. Since very few British intelligence officers spoke Greek, Turkish-Cypriot policemen who spoke it were used extensively by the Special Branch as interrogators.[18] Throughout the EOKA campaign, its leader, Grivas-Digenis, issued several leaflets presenting detailed information on armed attacks against Greek Cypriots by Turkish-Cypriot policemen and on the torture of EOKA prisoners by these policemen in the context of Britain's anti-EOKA campaign. This information included dates, locations and names.[19] The first Turkish-Cypriot policeman to be deliberately targeted for execution because of specific acts against EOKA was Police Sergeant Abdullah Ali Riza. He was shot dead by EOKA outside his house in Paphos on 11 January 1956.[20]

EOKA's use of force against certain Turkish-Cypriots was not unlike the violence it employed against specific categories of Greek Cypriots who had been actively engaged in the anti-EOKA campaign of the British forces. EOKA targeted and executed Greek-Cypriot policemen and colonial bureaucrats who committed specific offenses against the organization, often involving the betrayal of EOKA members.[21] EOKA actually executed a much larger number of Greek Cypriots than it did Turkish Cypriots.

In the document found in Loizides's briefcase, EMAK established its policy toward Greek policemen and bureaucrats working for the colonial government. EMAK stated that it understood their situation as government employees, and, therefore, it did not ask them to join the organization or quit their jobs. EMAK asked them, however, to refuse to collaborate with the colonial authorities or become instruments of the campaign against EMAK (later EOKA). EMAK warned these policemen and bureaucrats that they would be punished if they did.[22]

The Greek-Cypriot community conformed to EOKA's overall policy of not involving the Turkish-Cypriot community, as such, in the conflict. The policy was sabotaged, however, by the Anglo-Turkish alliance against EOKA. As a consequence, by 1957, EOKA was forced to reverse its original policy and fight a struggle on two fronts, one against the British and one against the Turkish Cypriots. In the final analysis, the Greek side had to fight a powerful Anglo-Turkish alliance at the local, regional and international levels, and on the political, diplomatic, and military fronts.

The Turkish-Cypriot leadership did everything in its power to assist the colonial government in its military campaign against EOKA and further its efforts to suppress the popular movement supporting and sustaining the organization.[23] In the fall of 1955, the British authorities formed the "Auxiliary Police Force" and the "Mobile Reserve Force," both manned exclusively by Turkish Cypriots. The objective of these two forces, totalling 3,000 policemen, was to fight along with the British against the EOKA movement. In essence, this meant fighting the Greek-Cypriot community. The target of the force became the Greek-Cypriots in general. EOKA and the Greek Cypriots were left with no choice but to fight back against this Anglo-Turkish military front. In the process, the dispute in Cyprus, which started as an anti-colonial movement, increasingly assumed the character of an ethnic conflict between Greeks and Turks. This was precisely what the British and the Turks had expected.

The Turkish-Cypriot leadership and the Turkish government considered EOKA to be their arch enemy. Not only was the organization advancing the cause of *Enosis,* which was anathema to the Turks, but it was killing Turks as well. Irrespective of what acts Turkish policemen had committed against Greeks, even if they had killed or tortured them, the killing of a Turkish-Cypriot policeman by EOKA was interpreted as an attack against the Turkish-Cypriot community. From the Turkish perspective, EOKA killed these policemen precisely because they were Turks. Regardless of what EOKA's intentions toward the Turkish-Cypriot *community* might have been, the perception of the Turkish-Cypriot leadership was that EOKA was a deadly enemy that had to be dealt with accordingly. On the other hand, Greek Cypriots deeply resented the fact that Turkish Cypriots were siding with the British and fighting along with them against an anti-colonial movement.

EOKA was unprepared for the formation of the Anglo-Turkish alliance and the active role the Turkish-Cypriot community had started playing in the fight against the organization. This constitutes additional evidence that EOKA had not planned to harm the Turkish-Cypriot community. It was not until 1957, two years after the EOKA campaign had started, that Grivas-Digenis drew up specific plans on how to confront the increasing Turkish violence against the Greeks.[24] This violence was fomented by the Turkish government mainly through two secret organizations in Cyprus—*Volkan* initially, and later TMT—and was encouraged by the British authorities. This explains why the Turkish Cypriots were able to sustain an aggressive posture against EOKA and the Greek-Cypriots between 1955 and 1958, even though they were outnumbered four to one. When EOKA began systematic retaliation against Turkish Cypriots during the summer of 1958, intercommunal violence killed 56 Greeks and 53 Turks. The higher number of casualties among the Greek majority suggests that the Turkish Cypriots were fighting the Greek Cypriots from a much stronger position than their numerical inferiority would suggest.

The Greek-Cypriot nationalist leadership and its supporters in Greece failed to anticipate the possibility that the EOKA campaign could become a catalyst for the strengthening and consolidation of an Anglo-Turkish alliance against the Greeks at all levels and in all fora. Indeed, it appears that the Greek side misread Turkey's intentions with regard to the Cyprus issue and believed that Turkey would have no reason to interfere in the dispute if the Turkish-Cypriot community in general were not harmed and were kept out of the fight against the British. However, both Britain and Turkey had different plans. They were close allies in NATO and even closer allies in the Baghdad Pact, an alliance of Britain, Turkey, Iraq, Iran and Pakistan, which was part of the West's "Northern Tier" strategy of containment of the Soviet Union. Britain and Turkey were also the major powers in the Baghdad Pact. Britain signed the pact on 30 March 1955, bringing it even closer to Turkey at precisely the time EOKA was starting its anti-British campaign in Cyprus. British and Turkish interests were converging to such an extent at the time that British Prime Minister Anthony Eden decided to give Ankara a critical voice in determining the future of the island. He, therefore, invited Turkey to participate, along with Britain and Greece, in the Tripartite Conference on Cyprus in London in

August 1955 (discussed in chapter 5). Turkey adopted the British position on the Cyprus issue by opposing EOKA and self-determination for the island, and by advocating the continuation of colonial rule.[25] To a very considerable degree, this Anglo-Turkish alliance enjoyed the support of NATO and the United States, and that of the anti-communist bloc in Europe and the Middle East. Thus, viewed from the broader context of military alliances at the peak of the Cold War, Greek Cypriots and Greeks put themselves in an impossible diplomatic position. On the battlefield in Cyprus itself, EOKA's brilliant performance in the art of guerrilla warfare proved extremely difficult for the British forces to handle. But it was a completely different story in the politico-diplomatic field where Makarios and the Greek government were unable to outmaneuver the formidable Anglo-Turkish front.

It was a contest that created a nightmare for Greek diplomacy as it followed a hopelessly contradictory course. On one hand, Greece was antagonizing the NATO alliance, which was vital to its national interests. On the other, it was supporting the Greek-Cypriot struggle for *Enosis*, a struggle which embodied the aspirations of the Greek nation and had captured the imagination of the Greek people. In the end, the Anglo-Turkish front and Cold War diplomacy won. The Greeks were the big losers when they signed the Zurich-London agreements in February 1959. These agreements were a diplomatic triumph for Turkey and a debacle for the Greek side. In addition, neither the Greek-Cypriot leadership nor the Greek government realized that Cyprus was one of the territories of the British Empire where the imperial policy of "divide and rule" ideally suited British objectives. In Cyprus, it was certain that the minority population—the Turks—could be counted on as an ally of the British in support of the continuation of colonial rule against the wishes of the majority—the Greeks.

When the armed struggle of EOKA was being planned, it was a grave miscalculation for the Greek-Cypriot leadership and the Greek government to misread the intentions of Turkey and Britain and fail to anticipate the Anglo-Turkish alliance concerning Cyprus. It was a miscalculation with disastrous consequences.

PAN-TURKISH IDEOLOGY AND CYPRUS

While the ideology of Greek irredentism (the *Megali Idea*) and the *Enosis* movement in Cyprus have received an extraordinary amount of scholarly attention, very little has been written about the ideology behind Turkey's policy on the Cyprus issue. Turkey's Cyprus policy is presented by Turkish officials and authors that do comment on it as primarily a reaction to the *Enosis* movement, which is seen as a manifestation of the *Megali Idea*. However, this policy has not emerged solely as a response to the *Megali Idea*.[26] Certainly, it has not evolved in an ideological vacuum. The most critical factor in the development of Turkey's policy toward Cyprus has been Pan-Turkish ideology. This ideology has been increasingly influenced by Turkish Islam which has played the other major role in the formulation of Turkey's Cyprus policy. Cyprus has, of course, been high on the Pan-Turkish agenda, but this does not necessarily imply that Pan-Turkish ideology emerged as a response to Greek irredentist nationalism.

Pan-Turkism is an extreme form of Turkish nationalism which promotes Turkish irredentism. It originated in the nineteenth century during the last decades of the Ottoman Empire.[27] The overall objective of Pan-Turkism, utopian as it may appear, is to somehow unite or bring under one roof the *Diş Türkler*—the "Outside Turks." According to Professor Jacob Landau, *Diş Türkler* "is a term frequently employed by Pan-Turkists in Turkey in recent years; it covers a wide range of groups comprising people of Turkic origins."[28] *Diş Türkler* are found in an area extending from Yugoslavia, Bulgaria, Greece and Cyprus to Iraq, Iran and the southern and central Asian regions of the Soviet Union, including Azerbaijan, Turkmenistan, Kazakhstan and Uzbekistan. In the early 1940s, when the Pan-Turkists were especially active, the "Outside Turks" living in Greece and Cyprus represented a very tiny percentage of the *Diş Türkler*, as they do now. At that time, the Pan-Turkists estimated that the overall number of "Outside Turks" was about 42 million, of whom only 200,000 or 0.4 percent lived in Greece and Cyprus.[29]

Pan-Turkism tends to glorify symbols of the Turks' ancient past as they marched westward from the central Asian region of the Altai and Ergenekon mountains to conquer Anatolia, most of the Middle East and the Balkans. One of the most distinct Pan-Turkish symbols is the *bozkurt*, the mythical grey wolf of the Asian steppes which, according to Turkish legend, led the early Turkish tribes in their march of conquest.[30] In Turkish lore, the Turkish tribe of Oguz Kağan had to leave the Ergenekon mountains and move westward early in the eighth century. A grey wolf led the tribe over a mountain path.[31] The *bozkurt*

Figure 1: The cover of the Pan-Turkish journal *Bozkurt*, first published between 1939 and 1942. The slogan on the top reads: *Her Irkin Üstünde Türk Irki* (The Turkish Race Above Any Other Race.) The head of the *bozkurt* (grey wolf) appears to the left under the title. *Bozkurt* was revived in 1972 and was published in Ankara and then in Konya until 1977.

became a fundamental symbol of Pan-Turkism in the twentieth century and it is still used by contemporary Pan-Turkists. An article published in the preeminent Pan-Turkish journal *Türk Kültürü* (Turkish Culture) in May 1967 is entitled *Bugünkü Mânâsi ile "Bozkurt"* (The Contemporary Meaning of the *"Bozkurt"*). The article presents three main guiding principles for Turkey, principles emanating from the symbol of the *bozkurt*. They are: (1) *Ata olorak bozkurt* (The *bozkurt* should be the father), (2) *Rehber olorak bozkurt* (The *bozkurt* should be the leader), and (3) *Kurtarici olarak bozkurt* (The *bozkurt* should be the savior).[32] This article also calls for Turkey's solidarity with those Turks who are "oppressed by the Greeks in Cyprus, by the Kurds in Iraq and by the Russians in the Soviet Union."[33]

From the 1930s to the 1970s, two of the most ardent disseminators of Pan-Turkish ideology were Hüseyin Nihal Atziz (1905-1975) and his brother Nejdet Sançar (1910-1973). Neither Hüseyin Nihal Atziz nor his brother concealed their racist views.[34] Both believed in the racial purity and racial superiority of the Turks and had little tolerance for minorities. At the same time, they were fiercely anti-communist.[35] The views of Reha Oğuz Türkkan, another important figure of Pan Turkism, were similar. Türkkan also believed in Turkish racial superiority and he and Hüseyin Nihal Atziz were engaged in a bitter feud accusing each other of not being a "pure" Turk.[36] Atziz and Türkkan founded and published some of the most influential periodicals in the history of Pan-Turkish literature in the 1930s, 1940s and 1950s. Atziz first published *Orhun* and then *Orkun*. Türkkan published *Ergenekon*, *Bozkurt* and *Gök Börü*. Another dedicated Pan-Turkish author was Ilhan Eğemen Darendelioğlu who initially published *Yeni Bozkurt* in 1948 and later became the editor of *Toprak* which was published for 22 years (1954-1976). The Pan-Turkish symbol of the *bozkurt*, the grey wolf, was depicted on the cover of *Ergenekon*, *Bozkurt* and *Orkun*. The slogan on the cover of *Ergenekon* and *Bozkurt* was *Her Irkin Üstünde Türk Irki* (The Turkish Race Above Any Other Race). (See figure 1 for the cover of *Bozkurt*.)

Over the years, Pan-Turkish ideology has experienced highs and lows. It has had to compete with the official ideology of Kemalism, the political and social philosophy of Kemal Atatürk. This ideology purportedly put an end to Turkish irredentist claims against all neighboring countries. It was born out of the demise of the multireligious and multiethnic Ottoman Empire, as Atatürk saw the need to downplay irredentism. He did not envision a neo-Ottoman Turkey—*Büyük Türkiye*, or "Greater Turkey" (literally "Great Turkey")—which was the goal of the Pan-Turkists. Atatürk's priority was to build a homogeneous and secular Turkish nation-state which was moving away from irredentist objectives. Since the death of Atatürk in 1938, however, supporters of Pan-Turkism have become quite vocal. This was especially true during the Second World War. Pan-Turkism lost part of its thrust following the defeat of Nazi Germany, but it remained a latent force in Turkish politics during the 1950s. From 1950 to 1960, the years the Democratic Party governed Turkey, Pan-Turkish groups

were tolerated and were even accepted as long as they did not challenge the ruling party or interfere with the government's foreign policy. Indeed, the government, acting selectively, encouraged the activities of some Pan-Turkish groups that operated under the guise of
nationalism.[37]

Since the 1960s, Pan-Turkism has been in the mainstream of Turkish
politics.[38] It could increase its influence in the 1990s, given the catalytic developments in the Soviet Union, especially in the southern Soviet
republics. It is in these republics that the major concentration of
Turkic-speaking Muslims is found.[39] While it is unpredictable what
direction these republics will take in a decentralized Soviet Union,
Turkey might still be faced with the dilemma of having to decide
whether to focus more attention on Muslim Asia and the Middle East
or move closer to Europe and the West. The campaign of the Turkish
elite to pursue membership for Turkey in the European Community is
incompatible with an eastward-looking Turkey. In addition, Pan-
Turkism has been opposed by westernized liberal and leftist intellectuals in Turkey who especially dislike its fascist overtones and associate it
with the most reactionary political forces in the country, such as the
Nationalist Action Party of Alparslan Türkeş. Turkish-born academics
living abroad have also been critical of Pan-Turkism. Still, Pan-
Turkism has proven to be a resilient ideology that refuses to die.

Within the wider context of Pan-Turkish ideology, there have been
divergent views—some more extremist and others more
pragmatic—concerning what Turkey as a nation-state could hope to
accomplish in pursuing a policy aimed at the creation of a Greater
Turkey. However, there has been a remarkable consensus in the attitude of Pan-Turkists toward Cyprus and Greece. Since Pan-Turkism
emerged, its position has been that Cyprus is a Turkish island, despite
its Greek majority. Pan-Turkish groups in Turkey have had Cyprus on
their agenda since the beginning of the century.[40] In the decade following the Second World War, *Orkun*, the most important Pan-
Turkish journal of the 1940s and 1950s, paid special attention to
Cyprus and advocated that the island should be united with Turkey.[41]

As far as Greece is concerned, the Pan-Turkish position has always
been that it is a hostile power and its objective is to encircle Turkey.
Pan-Turkists imagine that the encirclement of Turkey, from the
northern Aegean to Cyprus and the eastern Mediterranean, would be
complete if Cyprus were united with Greece and what they describe

as a "noose to strangulate Turkey" were created. From the Turkish
viewpoint, such encirclement would deprive Turkey of its access to
the sea, and Turkey's southern ports, especially Mersin and
Alexandretta, would then be extremely vulnerable to a Greek block-
ade.[42]

While the Turkish elite, especially the military, have subscribed to
Kemalist ideology, they have simultaneously embraced the two fundamental positions of Pan-Turkism: that Cyprus is Turkish (*Kibris
Türktür*) and that Greece aims at encircling Turkey. These two positions have become guiding principles of Turkish policy vis-à-vis
Cyprus and Greece since the early 1950s. Indeed for the last 40 years,
the army and the political forces in Turkey—with the exception of the
tiny Marxist left—have forged a basic consensus in their perception of
Cyprus and Greece, a consensus rooted in Pan-Turkish precepts. This
has occurred irrespective of other serious disagreements they have had
with the Pan-Turkists. With regard to Cyprus, this consensus has
found expression in two basic arguments. One is of an ethnological
nature and the other is based on historic and demographic claims. The
ethnological argument was advanced officially by the Turkish government in a memorandum circulated in August 1955. Under the sub-
heading "Population," it said the following:

The total population of the island [in 1955] is about 500,000. Of this, about
120,000 are of indubitable Turkish origin and culture, as a perfectly natural
consequence of three centuries of the existence of Cyprus as an integral part
of Turkey. 11,000 are of various races and faiths. The remaining 370,000 are
claimed by the Greek government to be Greeks. In fact, from the ethnic
point of view, almost the whole of this community belongs to the category of
peoples dispersed in the eastern Mediterranean who are referred to as
"Levantines." This Cypriot branch of the "Levantines" has nothing in common with the Greeks other than the Greek Orthodox faith under the influence of which it has adopted a certain dialect of the Greek language.[43]

Before discussing the substance of this Turkish thesis on Cypriot population, it should be noted that the Turkish-Cypriot component of the
population is inflated by at least 20 percent in the memorandum. In
1955, the Turkish-Cypriot population of Cyprus did not exceed
100,000. According to the last British colonial report on Cyprus in
1959, 78.8 percent (442,000) of the total population of 561,000 was
Greek and 17.5 percent (98,000) was Turkish.[44] It is inconceivable,
therefore, that the Turkish-Cypriot population in 1955, four years earlier, could have exceeded 100,000 people. Dr. Fazil Küçük, the most
prominent Turkish-Cypriot leader from the late 1940s to the late

1960s, put the number of Turkish Cypriots at about 100,000 in 1954. In a telegram he sent on 22 August 1954 to UN Secretary-General Dag Hammarskjöld on the Cyprus issue, Dr. Küçük declared: "100,000 Cyprus Turks strongly protest the Greek government position regarding the union of Cyprus with Greece and vehemently reject *Enosis*, self-government or a plebiscite."[45]

In February 1956, six months after the Turkish government circulated the August 1955 memorandum putting the number of Turkish Cypriots at 120,000, another official government document estimated their number to be 100,000.[46] The wide discrepancy in the Turkish-Cypriot population figures released by the Turkish government within a period of one year reflects the overall unreliability of Turkish demographic data on Cyprus. Most of the time, these data, which include statistics on population, emigration and immigration, have been contrived for purposes of political expediency.

It is apparent that the August 1955 memorandum reflects Pan-Turkish ideas on race and blood purity. The memorandum maintains that the minority population consists of pure Turks who are of "indubitable Turkish origin and culture." On the other hand, it says that the people comprising the majority population, those of the "Greek Orthodox" faith that are "claimed by the Greek government to be Greeks," are not actually Greeks. Rather, according to the memorandum, they belong to a "category of peoples"—a racially mixed group of people—called "Levantines." In the eastern Mediterranean and the Middle East, the term "Levantine" usually refers to a person who has no particular ethnic ties, national self-awareness or national identity. The logical conclusion of the Levantine thesis, as it is advanced in the memorandum, is that the majority population of Cyprus is not entitled to demand the right to self-determination and union with Greece because this population is not Greek but Levantine.[47] The memorandum also develops a series of ethnological, historical and legal arguments to support the thesis that 80 percent of the population of Cyprus is not entitled to the right to self-determination.[48] The Turkish government has persistently opposed any form of self-government for Cyprus based on the principle of majority rule.[49]

The Levantine theory of the racial origins of the Greek Cypriots is not an aberration of the 1950s. It is a theory which is still reflected in Turkish intellectual thought as it remains preoccupied with questions of racial purity, including the "genetic" purity of the Greek people.

Two decades after the Levantine thesis emerged, the *Turkish Yearbook of International Relations, 1974,* which was published in 1976, included an article which in essence "Levantinizes" not only the Greek Cypriots, but all the Greeks of today, as well. The article, "Certain Basic Misconceptions in the Field of History: Ancient Greeks, the West and the Modern World," employs theories on race and genetic purity which resemble those of Pan-Turkism. It says that its aim is to scientifically prove that the contemporary Greek people are not really Greeks. The article asks whether "we should think of the modern Greeks as the genetic products" of ancient Greece.[50] The answer to this question, according to the author, is that there is no "sufficient proof of direct genetic connection between the ancient and modern Greeks."[51] The writer of the article claims that the influence of ancient Greeks on modern Greeks has been limited to the "tricks in politics and diplomacy" that the modern Greeks have inherited from them.[52] It is noteworthy that this article was written by Dr. Yaman Örs, a medical doctor on the Faculty of Medicine at the University of Ankara. Moreover, it is not without significance that such an article has been published in the *Turkish Yearbook of International Relations,* one of the most prestigious Turkish publications on foreign affairs published in English.

Turkish officials use historical and demographic arguments more often than ethnological theories to advance Turkey's position regarding Cyprus. Arguments based on these factors state that the Greek majority in Cyprus represents an artificial construct. According to the prevailing view in Turkey in 1955, the composition of the population in Cyprus should not have been a criterion for determining the island's future. "The majority of the population had once been Turkish," the argument went, "but over the years, since British occupation, heavy migration from Greece combined with emigration of Turkish Cypriots to Turkey had given rise to the Greek majority."[53] Reflecting this logic, Acting Turkish Foreign Minister Fatin Rüstü Zorlu said in 1955:

It is not admissible to try to consider the island of Cyprus from the point of view of the present day population. When we take into account the population of Cyprus it is not sufficient to say, for instance, that 100,000 Turks live there. One should rather say 100,000 Turks out of 24 million Turks live there and that 300,000 Turkish Cypriots live in various parts of Turkey.[54]

In 1955, the Turkish government also said:

Fewer than 370,000 non-Turks who live on an island extension of the

Turkish mainland [Cyprus] wish to transfer that island to the sovereignty of a power [Greece] potentially hostile to their 24 million neighbors. The Turkish government cannot allow that to happen. Self-determination is for nations, not for "pocket majorities."[55]

Turkey perceived the Greek Cypriots as a "pocket majority" or "pocket population"—a philosophy reflecting the situation under the Ottomans when the Greeks formed "pocket majorities" throughout the empire. But it also viewed the Greek Cypriots as a *minority* amidst the 24 million Turks living in Turkey in 1955 since Cyprus was considered to be an integral part of Turkey.

The voluminous historical and demographic data on Cyprus that has been made public, including British colonial archives, indicate that there was no significant emigration from Greece to Cyprus and no mass migration of Turkish Cypriots to Turkey during colonial rule. However, the belief in the "Turkishness of Cyprus" runs deep among the Turks, who are still using the same argument Zorlu used in 1955 to support their conviction. In this respect, the following statement by then-Turkish prime minister and current president of Turkey, Turgut Özal, in 1986 is quite characteristic:

The island [Cyprus] has never been Greek in its history. It belonged to the Venetians and then was taken over by the Ottomans. Later the British rule came. I believe it was first during the Ottoman period and later under the British rule that the Greeks immigrated to the island. And I said, if you want to call the island something, it is more Turkish than Greek. It was governed for many hundreds of years by the Ottomans.[56]

In other words, the thrust of Özal's argument is the same as that expressed by the Turkish government in the 1950s. While his thesis avoids the aggressive language of Pan-Turkists, the use of Ottoman historic justification for the belief that Cyprus is Turkish leads to the same irredentist claims on Cyprus as those advanced by the Pan-Turkists. Özal's statement that the island is "more Turkish than Greek" reflects the "pocket majority" philosophy prevalent during the Ottoman Empire with regard to the Greeks. Consequently, in his view, the Greek Cypriots cannot have the normal democratic rights of a majority since Cyprus is part of the Turkish nation and, in the broader context of that nation, they constitute a minority. In the final analysis, the irredentist position expressed by the Menderes government 35 years ago resonates in Özal's view of Cyprus today.

Such arguments become cyclical as they are echoed by Turkish Cypriots and recycled from Cyprus back to Turkey. The leading legal scholar of the TRNC and close advisor to Denktash, Necati Münir Ertekün, wrote a book in 1984 which reflects the widespread Turkish belief that Cyprus rightfully belongs to Turkey. He opened his book with the following statement:

The island of Cyprus, which is geographically an extension of the Anatolian peninsula, was part of the Ottoman Empire from 1571 until 1878. . . . [Under Ottoman rule], the Turks also generally assisted the Greek-Cypriot population to organize themselves into a social and cultural entity and so to live as free citizens. [In 1878], Turkey consented to assign the island of Cyprus to be temporarily occupied and administered by Britain. . . . In 1914, when the Ottoman Empire entered the First World War on the side of Germany, Cyprus was annexed by Britain. . . . The Turkish community of Cyprus . . . firmly retorted to the Greek *Enosis* campaign by demanding that, if the island was to change hands again, it should be given back to Turkey.[57]

It is precisely these types of ethnological, historical and demographic arguments that have been used persistently by Turkey to rationalize and justify its policies vis-à-vis Cyprus. They have all led to one conclusion: that Cyprus is Turkish (*Kibris Türktür*). The ideology that Cyprus is Turkish has been the driving force behind the actions of Pan-Turkish groups in Turkey since the early 1950s. When Acting Turkish Foreign Minister Fatin Rüstü Zorlu went to London at the end of August 1955 to take part in the London Tripartite Conference on Cyprus, he made the Turkish stand on Cyprus clear to British Foreign Secretary Harold MacMillan. In a recently declassified Foreign Office document, MacMillan recounts his meeting with Zorlu which took place on 27 August 1955. MacMillan wrote:

. . . . Mr. Zorlu's reply was that Cyprus could not be regarded as an ordinary territory for normal constitutional development. . . . The Turks regarded Cyprus as part of their own territory ("notre terre").[58]

The official Turkish position at the Tripartite Conference left little doubt that the *Kibris Türktür* ideology had taken hold of Turkish foreign policy.

NOTES

[1]On the asynchronous socioeconomic development and political mobilization of the Greek-Cypriot and Turkish-Cypriot communities, see Michael Attalides, *Cyprus: Nationalism and International Politics* (New York: St. Martin's Press, 1979), 22–56; Richard A. Patrick, *Political Geography and the Cyprus Conflict: 1963–1971*, Department of Geography, Publication Series No. 4 (University of Waterloo, 1976), 28–29. On the emergence of Greek-Cypriot nationalism and the process of political mobilization, see Kyriacos

C. Markides, *The Rise and Fall of the Cyprus Republic* (New Haven: Yale University Press, 1977), 5-21.

[2]On the emergence and development of modern Greek nationalist ideology, its irredentist characteristics and the complicated relationship between this ideology and the Greek Orthodox Church, see the treatise by Paschalis M. Kitromilides, "Imagined Communities and the Origins of the National Question in the Balkans," in *Modern Greece: Nationalism and Nationality,* eds. Martin Blinkhorn and Thanos Veremis (Athens: Sage-ELIAMEP, 1990), 23-66. On the relationship between the ideology of *Enosis* and modern Greek nationalism, see also Paschalis Kitromilides, "The Dialectics of Intolerance: Ideological Dimensions of Ethnic Conflict," in *Small States in the Modern World,* eds. Peter Worseley and Paschalis Kitromilides (Nicosia: The New Cyprus Association, 1979), 143-170.

[3]See Frank G. Weber, *The Evasive Neutral: Germany, Britain and the Quest for a Turkish Alliance in the Second World War* (Columbia, Missouri, and London: University of Missouri Press, 1979). In this study, Weber's book has been the primary source for the discussion of Turkey's role during the war, especially its attitude toward Cyprus. The chapter "Turkey and the Russian Campaign: Cyprus and Caucasus" offers valuable insight into Turkish thinking about the eastern Mediterranean and Cyprus in a post-war settlement. See pp. 107-141.

[4]On the Turko-German pact of 1941, as well as on Turkish neutrality during the Second World War, see George Lenczowski, *The Middle East in World Affairs* (Ithaca: Cornell University Press, 1980), 129-134.

[5]Weber, *The Evasive Neutral,* 110-117.

[6]Ibid., 115-118, 122; Jacob M. Landau, *Pan-Turkism in Turkey: A Study of Irredentism* (Hamden, Conn.: Archon Books, 1981), 109-112.

[7]Weber, *The Evasive Neutral,* 113.

[8]On the role of the "Cyprus Regiment" and that of Greek-Cypriot volunteers in the British army's war effort, see Doros Alastos, *Cyprus: Past, Present and Future* (London: Committee for Cyprus Affairs, 1943), 61-66.

[9]Weber, *The Evasive Neutral,* 117-120.

[10]Ibid., 119-120.

[11]Quoted in Kemal H. Karpat, *Turkey's Politics: The Transition to a Multi-Party System* (Princeton: Princeton University Press, 1959), 266.

[12]On the British policy of drawing the "Turkish factor" more deeply into the Cyprus conflict, see Robert Stephens, *Cyprus: A Place of Arms* (London: Pall Mall Press, 1968), 137-156; Charles Foley, *Legacy of Strife: Cyprus from Rebellion to Civil War* (Baltimore: Penguin, 1964), 30, 89, 119-129;

Thomas Ehrlich, *International Crises and the Rule of Law: Cyprus, 1958-1967* (Oxford: Oxford University Press, 1974), 19; Stanley Kyriakides, *Constitutionalism and Crisis Government* (Philadelphia: University of Pennsylvania Press, 1968), 44, 137-140; Leontios Ierodiakonou, *To Kypriako Problema* (The Cyprus Question) (Athens: Papazisis, 1975), 94-138, 167-168, 189-202, 239-249, 277-281.

[13]See Speros Papageorgiou, ed., *Archeion ton Paranomon Egraphon tou Kypriakou Agonos: 1955-1959* (Archive of Illegal Documents of the Cypriot Struggle: 1955-1959), 2nd ed. (Nicosia: Epifaniou Publishers, 1984), 152-153.

[14]Ibid.

[15]On EOKA's policy of not disturbing the Turkish-Cypriot community, and on the Anglo-Turkish collaboration against EOKA, see George Grivas-Digenis, *Apomnemoneumata Agonos EOKA, 1955-1959* (Memoirs of the EOKA Struggle, 1955-1959) (Athens, 1961), 51-52, 256-262; and Halil Ibrahim Salih, *Cyprus: An Analysis of Cypriot Political Discord* (New York: Theo. Gans & Sons, 1968), 60-61, 167; Stephens, *Cyprus: A Place of Arms,* 146.

[16]The leaflet was EOKA's primary means of communicating with the Cypriot people. They were mimeographed and circulated in public places by masked men. In churches, they were usually thrown from the balcony by high school girls. The overwhelming majority of Greek Cypriots obeyed the instructions and orders of the leaflets faithfully.

[17]See Grivas-Digenis, *Apomnemoneumata*, 51-52.

[18]On the British Special Branch in Cyprus, its use of torture and the service of Turkish policemen as interrogators, see Salih, *Cyprus: An Analysis*, 58-59.

[19]See sample of EOKA leaflets published in Papageorgiou, *Archeion ton Paranomon Egraphon*, 184-196.

[20]Stanley Mayes, *Makarios: A Biography* (New York: St. Martin's Press, 1981), 88-89.

[21]On EOKA's policy of targeting and executing Greek policemen and colonial bureaucrats, see Markides, *The Rise and Fall of the Cyprus Republic*, 19-20.

[22]See Papageorgiou, *Archeion ton Paranomon Egraphon*, 153.

[23]Grivas-Digenis, *Apomnemoneumata*, 98, 148-151, 255-262; Salih, *Cyprus: An Analysis*, 58-61, 167; Nancy Crawshaw, "Cyprus: A Failure of Western Diplomacy," in *Greek Connections: Essays on Culture and Diplomacy,* ed. John T. Koumoulides (Notre Dame: University of Notre Dame Press, 1987),

103. See also the references in note 12.

[24]On EOKA's plans to confront the Turkish Cypriots, see George Grivas-Digenis, *General Grivas-Digenis on Guerrilla Warfare* (New York: Frederick Praeger, 1962), 43-45, 96-99.

[25]On the Anglo-Turkish alliance, the Baghdad Pact, and the pro-Turkish stand of Sir Anthony Eden, see Stephens, *Cyprus: A Place of Arms*, 136-143.

[26]On the genesis of Pan-Turkish ideology and its development during the last decades of the Ottoman Empire, see Landau, *Pan-Turkism in Turkey*, 1-70.

[27]The discussion on Pan-Turkism is primarily based upon the work of Landau, *Pan-Turkism in Turkey*. The work of Mehmed Ali Ağaoğullari was also utilized. See Mehmed Ali Ağaoğullari, "The Ultranationalist Right," in *Turkey in Transition*, eds., Irvin Cemil Schick and Ertuğrul Ahmed Tonak (Oxford: Oxford University Press, 1987), 177-217.

[28]Landau, ibid., 7.

[29]Ibid., 116.

[30]On the *bozkurt* as a symbol of Pan-Turkism and ultranationalism, ibid, 87, 88, 125, 126, 150; Ağaoğullari, "The Ultranationalist Right," 186.

[31]Lord Kinross, *The Ottoman Centuries: The Rise and Fall of the Turkish Empire* (New York: Morrow Quill Paperbacks, 1977), 16.

[32]Altan Deliorman, "Bugünkü Mânâsi ile 'Bozkurt' " (The Contemporary Meaning of the "Bozkurt"), *Türk Kültürü* 5, no. 55 (May 1967): 470-475.

[33]Ibid., 472.

[34]On the racist overtones of Pan-Turkism, see the chapter "Racialism—*Irkçilik*—and Pan-Turkism," in Karpat, *Turkey's Politics: The Transition to a Multi-Party System*, 262-270; Ağaoğullari, "The Ultranationalist Right," 181-183, 188-191, 210-211; Landau, *Pan-Turkism in Turkey*, 3, 87-92, 94-95, 126-127, 180, 184, 188.

[35]On the strong anti-communist component of Pan-Turkish ideology, see Landau, ibid., 79-81, 88-90, 94-95, 113, 115-116, 119-125, 129, 144-149, 151, 156, 159, 161-165; Ağaoğullari, ibid., 188-189, 191, 194, 196-197, 202-203.

[36]Landau, ibid., 95.

[37]See A.N. Kirmaci, "Nationalism-Racism-Turanism in Turkey," in *Political and Social Thought in the Contemporary Middle East*, ed. Kemal H. Karpat (New York: Praeger, 1968), 361.

[38]See chapter 5, "Pan-Turkism in the Republic of Turkey: Back into the Mainstream," in Landau, *Pan-Turkism in Turkey*, 144-175, 185. See also

Ağaoğullari, "The Ultranationalist Right," 200, 205, 206; Birand, *The Generals' Coup in Turkey,* 19, 31, 50-52.

[39]On the ascendancy of Turkish nationalism in the southern republics of the Soviet Union, see Daniel Pipes, "Moscow's Next Worry: Ethnic Turks," *New York Times,* 13 February 1990. On the sympathetic sentiment in Turkey toward the Azeri Turks in the Azerbaijan region of the Soviet Union, see *New York Times,* 24 and 26 January 1990.

[40]On the attention given to Cyprus by Pan-Turkish groups, see Landau, *Pan-Turkism in Turkey,* 48, 73, 77, 115, 118, 132, 150-151, 154-155, 156, 157, 159, 161, 164, 186; Ağaoğullari, "The Ultranationalist Right," 189, 191, 213.

[41]Landau, ibid., 127.

[42]On Turkish thinking that Cyprus is vital for Turkish defense and on the fear of "Greek encirclement," see *Turkey and Cyprus: A Survey of the Cyprus Question,* 12-21, 24, 54-55. See also Suat Bilge, "The Cyprus Conflict and Turkey," 142, and Kemal H. Karpat, "War on Cyprus," 186-187, in Karpat, *Turkey's Foreign Policy in Transition.* For a Turkish map illustrating the "Greek encirclement" of Turkey, see Derviş Manizade, *Kibris: Dün, Bugün, Yarin* (Cyprus: Yesterday, Today, Tomorrow) (Istanbul: Kibris Türk Kültür Derneği, Yaylacik Matbaasi, 1975), 200; *Turkey and Cyprus: A Survey of the Cyprus Question,* 37-38, 55.

[43]*Turkey and Cyprus: A Survey of the Cyprus Question,* 24.

[44]Colonial Office, *Cyprus: Colonial Report,* 1959, 16.

[45]See *Cyprus 1946-1968* (New York: Facts on File, Inc., 1970), 18.

[46]The figure of 100,000 Turkish Cypriots was included in the "Request for Indictment Presented to Marshal Law Tribunal No. 2," Document No. 1150-955/499, Istanbul, 9 February 1956. The indictment pertained to 23 individuals charged with involvement in the anti-Greek riots of 6 September 1955 in Istanbul and Izmir. (Hereinafter referred to as *Indictment 1150.*) The text of the indictment was included in a report by the U.S. Consul General in Istanbul: "American Consul General in Istanbul to Department of State," Telegram No. 563, Despatch No. 306, 20 February 1956. (Hereinafter referred to as *American Consul General, Istanbul, Despatch 306.*)

[47]*Turkey and Cyprus: A Survey of the Cyprus Question,* 35.

[48]Ibid., 22-45.

[49]Ibid., 18, 19, 35, 40, 42, 48-49, 56-57, 68-69.

[50]See Dr. Yaman Örs, "Certain Basic Misconceptions in the Field of History.

Ancient Greeks, the West, and the Modern World," in *The Turkish Yearbook of International Relations, 1974,* vol. 14 (University of Ankara: Institute of International Relations, Faculty of Political Science, 1976), 106, 112-113.

[51]Ibid., 113.

[52]Ibid.

[53]Frank Tachau, an American scholar who lived in Turkey in the 1950s, cites this argument as a standard one among many Turks. See Frank Tachau, "The Face of Turkish Nationalism as Reflected in the Cyprus Dispute," *Middle East Journal* 13 (Summer 1959): 268.

[54]*Turkey and Cyprus: A Survey of the Cyprus Question:* 53-54.

[55]Ibid., 18.

[56]See the interview with Turgut Özal in the *International Herald Tribune,* 2 June 1986.

[57]Necati M. Ertekün, *The Cyprus Dispute and the Birth of the Turkish Republic of Northern Cyprus* (Lefkoşa (Nicosia): K. Rustem & Brother, 1984), 1-2.

[58]Great Britain, Foreign Office, "Conversation between Secretary of State and the Turkish Minister for Foreign Affairs on August 27, 1955," RG 1081/894, Confidential, 31 August 1955.

5
Pan-Turkism in the 1950s: The Kibris Türktür Society

The activism of Pan-Turkish circles concerning the Cyprus issue has been evident in Turkey since the late 1940s and early 1950s. According to Jacob Landau, Cyprus has been "one of the pet issues of Pan-Turkists in Turkey since the end of the Second World War."[1] By the time Hüseyin Nihal Atziz's weekly journal, *Orkun*, was giving special emphasis to the Cyprus issue in 1951, a Pan-Turkish group focusing exclusively on Cyprus was already active. Founded in Istanbul in 1946, it was called *Kibris Türk Kültür Dernegi* (Cyprus Turkish Cultural Association, or CTCA).[2] The term *"Türk Kültür"* has generally been used by associations and publications in Turkey with Pan-Turkish tendencies. The establishment of CTCA coincided with the formation of *Türk Kültür Ocagi* (Hearths of Turkish Culture) and *Türk Kültür Dernegi* (Association for Turkish Culture).[3] The founders of CTCA included two Turkish Cypriots living in Turkey—Halil Fikret Alasya, an author and teacher, and Hasan Nevzat Karagil, a lawyer. On 1 October 1952, Alasya and members of his group met with Turkish Prime Minister Adnan Menderes and discussed the Cyprus question.

One of the most active Pan-Turkish groups of the early 1950s in Turkey was the *Türkiye Milliyetçiler Dernegi* (Association of the Nationalists of Turkey). The organization became known as the *milliyetçis* (nationalists). By the end of 1952, the *milliyetçis* had established more than 80 branches throughout Turkey. With the Greek-Cypriot agitation for *Enosis* in Cyprus on the rise, the *milliyetçis* found it to be an opportune time to advance the cause of the "Outside Turks" of Cyprus. They did it by propagating the idea that the Turkish minority in Cyprus "was in danger of being persecuted by the majority that was both Greek and communist."[4] During the 1950s, the *milliyetçis* established contacts with various groups in Turkey that had been active concerning the Cyprus issue, thereby promoting the Turkish cause in Cyprus and "injecting a Pan-Turk element into those activist groups."[5]

The Pan-Turkish groups, which were becoming increasingly active in the early 1950s, suffered a setback in 1953 when the *milliyetçis* started demanding the formation of a political party to advance the cause of Pan-Turkism. The ruling Democratic Party was unwilling to allow the *milliyetçis* to go that far. As a consequence, in January 1953, the government ordered the closure of all branches of the Association of the Nationalists of Turkey. Other nationalist groups with Pan-Turkish tendencies quickly took the place of the *milliyetçis* and kept up their activities focusing on the Cyprus issue.[6]

The Turkish group that was by far the most active with regard to the Cyprus issue in the 1950s was the *Kibris Türktür Cemiyeti* (The Cyprus is Turkish Society) which came to be known as *Kibris Türktür* (Cyprus is Turkish). Before it acquired legal status, it was called the Cyprus is Turkish Committee, also referred to as *Kibris Türktür*. Despite the fact that *Kibris Türktür* played a more important role than any other organization in Turkey with regard to the Cyprus issue, very little is known about this group. In its own way, it left its mark on the Turkish politics of the 1950s and also influenced Turkey's contemporary policy toward Cyprus and Greece.

ORIGINS OF KIBRIS TÜRKTÜR

The origins of *Kibris Türktür* are to be found within the circles of two important political groupings in Turkey in 1954: the *Millî Türk Talebe Federasyonu* (Turkish National Student Federation, or TNSF), and the publishers and editors of the major Turkish newspapers in Turkey.[7]

On 5 March and 21 April 1954, members of TNSF held meetings on the Cyprus issue at the student organization's headquarters in the Eminönü district in Istanbul. At the meetings, TNSF decided to arrange exchanges between Turkish students and Turkish-Cypriot students in order to strengthen the ties between Turkey and the Turkish Cypriots. Following the July 1954 British proposal to grant self-government to Cyprus, TNSF issued a pamphlet which stated: "It is our sacred duty to resist any action which will disturb the tranquility of the island which is an inseparable part of our own country and a sacred legacy of our grandfathers."[8]

The third week of August 1954, the Turkish Secretariat of the European Youth Campaign, in cooperation with TNSF, organized a national seminar in Istanbul to discuss the concept of European Union. Twenty Anatolian newspaper editors were invited to attend the seminar which started on 22 August and took place at the TNSF office. Two days earlier, on 20 August, however, Greece had raised the Cyprus issue at the United Nations. Thus, in the end, the focus of the seminar became the Cyprus issue.

The TNSF Executive Committee also invited all the newspaper owners and editors in Istanbul, where most of the major newspapers in Turkey are published, to attend a general meeting on the Cyprus issue at 5 p.m. Tuesday, 24 August, at the TNSF office. In addition, the meeting was attended by the editors of Anatolian newspapers and the TNSF leadership. It was presided over by Sedat Simavi, the owner of *Hürriyet*, the mass-circulation newspaper of Istanbul which was known for its anti-Greek editorials.[9] After four hours of debate, the participants decided to form an association to advance the Turkish cause in Cyprus. They named the association the Cyprus is Turkish Committee. They then elected an Executive Council which consisted of Hikmet Bil, an attorney who was the editor of *Hürriyet*; Ahmed Emin Yalman, a prominent journalist and the editor of the Istanbul daily *Vatan* who was known as Ahmed Emin; Kâmil Önal, a correspondent for a newspaper named *Hürriyet*, which was published in Hatay, and for the Ankara newspaper *Zafer*, the organ of the ruling Democratic Party; Orhan Birgit, a journalist for the Istanbul newspaper *Yeni Sabah*; Hüsamettin Ganoztürk, a medical student and the president of TNSF; Ziya Somar; and Hasan Nevzat Karagil, the Cypriot-born attorney who was also the vice-president of *Kibris Türk Kültür Derneği* (Cyprus Turkish Cultural Association, or CTCA). Karagil was elected president of the Cyprus is Turkish Committee (known as *Kibris Türktür.*)

IDEOLOGY

The charter of *Kibris Türktür* made it clear that the organization's objectives were to advance Turkey's irredentist nationalism. The charter stated that the aim of the organization was:

. . . to acquaint world public opinion with the fact that Cyprus is Turkish, to defend the rights and privileges of Turks with regard to Cyprus and [do it] from every point of view, and to condition Turkish public opinion.[10]

From its inception, *Kibris Türktür* incorporated three complementary viewpoints into its ideology. These viewpoints were reflected in the ideological make-up of its founding members and the members of its first Executive Council. The first viewpoint was a Pan-Turkish irredentist stance that was made quite obvious by the new organization's name, *Kibris Türktür* (Cyprus is Turkish). The official symbol of *Kibris Türktür* was a green map of Cyprus cradled by the crescent of the Turkish flag. All founding members of the organization espoused the principle, as expressed in its charter, that Cyprus is rightfully an integral part of the Turkish nation.[11] The second viewpoint, which was complementary to the first, was a strongly anti-Greek position, and the third was vehement anti-communism, which also constitutes a basic characteristic of Pan-Turkism.

What Pan-Turkists feared most was a Cyprus that was both Greek and communist. The most virulent anti-Greek propaganda campaign was waged in the mass circulation Istanbul newspapers *Hürriyet* and *Istanbul Ekspres*, the prestigious Istanbul daily *Vatan*, and the Ankara newspaper *Zafer*, the mouthpiece of the ruling Democratic Party. *Hürriyet* and *Vatan* published the most inflammatory articles against Greece, the Greek Orthodox Patriarchate in Istanbul and Archbishop Makarios. They also propagated the Pan-Turkish view that, not only was Cyprus Turkish, but western Thrace (Greek Thrace) and the Aegean islands were as well.[12] All four of these newspapers devoted a great deal of editorial space to apocalyptic articles highlighting the grave danger to Turkey that a "Greek and communist" Cyprus would pose. This was one more reason, the argument went, for Cyprus to become Turkish if the British decided to leave the island. This way, it was argued, Turkey not only would get back what was historically hers—Cyprus, but a great service would be done to the free world by making sure that the island would never become a communist base in the eastern Mediterranean. Speculating on what might happen if Cyprus did not become Turkish, Prime Minister Menderes said in the summer of 1955 that "the surrender by Britain of her sovereignty over Cyprus is likely to result in the destruction of NATO's whole defense system in the Mediterranean."[13] Likewise, Ahmed Emin, editor of *Vatan* and member of the *Kibris Türktür* Executive Council, argued that the *Enosis* movement in Cyprus was inspired and directed by the communists and Moscow. The "ridiculous idea of self-determination applied to small areas of territory here and there" was threatening vital interests of the free world, he said.[14]

The Turkish thesis that the church-led nationalist movement in Cyprus and EOKA's armed struggle against the British were part of a communist plot was presented in detail in the indictment of 9 February 1956 against the organizers of the anti-Greek riots in Istanbul and Izmir on 6 September 1955. These riots, which were instigated by the Turkish government and organized by *Kibris Türktür*, resulted in the destruction of most of the Greek Orthodox churches and Greek commercial establishments in Istanbul and many Greek homes in the city. Martial law was imposed immediately after the riots. The indictment, containing an introduction to the events of 6 September 1955, was prepared by a top Turkish military officer, Major General Namic Arguç, who was Martial Law Commander of the Beyoğlu Region of Istanbul. In the introduction, under the subtitle "The Cyprus Problem," it was argued that the Communist Party of Cyprus (AKEL), acting on instructions from Moscow and the Comintern, had formed a close alliance with the Greek Orthodox Church and the Cypriot nationalists. In this way, it said, the communists had come to control the *Enosis* movement and EOKA.[15] The communist objective was to undermine NATO's southern flank by using the *Enosis* movement in Cyprus to destroy Greek-Turkish friendship, the indictment added.

Certainly, the communists and the Soviet Union wished to see NATO undermined by the Cyprus dispute. The notion, however, that the nationalist movement in Cyprus, the leadership of the Greek Orthodox Church and EOKA were controlled by communists is absurd *in extremis*. In fact, quite the opposite was true. The *Enosis* movement, which was developed under the aegis of the church and culminated in the EOKA movement, was guided and controlled by a fiercely anti-communist leadership from beginning to end.

Even Rauf Denktash has acknowledged that fact lately. He wrote in 1982:

EOKA's ranks were closed to Turkish Cypriots and to members of AKEL, the Greek Cypriot Communist Party. . . . Anyone who opposed it [EOKA's *Enosis* campaign] would be treated like a "traitor" and eliminated; all members of AKEL were traitors.[16]

What is important, nonetheless, is that this ideological myth of a communist-controlled *Enosis* movement in Cyprus became a central theme around which Turkish arguments about Cyprus revolved.[17] The *Kibris Türktür* position that Turkey's vital interests were threatened by a "Greek and communist" Cyprus reflected not only the official Turkish view, but a widespread belief held by Turks in general. The nationalist leadership in Cyprus underestimated the extent of Turkish opposition to *Enosis*. The AKEL communists were also unable to realize that Turkey was determined to adhere to its policy of opposing a communist-dominated and pro-Soviet Cyprus. As it turned out, AKEL came to favor an independent Cyprus. But it also followed a staunchly pro-Soviet line and based its Cyprus policy on the Marxist precept of "class solidarity" between Greek- and Turkish-Cypriot workers. If the Greek-Cypriot nationalist call for *Enosis* was anathema to Turkey, AKEL's ideology and its pro-Soviet stand were double anathema and were bound to cause a reaction from the Turkish side.

THE BLESSINGS OF THE MENDERES GOVERNMENT

Very quickly, the activities of *Kibris Türktür* were sanctioned by the Turkish government. The Turkish newspapers of 25 August 1954, the day after the birth of *Kibris Türktür,* gave wide publicity to the fact that such an organization had been established. The government organ, *Zafer,* after praising the formation of *Kibris Türktür* in its main editorial, wrote: "A communist base [Cyprus] operating under Comintern directive, established 60 kilometers from Turkish territory, will never be tolerated." More importantly, on 28 August, four days after *Kibris Türktür* was established, its Executive Council was received by Prime Minister Menderes in the *Vilayet* (governor's mansion) in Istanbul.[18] Also present at the meeting were Deputy Prime Minister and Foreign Minister Fuat Köprülü, Minister of State and Acting Foreign Minister Fatin Rüstü Zorlu, Minister of State Mukerrem Sarol and Istanbul Governor Fahrettin Gökay. The meeting was arranged by *Vatan* editor Ahmed Emin, who seemed to be well-acquainted with Menderes. The speediness with which the meeting was arranged, the presence of Menderes, Köprülü and Zorlu—the three most important figures in the government—and the length of the meeting indicated the importance which the Menderes government attributed to *Kibris Türktür.*

Orhan Birgit, a member of the *Kibris Türktür* Executive Council who attended the meeting, describes how the Executive Council felt about the importance of having the government help *Kibris Türktür* clarify its legal status (emphasis added):

Because we were to perform this national service [on the Cyprus issue] *under the direction of the Turkish government* which was to defend its thesis in the UN and thus achieve success, Ahmed Emin Yalman, one of us, a good friend and rather a confidante of the prime minister—*in order to fix our status*—was to speak to Menderes and pass on to us whatever was necessary.

. . . Ahmed Emin Yalman spoke to Menderes, and the prime minister, who was pleased at the forming of the society, announced he would receive us.[19]

Birgit then explains that the meeting with the Turkish government leadership was very cordial. At one point, Birgit states, Menderes, who was sitting next to him on the same divan, became so cordial that he patted him on the shoulder and said, "The Greeks should see how the opposition and the ruling party [of Turkey] are united on the Cyprus issue."[20] Evidently, Menderes was referring to the fact that *Kibris Türktür* also enjoyed the support of the opposition, Ismet Inönü's Republican People's Party (RPP). The Executive Council of *Kibris Türktür* had members, such as Hikmet Bil, who maintained good relations with RPP. In addition, from the very beginning, *Kibris Türktür* had developed close ties with student organizations and labor unions, some of which had strong ties with the opposition. Menderes, therefore, had good reason to state that *Kibris Türktür* exemplified Turkey's united stand on the Cyprus issue.

According to Birgit, a considerable part of the conversation at the meeting between Turkey's top leaders and the *Kibris Türktür* Executive Council revolved around classified information. He tells what Menderes said in response to Köprülü's reaction to the discussion of secrets in this classified information:

The prime minister, notwithstanding Köprülü's gesturing to him that he should not reveal them [the secrets] said, "We have no secrets from our children. These secrets must remain sacred yesterday, today and tomorrow. They are as if forgotten."[21]

One can only speculate about the nature of the classified information discussed at the 28 August 1954 meeting. Conceivably, the discussion could have included plans for dealing with the Greek minority in Istanbul and the Patriarchate, and for activating Turks and Turkish Cypriots to mobilize public opinion concerning Turkey's cause in Cyprus. What is most remarkable is the fact that Turkey's top leaders confided classified information to the members of an organization established only four days earlier during their very first meeting with the organization's Executive Council. From then on, *Kibris Türktür* was to act with the government's blessing, and often in cooperation with it, in its campaign on the Cyprus issue.

Toward the end of the 28 August meeting, Menderes told the *Kibris*

Türktür Executive Council that he "had confirmed in a definite language that Cyprus could never be Greek" during a recent conversation with the British ambassador to Turkey. Then Hikmet Bil told the prime minister that, following their meeting, the Executive Council and the Turkish National Student Federation would meet with the press and representatives of political parties, labor unions and student groups at the TNSF office in Istanbul. Bil asked Menderes if he would allow him to tell the people who would be attending the meeting what the prime minister had said about Cyprus. Menderes gave Bil permission to do so, and added, "There is absolutely no question of Cyprus being annexed to Greece. My best wishes to you."[22]

During the meeting at the TNSF office, in an atmosphere of great enthusiasm, *Kibris Türktür* President Hasan Nevzat Karagil told the participants about the meeting with Menderes and conveyed the prime minister's statement that Cyprus could never be Greek. Since Archbishop Makarios and the Greek Orthodox Church of Cyprus were leading the *Enosis* campaign, the *Kibris Türktür* Executive Council decided that a letter should be sent to the spiritual leader of the Greek Orthodox Church, Patriarch Athenagoras, stating that it was not proper for the church and its bishops to get involved in politics.[23] Up until then, relations between the Patriarchate and the Menderes government had been rather friendly. Patriarch Athenagoras had established positive ties with the government, especially with Deputy Prime Minister and Foreign Minister Fuat Köprülü. The *Kibris Türktür* letter to the Patriarch was the first sign, an ominous one, that Turkey was determined to implicate the Greek minority in Istanbul and the Patriarchate in developments in Cyprus. The Patriarchate, however, did not have anything to do with the nationalist agitation carried out by the Greek Orthodox Church of Cyprus, an autocephalous church which is not under the jurisdiction of the Patriarchate. In fact, both the Patriarchate and the Greek minority in Istanbul had negative feelings toward Makarios as a political persona. They watched the *Enosis* movement in Cyprus with grave apprehension as if they had a premonition of what was to come.[24] Nonetheless, the Turkish campaign against the Patriarch became so intense in the 1950s that the Turkish press would find reason to attack him no matter what he did. For example, after an earthquake in Turkey in the spring of 1957, Patriarch Athenagoras donated 40,000 Turkish lira ($14,000) to the earthquake relief fund in the name of the

Greek Orthodox Church and the Greek community in Istanbul. His gesture was intended to demonstrate his sympathy for the victims, but he was attacked by *Hürriyet* which claimed that he had exceeded his powers by intervening in worldly affairs.[25]

THE EXPANSION PHASE

On 2 October 1954, the Cyprus is Turkish Committee submitted its constitution to the Istanbul District Administration and acquired legal status under the name Cyprus is Turkish Society (*Kibris Türktür Cemiyeti*), but it continued to be known as *Kibris Türktür*. The members of the new society's organizing committee were Mes'ut Ulkü, general president of the Turkish National Student Federation (TNSF), Gürcan Ketem, member of the TNSF Executive Board, Ali Ihsan Çelikkan, secretary of the Turkish Secretariat of the European Youth Campaign, Kemal Demirel, journalist, and Ismail Hakki Zarakoglu. The composition of the organizing committee was indicative of the important role played by the student movement in *Kibris Türktür*, as was the fact that the building housing the TNSF office in Istanbul also became the headquarters of *Kibris Türktür*. The organizing committee called *Kibris Türktür*'s first meeting under its new legal status to elect a temporary Executive Committee. Hikmet Bil was elected to serve as president, in accordance with Article 32 of the organization's constitution.

On 27 April 1955, the Executive Committee of the society took its final form and became known as the Central Executive Committee. Hikmet Bil became president, Hüsamettin Ganoztürk was chosen as vice-president, Kâmil Önal became general secretary and Nedim Üsdiken, a medical student, was made treasurer. Ahmed Emin, Orhan Birgit and Sedat Bayur were also selected to be members of the Central Executive Committee.[26] The Central Executive Committee usually held its meetings in Istanbul at the headquarters of *Kibris Türktür* in the building housing the Turkish National Student Federation.

From the fall of 1954 on, *Kibris Türktür* had embarked on an expansion drive throughout Turkey and the organization spread quickly throughout the country. By the beginning of 1955, it had established about 50 branches in various regions of Turkey. Branch offices were opened in 13 districts of the Istanbul region, including Bakirköy, Büyükçekmece, Fatih, Kadiköy, Karagümrük, Paşabahçe and Topkapi. Each district branch was run by a local Executive

Committee of eight members who reported directly to the Central Executive Committee.

Next to those in Istanbul, the most important branch of *Kibris Türktür* was the one in Izmir (Smyrna) which was established in the summer of 1954.[27] It operated under an eight-member Executive Committee. Its president was Fikret Florat, an Izmir lawyer. The secretary of the Izmir branch was Burhanettin Asutay, a well-known labor leader and president of the *Ege* (Aegean) Labor Federation. Also serving in the Executive Committee was Nuri Erdol, editor-in-chief of the Izmir afternoon paper *Gece Postasi*. In March 1955, a *Kibris Türktür* branch also opened in the Izmir suburb of Karşiyaka. In August, another one opened in Urla, a small town 20 miles west of Izmir where Bulgarian Muslim refugees resided. *Kibris Türktür* also established branches in a number of other cities including Ankara (the capital), Adana, Antalya, Balikesir, Gaziantep, Konya, Mersin, Malatya, Samsun, Sinop and Tarsus. By July 1955, *Kibris Türktür* claimed to have over 100,000 members.[28]

THE LEADERSHIP

By examining the composition of *Kibris Türktür*'s Executive Committees in Istanbul and Izmir, it is possible to shed some light on the reason this newly founded organization was so effective in its efforts to agitate and mobilize the masses and organize large demonstrations to make its beliefs on Cyprus and the Turkish Cypriots known. In 1955, *Kibris Türktür* organized rallies that attracted over 100,000 people and received wide publicity in the press. The three most influential members of the organization's Central Executive Committee were Hikmet Bil, Kâmil Önal, and Ahmed Emin. A sketch of their social and political backgrounds will be useful in explaining some of the actions of the organization, particularly those related to Turkish irredentism.

As president of *Kibris Türktür*, Hikmet Bil emerged as the most important figure of the organization. As the editor of *Hürriyet*, he was responsible for the newspaper's vehement editorials against the Greeks of Cyprus, the Patriarchate, the Greek minority in Istanbul and Greece in general.[29] Bil's background is not very clear. He was born in the Turkish city of Izmit and graduated from law school before becoming a journalist. According to a confidential report to the State Department by the U.S. Embassy in Ankara, he was "possibly connected with a nationalist organization which the government dissolved in 1953."[30] In all likelihood, this was a reference to *Türkiye Milliyetçiler Derneği* (Association of the Nationalists of Turkey), the Pan-Turkish organization closed down by the Menderes government in January 1953. Hikmet Bil's possible ties with the *milliyetçis* might explain why he espoused the Pan-Turkish views evident in *Hürriyet* editorials.

As editor of *Hürriyet*, he was also well-connected with the leadership of the ruling Democratic Party, especially with Prime Minister Menderes to whom he apparently had direct access. According to the U.S. Embassy in Ankara, Hikmet Bil's frequent travelling abroad and the fact that *Kıbrıs Türktür* printed large quantities of several different handbills for demonstrations were signs that the organization was well-connected and had some funds. A U.S. Embassy source reported that Menderes's office had at one time given Bil 50,000 Turkish lira ($17,857).[31]

Hikmet Bil is also believed to have been connected with Ismet Inönü's opposition Republican People's Party.[32] Menderes himself alluded to Bil's ties with the opposition when he first met with the *Kıbrıs Türktür* Executive Council on 28 August 1954. *Kıbrıs Türktür* cooperated with local labor unions in Istanbul and Izmir. Several of the labor leaders who were members of district branches of *Kıbrıs Türktür* in these cities were supporters of RPP.

The ties between *Kıbrıs Türktür* and RPP became an issue in the debate in the Grand National Assembly on 12 September 1955 in the aftermath of the anti-Greek riots of 6 September 1955. Menderes referred to the instrumental role *Kıbrıs Türktür* had played in the riots, but Inönü made no reference at all to the organization in conjunction with them. Inönü put the blame for the riots directly on the government and on Prime Minister Menderes personally.[33] Menderes responded angrily by saying that RPP was the primary force behind the establishment of *Kıbrıs Türktür,* which carried out the riots.[34] Menderes had given a great deal of support to *Kıbrıs Türktür,* but it is not unlikely that one reason he did so was to counter Inönü's persistent criticism that the government was passive in defending Turkish rights in Cyprus.[35]

An additional indication that Inönü's RPP was supportive of *Kıbrıs Türktür* is reflected in the comments in the Ankara newspaper *Ulus,* the official organ of RPP, in the aftermath of the riots. *Ulus* came to the defense of Hikmet Bil following his release from jail, where he had spent several months after being arrested for his involvement in the riots. On 5 January 1956, Hüseyin Cahit Yalçin wrote the following in *Ulus* in reference to the riots: "Initially, the *Kibris Türktür* Society and the communists were held responsible for the incidents. However, it appears that a chairman of the Democratic Party district organization and its members were among the pillagers and plunderers. Recently, the innocence of the chairman of *Kibris Türktür* was established and he has been released from jail."[36] The important point is that *Kibris Türktür* had close ties with the opposition and even closer ties with the government. It was a truly nationalist group uniting the two sides on the Cyprus issue, and Hikmet Bil personified this unity.

The second most influential figure of *Kibris Türktür* was Kâmil Önal, the controversial general secretary of the organization. Önal was an adventurer who emerged as the main *agent provocateur* of the group. He was born in 1925 in Antakya in the district of Alexandretta (Hatay).[37] At the time, this district was part of French-mandated Syria. Developments in Alexandretta during Önal's childhood apparently left their imprint on him. He was 14 years old when Alexandretta was annexed by Turkey in 1939. (What happened in Alexandretta was what the Greeks would call *enosis*—union of Alexandretta with Turkey.[38]) In 1946, Önal graduated from the Reserve Officers School as an infantry lieutenant. Following his discharge from military service, he became a journalist and worked for newspapers in Antakya, Antalya and Mersin. He was also a correspondent for *Zafer*, the mouthpiece of the ruling Democratic Party.[39] At some time in the early 1950s, he was recruited by Turkey's National Intelligence Organization. According to the French author François Crouzet, "Kâmil Önal had been an agent for the Turkish counterespionage."[40] Working as a paid informer, Önal carried out several missions to the Middle East, mainly to Lebanon and Syria. His objective was to gather information about Kurdish, Armenian and communist groups in Syria and Lebanon and report his findings to Turkish intelligence.[41] At the time he became involved with *Kibris Türktür* in August 1954, he was working for the Ankara News Agency. He was present at the 24 August 1954 meeting founding *Kibris Türktür*. During the meeting, he gave an emotional speech reminding the participants that Alexandretta had been "united with Mother Turkey" during his childhood years. He proclaimed that he wanted to work for a similar cause, "the cause of Cyprus uniting with Turkey."[42]

As general secretary of *Kibris Türktür*, Önal worked closely with Hikmet Bil and became his travelling companion on his trips to Cyprus and England. Önal also travelled extensively throughout Turkey organizing *Kibris Türktür* branches and spreading disinformation about Cyprus. In his speeches, he deliberately fabricated stories about Greek-Cypriot attacks on Turkish Cypriots. Thanks to Önal, this type of disinformation appeared in local newspapers throughout Turkey and created an atmosphere of intense nationalist excitement and heightened anti-Greek sentiment.

The third most influential figure in the Central Executive Committee was Ahmed Emin. He was in his seventies when he joined *Kibris Türktür* but he was one of the most, if not the most, renowned publishers and journalists in Turkey. He was an independent-minded man who had often defied authority in his long career as a journalist and as the editor of *Vatan*, and he had suffered because of it.[43] He was critical of the authoritarian tactics of the ruling Republican People's Party in the 1940s, and he was among the first to support the rebellion inside the party in the summer of 1945. The rebels in RPP were Celâl Bayar, Fuat Köprülü, Adnan Menderes and Refik Koraltan. They were either expelled from Ismet Inönü's RPP, or they resigned from it. In January 1946, they formed the Democratic Party. In 1950, it won the election and became the ruling party under the leadership of Adnan Menderes.

Ahmed Emin, therefore, had old ties with the Democratic Party and it was he who arranged the first meeting between *Kibris Türktür*'s Executive Council and Prime Minister Menderes on 28 August 1954. Ahmed Emin's influence was mainly exercised through his newspaper *Vatan*. Reflecting the independent spirit of its editor, *Vatan* did not hesitate to criticize the repressive press laws introduced by the Menderes regime in 1956. As a consequence, Ahmed Emin was jailed, causing an international outcry.[44]

Ahmed Emin's views on the Cyprus issue and Greek-Turkish relations thus acquired added significance. He was a fervent nationalist and anti-communist who supported the view that Cyprus, western Thrace and the Aegean islands belong to Turkey.[45] He advanced the thesis that the *Enosis* movement in Cyprus represented an expression of Greece's drive toward achieving the *Megali Idea*.[46] In addition, he repeated the illogical notion that the EOKA movement in Cyprus and "the violent activity of the Cypriot church is a mere camouflage for the initiative held by communists."[47] His statements raised a nightmarish specter for Turkey—a Greek, communist Cyprus which threatened the vital interests of the free world in the Middle East. Ahmed Emin's commitment to Turkish irredentism with respect to Cyprus and his solid anti-Greek views added credibility to the extremist positions of *Kibris Türktür* precisely because these views were coming from such a well-respected Turkish journalist. Thus, despite his independent spirit, Ahmed Emin contributed to the creation of extreme anti-Greek sentiment in Turkey throughout 1955 through his newspaper *Vatan*. It was quite natural, therefore, that he was an important member of *Kibris Türktür* which spearheaded the anti-Greek campaign at the time.

In addition to examining the background of key leaders of *Kibris Türktür*, it is useful to study the composition of the organization's Executive Committees in Istanbul and elsewhere to better understand the modus operandi of the organization. The coalition of the press, the student movement and sectors of organized labor, as represented in the Executive Committees of *Kibris Türktür*, enabled the organization to perform the role of a very effective agit-prop (agitation and propaganda) organization on the Cyprus issue. The three components of the coalition were able to bring about mass mobilization in support of Turkey's cause in Cyprus.

The extremely close ties of *Kibris Türktür* with the press served as the propaganda channel of the organization. It is significant that four out of the seven Central Executive Committee members in Istanbul were editors or journalists. In Izmir, an important member of the Executive Committee was the editor of a major newspaper. *Kibris Türktür* could thus be certain that its activities and proclamations would receive very wide publicity indeed. Through the inflammatory propaganda of the press, Turkish public opinion was aroused and kept in a state of nationalist agitation for months. In 1955, the press contributed to establishing a high level of sentiment against the Greek minority in Turkey, the Patriarchate, and Archbishop Makarios. These targets had been precisely the ones focused on by *Kibris Türktür* since its inception and the campaign against them reflected the position adopted by both the Menderes government and the opposition on the Cyprus issue.

The activities of *Kibris Türktür* were integrated into those of the Turkish National Student Federation. The TNSF was strongly represented in the Central Executive Committee of *Kibris Türktür*, in the 13 Executive Committees of the organization's branch offices in

Istanbul, and in its organizing committee. The Turkish student movement was a dynamic group which was essential for mass mobilization. With the headquarters of *Kibris Türktür* in the building housing TNSF in Istanbul and branches of TNSF in other major Turkish cities serving as centers of *Kibris Türktür* activity, the student movement served as the organizational means through which *Kibris Türktür* brought the masses into the streets to demonstrate in support of its cause in Cyprus. The top leadership of TNSF, including Mes'ut Ulkü, Hüsamettin Ganoztürk, Gürcan Ketem and Ali Ihsan Çelikkan, became the agents of *Kibris Türktür* in its mass mobilization campaign.

This campaign was greatly assisted by labor unions, even though the ties between *Kibris Türktür* and labor were not as close as those between the organization and TNSF. Cooperation between labor and *Kibris Türktür* was important, especially in Izmir and Istanbul. In Izmir, the secretary of the *Kibris Türktür* branch was a prominent labor leader and, in Istanbul, leaders of local labor unions sat on the Executive Committees of four or five *Kibris Türktür* branches.[48] From the organizational point of view, labor unions provided *Kibris Türktür* with the means to reach out to Turkish workers in major urban centers and bring them into the streets to participate in demonstrations. Local labor union offices, especially those of organizations representing the textile industry, were utilized by *Kibris Türktür* in the planning of demonstrations concerning Cyprus.

In political terms, the position of *Kibris Türktür* became much stronger by 1955 than it had been the previous year because it had the blessings of the government while keeping strong ties with the opposition. However, the ties *Kibris Türktür* had with the government were much more significant than those with the opposition. If the Menderes government had wanted to, it possessed the authority and the power to curb the activities of *Kibris Türktür* or even close it down as it had done with other groups and organizations. Moreover, the Menderes government had imposed very strict press laws, and, if it so wished, it could definitely have prevented *Kibris Türktür's* activities and proclamations from being reported in the press. Instead, the government—especially Prime Minister Menderes and Acting Foreign Minister Zorlu—embraced *Kibris Türktür* from the very beginning. Under a regime that was becoming increasingly authoritarian and repressive, the support of the Menderes government for *Kibris Türktür* gave the organization freedom of action that few other groups enjoyed at the time.

However, *Kibris Türktür* was not purely a creation of the government. Had it been a mere puppet of the Menderes government, it would not have been so successful in mobilizing the masses, the students, the workers and the professionals to take to the streets. For one thing, by 1955, popular discontent against the government was on the rise. It was the combined support *Kibris Türktür* enjoyed from both the government and the opposition that enabled it to rally the nation around the cry "Cyprus is Turkish and Turkish it Shall Remain." Indeed, the catalytic force which brought about the creation of *Kibris Türktür* was the convergence of two trends—Turkish irredentism and anti-Greek sentiment—both characteristics of Pan-Turkism. Dormant under Kemal Atatürk, Turkish irredentism and anti-Greek sentiment had been awaiting an opportunity to resurface. In 1959, Frank Tachau, an American scholar who had been in Turkey between fall 1954 and spring 1956, wrote an article entitled "The Face of Turkish Nationalism as Reflected in the Cyprus Dispute." In the article, Tachau said:

Turning again to the Cyprus dispute, we find that it demonstrates the official version of Turkish nationalism under the Republic and the actual operative ideas and loyalties of the people.

The strategic argument was undoubtedly the Ankara government's strongest point in setting forth the Turkish interest in Cyprus. Not so for the people. Time and again during my stay in Turkey, I was confronted by angry Turks heatedly trying to convince me that "Cyprus is Turkish." Their main argument was hardly ever strategic or military. If such considerations figured at all, they were invariably combined with, and usually overshadowed by, anti-Greek sentiment. I would hear countless stories of Greek atrocities against Turkish villagers in the bitter war of 1919-1923, followed by the assurance that the Turkish minority in Cyprus might expect similar treatment. My informants sometimes went so far as to assert that the Greeks still harbored ambitions for the reëstablishment of the Eastern Roman Empire with its capital Constantinople.[49]

It was precisely these deeply-held popular emotions which paved the way for *Kibris Türktür* to emerge as the organization that embodied the consciousness of the nation on the Cyprus issue, uniting both the government and the opposition. The anti-Greek riots in Istanbul and Izmir on 6 September 1955, which revolved around the Cyprus issue, were orchestrated by the government and executed by *Kibris Türktür*. They were vivid testimony to the fact that extremist Turkish nationalism had returned with a vengeance. According to a U.S. Embassy report from Turkey in the aftermath of the riots, a critical underlying factor behind the riots was "to be found in the latent anti-Greek feeling" prevailing in Turkey.[50]

It is also noteworthy that the establishment of *Kibris Türktür* and its campaign for a Turkish Cyprus, with the support of the government and the opposition, preceded the Greek Cypriots' resort to arms in 1955 with the establishment of EOKA. Turkey's activism and claims with regard to Cyprus were not merely a reaction to the armed struggle of EOKA, contrary to the commonly held view. *Kibris Türktür*'s campaign in Turkey demonstrates that an active Turkish irredentist movement to promote Ankara's position on the Cyprus issue was already in full swing a year before the EOKA campaign began. As for the Greek side, it overlooked Turkey's position on the Cyprus issue when it was planning to resort to arms.

NOTES

[1]Landau, *Pan-Turkism in Turkey*, 132.

[2]On the Cyprus Turkish Cultural Association being a Pan-Turkish group, ibid., 150.

[3]Ibid., 130.

[4]Jacob M. Landau, *Radical Politics in Modern Turkey* (Leiden: E.J. Brill, 1974), 201.

[5]On the Association of the Nationalists of Turkey and its activities regarding Cyprus, see Landau, *Pan Turkism in Turkey*, 131-132.

[6]Ibid.

[7]Information on the origins and establishment of *Kibris Türktür* is primarily based on the indictment against members of the *Kibris Türktür* Executive Committee for the role they played in the anti-Greek riots of 6 September 1955 in Istanbul and Izmir. See *Indictment 1150*.

[8]Ibid.

[9]On *Hürriyet*'s strong anti-Greek line and its popularity, see Alexandris, "To Melonotiko Zetema," 495-496.

[10]See *Indictment 1150*.

[11]Ibid.

[12]The anti-Greek campaign of the Turkish press in 1955 is described in several lengthy reports by the U.S. Embassy in Ankara, including: "American Embassy in Ankara to Department of State. Subject: The Istanbul-Izmir Disturbances of September 6, 1955." Despatch No. 228,

Confidential, 1 December 1955. (Hereinafter referred to as *American Embassy, Ankara, Despatch 228*.) French author François Crouzet characterized this campaign as "une campagne violemment antigrecque" (a violently anti-Greek campaign). See François Crouzet, *Le Conflit de Chypre: 1946-1959*, vol. 2 (Bruxelles: Etablissements Emile Bruylant, 1973), 689.

[13]See *Turkey and Cyprus: A Survey of the Cyprus Question*, 21.

[14]See Ahmed Emin Yalman, "Letter to the Editor," *The Times*, London, 1 September 1955.

[15]See *Indictment 1150*.

[16]Rauf R. Denktash, *The Cyprus Triangle* (London: George Allen and Unwin, 1982), 22.

[17]See *Turkey and Cyprus: A Survey of the Cyprus Question*, 12-13, 18-22, 35, 39, 68-69.

[18]An account of the meeting is found in *Indictment 1150*.

[19]Orhan Birgit's account of the meeting between Prime Minister Menderes and the *Kibris Türktür* Executive Council was published in *Akis*, 11 February 1956 and was also included in *American Consul General, Istanbul, Despatch 306*.

[20]Ibid.

[21]Ibid.

[22]Ibid.

[23]See *Indictment 1150*.

[24]On the absence of involvement by the Patriarchate and the Greek minority in Istanbul in the *Enosis* movement in Cyprus, see Alexandris, *The Greek Minority*, 252-256.

[25]Reported in: "American Consul General in Istanbul to Department of State. Subject: Political Developments in Istanbul, May 1957." Despatch No. 384, 13 June 1957.

[26]See *Indictment 1150*.

[27]The information on the Izmir branch of *Kibris Türktür* is taken from a report by the U.S. Consulate in Izmir: "American Consulate in Izmir to Department of State. Subject: Aftermath of the Izmir Disturbances on September 6." Despatch No. 29, Confidential, 4 October 1955.

[28]See Crouzet, *Le Conflit de Chypre*, 689.

[29]Alexandris, "To Meionotiko Zetema," 495-496.

[30]See *American Embassy, Ankara, Despatch 228.*

[31]Ibid.

[32]Ibid.

[33]See Ismet Inönü's speech in the Grand National Assembly on 12 September 1955 in the Turkish newspaper *Ulus,* Ankara, 13 September 1955.

[34]See *American Consul General, Istanbul, Despatch 306.*

[35]Information on RPP's criticism of the Menderes government for being passive on the Cyprus issue was based on: "American Embassy in Ankara to Department of State. Subject: Transmitting Copies of Embassy's Classified Briefing Paper on Turkey/Addendum: Anti-Greek Riots in Istanbul and Izmir." Despatch No. 153, Secret, 18 October 1955. (Hereinafter referred to as *American Embassy, Ankara, Despatch 153.*)

[36]*Ulus,* 5 January 1956.

[37]Information on Kâmil Önal's background is based on *Indictment 1150.*

[38]On the similarities between Turkish policy toward Alexandretta and Cyprus, see Stephens, *Cyprus: A Place of Arms,* 116-117.

[39]*American Consul General, Istanbul, Despatch 306.*

[40]Crouzet, *Le Conflit de Chypre,* 713.

[41]*Indictment 1150.*

[42]Ibid.

[43]On Ahmed Emin's independent-minded ideas, see Lewis, *The Emergence of Modern Turkey,* 300, 305.

[44]Lenczowski, *The Middle East in World Affairs,* 149.

[45]For the views expressed by Ahmed Emin in his newspaper, the Turkish newspaper *Vatan,* Istanbul, see "American Consul General in Istanbul to Department of State. Subject: The Riots of September 6-7 in Istanbul." Despatch No. 116, 14 September 1955. (Hereinafter referred to as *American Consul General, Istanbul, Despatch 116.*)

[46]See Ahmed Emin Yalman, "Letter to the Editor," *The Times,* London, 1 September 1955.

[47]Ibid.

[48]*American Embassy, Ankara, Despatch 228.*

[49]See Tachau, "The Face of Turkish Nationalism," 267.

[50]*American Embassy, Ankara, Despatch 153.*

6

The Cyprus Question and
the Anti-Greek Riots of September 1955

"On the evening of last September 6 [1955] one of the wildest eruptions of mob fury and hysteria in modern times broke out in Turkey's ancient city of Istanbul." This is how an American journalist, the roving editor of *Reader's Digest* who was an eyewitness to the event, began his description of the attack against the Greek minority in Istanbul.[1] Simultaneously, an anti-Greek riot took place on a smaller scale in Izmir.

The renowned Turkish author Aziz Nesin has written a series of articles on the anti-Greek riots in the Istanbul newspaper *Sabah*. He concluded:

That night [of 6 September 1955] resembled the night of Saint Bartholomew. The night of Saint Bartholomew began with the order of Charles IX. The night of 6 to 7 September began with the order of the Democratic Party. . . . Target of the plunder of that night were the Greeks of Istanbul.[2]

The magnitude of the catastrophe which befell the Greek minority in Istanbul is well-documented. The city's Greek minority and its communal institutions suffered an irreparable blow. Ninety percent of all Greek shops and 10 percent of all Greek homes were attacked and destroyed. Seventy-five percent of the Greek schools were attacked and most of them were destroyed. More significantly, 90 percent of the Greek Orthodox churches 73 out of 80 were attacked and gutted, while the two major Greek Orthodox cemeteries were desecrated.[3] Sixteen Greeks in Istanbul were either killed during the riots or subsequently died from wounds inflicted while they were in progress, and 32 were seriously injured.[4] A number of Greek women, between 50 and 200, were raped.[5]

While, in Istanbul, it was the Greek minority and the Greek

Orthodox religious institutions that came under attack, in Izmir it was the Greek state itself which was the target of the mob. The rioters attacked and burned down the Greek Consulate and the Greek Pavilion, along with its Greek flag, at the Izmir International Fair. They also attacked and destroyed several of the homes of Greek officers stationed at the NATO headquarters in Izmir. A number of Greek officers were abused and some Greek women were dishonored.

Short of being an outright military attack, what happened in Istanbul and Izmir represented an extremely serious injury to Greek interests and, more importantly, to Greek honor. Greece's national symbols, its religion, its military, and its diplomats all came under attack. Indeed, what happened in Istanbul and Izmir on that Tuesday night, 6 September 1955, was a watershed in Greek-Turkish relations.

As it turned out, Greece's passive and rather fatalistic response to the catastrophe had long-term consequences which are still felt today. The Greek press was vocal in its condemnation of the riots. But the Greek government—reacting to a considerable extent to severe U.S. pressure—adopted the attitude that the Istanbul and Izmir events were regrettable, but Greece should strive to avoid a severe break in Greek-Turkish relations for the sake of NATO solidarity. This position was best expressed by Deputy Prime Minister and Foreign Minister Stephanos Stephanopoulos of Greece while he was representing his country at the London Tripartite Conference. On the day after the riots, he stated:

The incidents which took place in Constantinople and Smyrna against the Greek minority are regrettable. The calmness shown by Greek public opinion in reaction to these disturbances proves how deep the roots of Greek-Turkish friendship are in the Greek soul.[6]

This line of argumentation reflected the thinking of the Greek Palace—King Paul and Queen Frederika. The armed forces, which played a decisive role in Greek politics and were the pillar of the throne, adopted a similar line. It was quite telling that the armed forces took such a passive stand considering that Greek military honor had come under direct assault in Izmir. Evidently, for the Greek armed forces fighting the threat of communism, confronting the Warsaw Pact countries—particularly Bulgaria—took priority over dealing with the problems of the Greeks in Turkey (and in Cyprus, for that matter). Turkey was not the enemy; the communists were. Anti-communism became the dominant ideology of the Greek officer corps in the

1950s, pushing aside traditional Greek nationalism. With such an ideological outlook characterizing the Greek armed forces from the end of the Second World War at least up until the Turkish invasion of Cyprus in 1974, the army was not in the mood to adopt a more resolute posture toward Turkey in the aftermath of the anti-Greek riots. Greece's passive response to the riots was not an unrelated factor in the determination of the fate of the Greek minority in Istanbul. Numbering 100,000 in September 1955, it has been reduced to about 3,500 today.[7]

Greece's passivity toward the plight of the Greek minority in Turkey and the destruction of its institutions and property has also had a very profound effect on the Cyprus issue, one that the Greek side was unable to foresee at the time of the riots. Indeed, at the time, the political and diplomatic implications of Greece's passivity were not understood in Cyprus. EOKA's objective was not to win militarily, but to achieve a political victory. On the political and diplomatic front, however, barely six months after EOKA's campaign had started, the most crucial source of support for the Greek Cypriots, Greece's diplomatic support, was already in retreat under Turkish pressure. The Greek side had lost a critical round in the streets of Istanbul and Izmir.

Following the military coup in Turkey on 27 May 1960, during which the Menderes regime was overthrown, the leaders of the Democratic Party were put on trial by the military government. Among the many charges they faced, they were charged with instigating the anti-Greek riots, and Adnan Menderes and Fatin Rüstü Zorlu were found guilty of masterminding them.[8] Yet, the critical agent through which the riots were carried out, *Kibris Türktür*, has been left out of the picture. The purpose of dealing with the anti-Greek riots here is precisely to emphasize that the exploitation of the Cyprus issue by *Kibris Türktür* was instrumental in creating the atmosphere which led to these riots. There is little doubt that the Turkish government also played a major role in planning the riots.

THE POWER OF RUMOR

As mentioned earlier, EOKA started its military campaign in April 1955 by attacking British military and police installations—symbols of colonial authority. Throughout its four-year campaign, its policy was to target these installations and avoid the indiscriminate killing of civilians. However, attacks on British police stations posed a problem for

EOKA because the attacks killed both Greek- and Turkish-Cypriot policemen, in addition to Britons. These attacks usually involved time bombs and grenades. The most serious incident in 1955 involving Turkish-Cypriot casualties occurred on 20 June when EOKA targeted one of the main symbols of British colonial rule, the Central Police Headquarters in Nicosia. On that day, a time bomb exploded at the headquarters killing one Greek-Cypriot civilian and seriously injuring four Turkish-Cypriot policemen. Ten Turkish-Cypriot policemen suffered minor injuries. The British came to depend increasingly on Turkish-Cypriot policemen in their fight against EOKA.

It was difficult for many Turkish Cypriots, especially their leaders, to accept EOKA's assurances that it harbored no ill intentions toward them. For the Turkish-Cypriot leadership, EOKA represented a deadly enemy. Ten days after the attack on the Central Police Headquarters, supporters of Turkish-Cypriot leader Dr. Fazil Küçük circulated leaflets which, in effect, called on the Turkish Cypriots to side with the British in the fight against EOKA. In response, EOKA circulated a leaflet which aimed at reassuring the Turkish Cypriots that EOKA was not their enemy.

Despite the violent turn of events in Cyprus with the onset of the EOKA campaign, the peaceful coexistence between the Greek- and Turkish-Cypriot communities had not yet been disrupted in summer 1955. The only area where one could detect tension between Greek and Turkish Cypriots was in Nicosia, the center of Turkish-Cypriot extremists who adopted the *Kibris Türktür* line. At the end of 1955, the year the EOKA campaign had begun, it was quite remarkable that no serious intercommunal violence had yet taken place. The foundations of peaceful coexistence between Greek and Turkish Cypriots were still holding even though they had sustained some cracks.

On 29 June 1955, British Prime Minister Anthony Eden invited Greece and Turkey to take part in the Tripartite Conference in London to discuss the Cyprus question. Britain did not invite Archbishop Makarios, the political representative of the Greek Cypriots, to take part in this conference, set to begin on 29 August 1955. What happened in Cyprus and Turkey in July and August of that summer set the stage for the anti-Greek riots of 6 September 1955 in Turkey. It was during this period that the activities of *Kibris Türktür* reached their peak.

The forthcoming Tripartite Conference prepared the ground for the diplomatic battle ahead among Britain, Greece and Turkey. Greece agreed to attend the conference, but made it clear that it was maintaining its position that the Cyprus question should be resolved by applying the principle of self-determination on the island. Archbishop Makarios opposed the conference outright. He suspected that it was a British diplomatic trap to have Greece recognize that Turkey was a legitimate party to the Cyprus dispute. This would undermine the Greek-Cypriot position that the point at issue was the principle of self-determination. For its part, Turkey adopted the stance that the Cyprus issue was neither a colonial question nor an issue of self-determination, or even self-government. Instead, Turkey maintained that it was a matter of defending the rights of the Turkish-Cypriot minority and safeguarding Turkey's vital interests in the eastern Mediterranean, which were seen as coinciding with those of NATO and the Baghdad Pact. If there were going to be a change in the colonial status of Cyprus, the island should be returned to Turkey where it "belonged," the Turks argued. The British position was much closer to Turkey's view that the question of Cyprus was not one of self-determination but, rather, one to be settled among three good NATO allies in a way which served the interests of the members of the alliance in the Middle East, especially those of Britain. However, Britain left the door open for a formula allowing for limited self-government in Cyprus. But even this was unacceptable to Turkey, for it feared that limited self-government might eventually lead to majority rule if Britain, for one reason or another decided to relinquish its sovereignty over the island.

Under these circumstances, the Turkish aim in July and August 1955 was to first demonstrate that the Turkish minority in Cyprus was so threatened by EOKA and the Greek majority that self-determination on the island would lead to the destruction of the Turkish community. Second, Ankara wanted to demonstrate that Turkish public opinion had very strong feelings about Cyprus and opposed self-determination and *Enosis* resolutely, and that, in general, Cyprus was Turkey's most important national cause. The Turks reasoned that these factors made it impossible for the Turkish government to deviate from the stand it had taken. They believed that this should have been understood by Greece, Britain and the United States.

On 21 July 1955, the president of *Kibris Türktür*, Hikmet Bil, arrived in Cyprus accompanied by Kâmil Önal, the general secretary of the organization. According to the court document indicting Bil and Önal for planning the anti-Greek riots of 6 September 1955, the *Kibris Türktür* governing board decided "to organize a trip to Cyprus and London" to *"assure a reaction to the [Turkish] cause abroad* (emphasis added)."[9] Accordingly, the two men travelled around Cyprus visiting Turkish-Cypriot communities. The well-known British journalist Charles Foley wrote that Bil had "come from Ankara with an important mission: to help reorganize the Turkish-Cypriot political party."[10] Foley met Bil at a reception given by the Turkish Consul in Nicosia. Accompanying Bil at the reception was the prominent Turkish-Cypriot leader Dr. Fazil Küçük. He was a respected physician who was known as Dr. Küçük. Bil repeated the irredentist argument of Pan-Turkists to Foley: "If and only if Britain decides to abdicate in Cyprus, then we shall put forward our claim to regain the island for Turkey. If necessary, we shall fight."[11]

Up until 1955, Turkish-Cypriot political organization had been anemic. It had revolved around the *Kibris Türk Millî Birlik Partisi* (Cyprus Turkish National Union Party, or CTNUP) founded in 1945 by Dr. Küçük. Four years after the founding of CTNUP, the Turkish Cypriots established an umbrella organization called *Kibris Türk Kurumlari Federasyonu* (Federation of Cypriot Turkish Associations). The president of this federation was Faiz Kaymak, a political associate of Dr. Küçük's.

By the mid-1950s, it became evident that a new Turkish-Cypriot party was needed. Under the direction of *Kibris Türktür* in Turkey, Dr. Küçük changed the name of his party to *Kibris Türktür Partisi* (Cyprus is Turkish Party, or CTP). Thus, a sister organization of Turkey's *Kibris Türktür* was established in Cyprus, and Hikmet Bil was keen to see that cooperation between the two became as close as possible. Indeed, in terms of objectives, Dr. Küçük's CTP adopted the *Kibris Türktür* agenda. British colonial authorities, who viewed the union of Cyprus with Greece as an anathema, found nothing objectionable in Bil's visit to Cyprus and the establishment of a political party aiming at the union of Cyprus with Turkey.

In addition to assisting Dr. Küçük's CTP organizationally, *Kibris Türktür* aided it financially. While in Cyprus, Bil and Önal met Faiz Kaymak, who was still the president of the Federation of Cypriot Turkish Associations. They made arrangements for *Kibris Türktür* to send money from Turkey to CTP through Kaymak. This was to materialize five weeks later when Kaymak visited Turkey. Önal arranged that 17,000 Turkish lira ($6,000) would be given to *Kibris Türktür*.[12]

Hikmet Bil and Kâmil Önal left Cyprus for London on 25 July 1955.[13] Several thousand Turkish Cypriots lived in London and, in addition, the Tripartite Conference was to take place there at the end of August. They stayed in the British capital for a week and set up the London branch of *Kibris Türktür* under Necati Sağer. Bil and Önal wanted the Turkish-Cypriot immigrants in London to organize demonstrations to counteract the Greek-Cypriot rallies that had been going on in that city in support of Makarios and self-determination in Cyprus. Bil was interviewed by the BBC while he was in London.

On 2 August, Bil and Önal left London for Paris. There were no Turkish immigrants in the French capital to mobilize into action, and it is unclear what the two men did while they were there. Then, Hikmet Bil visited Rome from 5 to 9 August and returned to Istanbul on 9 August 1955.[14] (It is not certain whether Önal was with Bil in Rome.)

By the time Bil and Önal returned to Istanbul, the political situation had deteriorated. Ismet Inönü's opposition Republican People's Party was accusing the government of authoritarianism, and, on 12 August, the opposition announced that it would boycott the forthcoming municipal elections. Party strife intensified when the Menderes government arrested Kâsim Gülek, the general secretary of RPP. At the same time, Turkish Deputy Prime Minister and Foreign Minister Fuat Köprülü charged that the opposition was employing tactics against the government resembling those of the communists and this behavior verged on high treason.[15]

It was in this atmosphere of rising domestic tension that the Cyprus issue began dominating the political scene. At the beginning of July 1955, the Turkish press intensified its anti-Greek campaign. The targets were Patriarch Athenagoras and the Greek minority in Istanbul. The Greeks in Turkey were asked to denounce the *Enosis* movement in Cyprus and, especially, Archbishop Makarios. By doing so, they would demonstrate whether their loyalty lay with Turkey or Greece.[16] While both the government and the opposition press in general kept up the anti-Greek campaign, *Hürriyet* and *Vatan* played a leading role in it as they raised the specter of Greek armies marching to reconquer Constantinople and Anatolia. The Turkish press reported that a Greek movement to revive the *Megali Idea* was imminent.[17]

Within this charged political atmosphere of acrimonious partisan strife and heightened nationalist and anti-Greek sentiment because of Cyprus, an ominous development occurred. It stands out as a classic case study of the power of politically motivated rumors thrust into an environment of heightened nationalist emotions. Out of nowhere, in the third week of August 1955, a rumor that something terrible was about to happen to the Turkish minority in Cyprus started sweeping through Turkey:

Greek terrorists in Cyprus were planning to attack and massacre the unarmed Turkish Cypriots. This attack was to take place on Sunday, August 28. On that date, the Greek Cypriots had announced that they would hold a general meeting in protest of the Tripartite Conference in London starting next day [August 29]. August 28 was to be the day they would carry out the massacre.[18]

This rumor could have been unimportant and irrelevant, as so many other rumors in the Middle East often are, had it not been for its catastrophic results. It played a pivotal role in creating the atmosphere which allowed the 6 September riots to take place. Given the grave consequences of this rumor, the way it was manipulated by *Kibris Türktür*, and the publicity it was given by both the government and the opposition in Turkey, it is important to first examine the degree of its validity.

Some political rumors contain a kernel of truth around which the rumor develops. Other rumors are baseless but nonetheless take root because a propitious political environment allows them to spread. The rumor about a 28 August massacre of the Turkish Cypriots by the Greek Cypriots was unfounded. In fact, it was manufactured by *Kibris Türktür*, but it swept through Turkey precisely because it was disseminated in a propitious political environment.

There exists no evidence that "Greek terrorists," meaning EOKA, had been preparing for an attack on the Turkish-Cypriot community. The British authorities fighting EOKA never presented any evidence to suggest that such an attack had been planned or even considered. In fact, an attack against the Turkish-Cypriot community ran counter to EOKA policy at the time. The attack rumor started on 13 August, only five weeks after EOKA's announcement in a leaflet that sought to reassure the Turkish-Cypriot community of its good intentions. When EOKA's leader, Grivas-Digenis, stated that the Turkish Cypriots were not in danger as a community, it was a matter of military honor as well as an order to EOKA guerrillas not to harm the Turkish-Cypriot community. EOKA was a highly disciplined organization which had its own code of honor. This held true throughout the EOKA campaign, and it was certainly true in the summer and fall of 1955 when EOKA kept its pledge not to attack the Turkish-Cypriot community. Therefore, the essence of the rumor, an EOKA attack and massacre of the Turkish-Cypriot community, was baseless, not only because no evidence whatsoever has been found to support such a serious charge, but also because it was contrary to EOKA's policy.

The second factor discrediting the rumor concerns the circumstances and the date the massacre was supposed to take place. According to the rumor, "Greek terrorists" planned to carry out the massacre on 28 August, the date the Greek Cypriots had announced a "general meeting" in protest of the Tripartite Conference in London. In reality, there were going to be meetings and rallies throughout Cyprus on that date which had been called, *not by EOKA*, but by the Communist Party of Cyprus, AKEL.[19] In fact, the pro-EOKA nationalists who dominated the Ethnarchical Council had rejected AKEL's plea that nationalists and communists hold joint rallies in protest of the Tripartite Conference.[20] There was, however, nothing anti-Turkish in AKEL's call for rallies on 28 August. Quite the contrary. AKEL was in favor of cooperation between the Greek and Turkish Cypriots. Indeed, one of the reasons AKEL did not embrace the EOKA campaign was that the communist party saw EOKA as an ignitor of Greek nationalist passions which would undermine the peaceful coexistence and "class solidarity" between Greek and Turkish Cypriots. When AKEL's rallies were held on 28 August, its leadership gave a warning, not to the Turks, but to EOKA. Disturbed by the anti-communist attitude of EOKA, AKEL leaders warned the organization not to attack or harass leaders of the communist labor movement.[21] There was no incident involving Turks before, during or after the rallies held by AKEL on 28 August.

The rumor, therefore, that the Greek Cypriots who had planned the meetings and rallies on 28 August intended to attack and massacre the Turkish Cypriots ran contrary to all facts related to these meetings. Throughout its history, AKEL had never advocated and, indeed, had always opposed attacking Turkish Cypriots. It was absolutely inconceivable that AKEL would have initiated an attack on the Turkish Cypriots on 28 August.

In Turkey, 28 August is associated with the battles between the

Turkish and Greek armies in Asia Minor in 1921 and 1922. Five days of patriotic celebrations begin on 26 August to mark Turkey's victory over Greece in 1922. That year the Turkish army, led by Kemal Atatürk, launched its "Great Attack" against the Greek army and drove it out of Anatolia. The celebrations culminate on 30 August, which is Turkey's Victory Day. Then, on 9 September, the Turks commemorate the day in 1922 that Atatürk entered Smyrna (Izmir) and literally drove the Greeks into the sea. Because these celebrations were underway in Turkey in the last week of August, patriotic emotions were heightened and memories of the war with the Greeks in Asia Minor were bitter and vivid. Rumors about an impending massacre of Turks in Cyprus during this period would have revived memories of this war and would have increased nationalist sentiment even further.

In the final analysis, the Turkish rumor that Greek Cypriots were planning a massacre of Turkish Cypriots on 28 August was a fabrication. Because the rumor was so transparent and lacking any basis in truth, the question arises as to how it emerged and how it spread so quickly throughout Turkey. There is documented evidence to indicate that the rumor was initiated by Dr. Küçük, the president of the Cyprus is Turkish Party, Kibris Türktür's sister organization in Cyprus. The epicenter of the rumor in Turkey then became Hikmet Bil who disseminated it throughout the country through the Kibris Türktür branches. On 13 August 1955, Dr. Küçük wrote a letter to Hikmet Bil in Istanbul in which he said that the Greek Cypriots had become intolerable. He also said the situation was getting worse and there were fears that the Greek Cypriots were getting ready for a massacre.[22] In addition, the letter said:

My request to you of this is that, as soon as possible, you inform all branches [of Kibris Türktür] of this situation and that we get them to take action. It seems to me that meetings in the mother country would be very useful. Because these Cyprus Greeks will hold a general meeting August 28. Either on that day or after the conclusion of the Tripartite Conference they will want to attack us. As is known, they are armed and we have nothing.[23]

It is not known whether Dr. Küçük communicated with Bil about the letter before he wrote it. However, upon receiving Dr. Küçük's letter on 16 August, Bil sent an urgent and secret circular to all branches of Kibris Türktür throughout Turkey.[24] In the circular, Bil referred to Dr. Küçük's letter from Cyprus about an impending attack and massacre of unarmed Turkish Cypriots on 28 August by armed Greek Cypriots belonging to EOKA. Then, Bil instructed the *Kibris Türktür* branches to do the following (emphasis added):

As might be suitable, with whatever additional observations that the headquarters wishes to make, please notify all organizations that our branches should choose whatever action they see fit, particularly with the view that *London and Athens should be intimidated by the manly voice* arising in the mother country.[25]

In this secret document, it is evident that Hikmet Bil used the massacre rumor as a pretext to ask *Kibris Türktür* branches to stage demonstrations in Turkey in view of the upcoming Tripartite Conference.

Dr. Küçük's close associate, Faiz Kaymak, arrived in Ankara on 17 August, the day after Bil sent his circular to the *Kibris Türktür* branches. Kaymak had met Hikmet Bil and Kâmil Önal in Cyprus three and a half weeks earlier. Upon his arrival in Ankara, Kaymak stated to the press that the Greek Cypriots were planning to attack the unarmed Turkish Cypriots. On 18 August, the Turkish press published Kaymak's statements. On that day, the president of the Union of Turkish Students in Istanbul, Tonguç Göker, also stated that the Greek Cypriots were planning a massacre of Turkish Cypriots on 28 August. This statement was published in *Hürriyet* the next day.[26] On 18 August, Kâmil Önal, the main agitator of *Kibris Türktür,* was in Adana organizing the local *Kibris Türktür* branch. He called a news conference in order to brief the press on developments in Cyprus. Önal told reporters a deliberately fabricated story about "Greek-Cypriot attacks on Turkish cemeteries."[27] He said that Greek Cypriots had set fire to several Turkish-Cypriot cemeteries in Cyprus. However, he said, when the Turkish Cypriots retaliated and set fire to one Greek-Cypriot cemetery, "the Greeks, because they are cowards, backed down."[28] The story, which had absolutely no factual basis, was published the next day on the front page of the local newspaper *Demokrat,* making the reports about an impending slaughter of Turkish Cypriots appear even more credible.

Five personalities, therefore, all associated very closely with *Kibris Türktür*—Dr. Fazil Küçük, Hikmet Bil, Faiz Kaymak, Tonguç Göker and Kâmil Önal—contributed in various ways to helping the rumor about the massacre reach the press and, therefore, the public. By the third week of August, the rumor that "Greek terrorists" in Cyprus were planning to massacre the Turkish Cypriots on 28 August had swept through Turkey.

Soon, Prime Minister Menderes, himself, gave credence to the massacre rumor in an important speech he gave on the Cyprus issue on Wednesday, 24 August 1955. The occasion was a farewell dinner for the Turkish delegation to the Tripartite Conference in London, headed by Acting Foreign Minister Fatin Rüstü Zorlu. Present at the dinner, at *Liman Lokantasi*, a well-known restaurant in Istanbul, were members of the cabinet, members of parliament, and editors and journalists from the major Turkish newspapers. To remind the Turkish nation of the bloody wars with the Greeks, Menderes referred to Cretan rebellions under the Ottoman occupation and to the Asia Minor campaign of the Greeks:

The reappearance in Cyprus today of those Greek methods which led to the fall of Crete reminds the Turks of the course taken by Greek irredentism from its inception to the present day. And we will feel impelled to once again ask of those who clamor for pocket majority rights in Cyprus today: "What brought you to the gates of Ankara in 1922."[29]

Menderes's reference to the Cretan campaign hit a very sensitive nerve in the Turkish psyche. Along with the Greek campaign in Asia Minor, the liberation of Crete by the Greeks evokes the most bitter emotions among Turks. Menderes exploited these emotions and masterfully brought them into play by alluding to them in conjunction with the rumor about an impending attack on Turks in Cyprus. He also said:

. . . . As a result of deliberate and systematic incitement, the situation in the island [Cyprus] has much deteriorated and there is a rumor that next Sunday [August 28] disturbances may take place which may lead to a massacre of the Turkish population. . . .[30]

Menderes was essentially repeating the information in the letter that Dr. Küçük had sent to Hikmet Bil on 13 August. The Turkish prime minister added:

. . . . We are therefore obliged to take seriously into account the possibility of an attack by them [Greek terrorists], which might be so sudden as to take the [British] administration unaware. It is also my duty to reassure our brother Turks in Cyprus, who are at present anxious and disturbed in their minds, that even if they find themselves unarmed and temporarily powerless before armed and numerically superior opponents, who have been violently inflamed against them, they will not be left undefended.[31]

In this way, Menderes put the prestige of his office behind the rumor and gave it credibility. In doing so, he made it an issue of high national priority. The next day, the prime minister's speech received front page coverage in the Turkish press. A whole nation was now convinced that the Turkish Cypriots were about to be slaughtered by the Greek

Cypriots who were led by a Greek Orthodox priest, Archbishop Makarios.

Following Menderes's speech, opposition leader Ismet Inönü expressed his support for the government's handling of the Cyprus issue and stated the following with regard to the massacre reports:

> The government statement has filled me with great misgivings about the safety of the Turkish population of Cyprus. We will fully support the government in all steps that will be taken for the protection of our brethren in Cyprus. During the time that the government is busy with the Cyprus issue, our domestic politics shall be impregnated with that issue.[32]

Thus, in one stroke, Inönü put partisan politics aside for a moment and came out in support of Menderes's Cyprus policy. It is even more significant that he added his great personal prestige and the backing of the opposition to the government's sober warnings of the impending attack. Government and opposition were in agreement. The massacre of the Turkish Cypriots in Cyprus seemed imminent.

Similar statements were being made in London. Upon his arrival there on 25 August, Fatin Rüstü Zorlu referred to "the incidents of bloodshed and the threats directed against the life and property of my fellow countrymen in Cyprus...." Zorlu warned that Turkish public opinion would not remain indifferent "in the face of those atrocities."[33] Dr. Fazil Küçük, who arrived in London on 26 August, declared in all seriousness (emphasis added):

> A handful of ambitious adventurers in Cyprus, using Hitlerite methods of propaganda, have concocted the so-called "Cyprus question." Unless Greek ambitions are stopped, *they could bring about a third world war*. . . . Cyprus was never Greek. . . . Historically, it is Turkish and geographically a part of Turkey.[34]

The statements by Zorlu and Küçük in London received wide publicity in Turkey, reinforcing the information disseminated by *Kibris Türktür*. Thus, in this way, within days of Dr. Küçük's letter to Hikmet Bil about a massacre, the rumor was elevated to the level of a top national issue by the Turkish government. In the process, the rumor united government and opposition, received the widest possible publicity and aroused the rawest of nationalist emotions. According to a U.S. consular report from Istanbul, the rumor, as reported in the press, "was regarded in Istanbul as primarily responsible in inflaming the public."[35] For months, Turkey's press had been carrying out an aggressive campaign against Patriarch Athenagoras and Turkey's Greek minority. It was inevitable, therefore, that the anti-Greek sentiment sweeping through Turkey would become even more intense as a result of this rumor. On 24 August, the day of Menderes's speech about the impending slaughter of Turkish Cypriots, the well-respected Turkish journalist Jihan Baban reported in the Istanbul newspaper *Tercüman* that Patriarch Athenagoras was supporting the Greek Cypriots and that he was an agent of those advocating the *Megali Idea*. These were serious charges and Baban demanded that the Patriarch be expelled from Turkey.[36]

Four days later, on 28 August, the day the massacre was supposed to take place, the prestigious newspaper *Cumhuriyet*, published in Istanbul, implied that the Patriarchate "harbored agents of anti-Turkish intrigue." It also charged that the Greeks of Istanbul had been trying to help finance EOKA's activities. According to *Cumhuriyet,* some Greek Orthodox bishops had collected "millions of lira" for that purpose.[37] Thus, the newspaper falsely and deliberately implicated Istanbul's Greek minority in the activities of EOKA, which it said was about to kill the "Turkish brothers" of Cyprus. On the same day, the mass-circulation newspaper *Hürriyet*, commenting on Menderes's speech about the impending massacre, gave this ominous warning:

If the Greeks dare touch our brethren [in Cyprus] then there are plenty of Greeks in Istanbul to retaliate upon.[38]

The position of the Patriarchate, the Greek Orthodox institutions and the Greek minority in Istanbul was becoming precarious indeed. Politically motivated rumors can bring about mass violence in any society where heightened ethnic, religious or racial tensions are combined with economic crises. Minorities become particularly vulnerable under such conditions. This is especially true in the Middle East, a region with a long history of ethnic and religious strife and group conflict. Memories of massacres are vivid for many groups in the area. Therefore, a rumor about an impending massacre of one's compatriots or co-religionists carries the potential of having an enormous psychological effect on the group involved and can give rise to profound anxiety leading to mass violence against minorities. That is precisely what transpired in Turkey in the late summer of 1955.

A baseless rumor about a 28 August massacre of Turkish Cypriots had taken hold of a whole nation—its leadership, its political parties, its press and its masses. On 28 August, Colin Legum wrote a prophetic report in the *Observer* of London. He wrote that there was "hysterical propaganda" in Turkey about an impending massacre in Cyprus. He said the Turks seemed to put faith in a totally unsubstantiated rumor that EOKA was planning to massacre the Turks of Cyprus. Just the repetition of such rumors could easily set Turkish mobs into motion, Legum concluded.[39] A U.S. Embassy report from Ankara to the State Department the day after the riots stated that the "favorable climate for violence [had been] promoted by increasingly bitter official statements and provocative press stories since [the] prime minister's speech of August 24."[40]

On Sunday, 28 August, the Greek-Cypriot communists held their rallies, and the day ended quietly for the Turkish community in Cyprus. EOKA's only violent activity that day was the shooting death of a Greek-Cypriot policeman of the Special Branch. In Turkey, however, nationalist sentiments were running high in anticipation of the 30 August and 9 September celebrations marking the victories over the Greeks in 1922. As for *Kibris Türktür*, it was moving ahead to bring matters to a climax. The organization was waiting and ready to exploit what a U.S. Embassy report called a "latent anti-Greek psychosis."[41] The three active components which gave the organization the ability to mobilize Turkish public opinion—the press, the Turkish National Student Federation and a number of labor unions—all came together on 6 September when the anti-Greek riots took place.

About the time the Tripartite Conference opened in London on 29 August, Kâmil Önal placed an "urgent" order at the Birlik Printing Office in Istanbul for 15,000 to 20,000 placards with the *Kibris Türktür* symbol on them.[42] The symbol was a map of Cyprus cradled in the crescent of the Turkish flag. Önal pressured the printer to have them ready as soon as possible. It was the first time *Kibris Türktür* had ordered so many placards at once. On Sunday, 4 September, on instructions from Kâmil Önal, the *Kibris Türktür* branches around Istanbul suddenly accelerated the distribution of the placards to shops owned by Turks.[43] If a shop displayed the placard in its window, it would indicate that the establishment was Turkish-owned and the shop would be spared from attack two days later during the demonstrations. The placards began appearing in the windows of Turkish shops and other Turkish establishments a few days before the riots.

The placard operation was directed from the headquarters of the Turkish National Student Federation in Istanbul on 4 September. That day, Hikmet Bil also asked Kâmil Önal and Hüsamettin Ganoztürk, the president of TNSF, to send some students to Taksim Square to

burn the "anti-Turk Greek-language newspapers."⁴⁴ At the time, there
were two Greek dailies in Istanbul, *Apogeumatini* and *Embros*. The
burning of these newspapers was to be a show of solidarity with a
Turkish-Cypriot demonstration in London which had been organized
by the *Kibris Türktür* London branch after consultation with the
Istanbul headquarters. In order to assure wider publicity for the Greek
newspaper-burning, Hikmet Bil instructed Ganoztürk to call the
newspapers *Vatan* and *Milliyet* and ask them to send photo reporters to
Taksim square to cover the event. Hikmet Bil, himself, called
Hürriyet.⁴⁵ This was another indication of how closely *Kibris Türktür*
was cooperating with the press in the anti-Greek campaign. Indeed,
the next day, 5 September, most of Istanbul's newspapers gave prominent coverage to the newspaper-burning in Taksim Square. This press
campaign continued unabated on 6 September. For instance, *Yeni
Sabah*, the Istanbul newspaper for which Orhan Birgit of the *Kibris
Türktür* Central Executive Committee was working, had as its main
headline: "*TNSF and Kibris Türktür Announce: September 9 is Day of
National Warning for the Greeks.*" Under this headline, there was the
title: "*The Terrorist who had Murdered a Police Officer was Arrested during
an Inspection of Makarios's Car.*" The item about the "terrorist" in
Makarios's car was contrived, as were other reports about Cyprus disseminated by *Kibris Türktür*. No such incident ever took place in
Cyprus. At the same time that the press was linking Makarios to what
it termed "EOKA murderers," the streets and walls of Istanbul were
being filled with anti-Makarios graffiti. Two main slogans written in
black paint appeared throughout the city: "*Kibris Türktür*" (Cyprus is
Turkish) and "*Katil Makarios*" (Makarios Murderer).

KIBRIS TÜRKTÜR AND THE ANTI-GREEK RIOTS

During the last few days of August and the first few days of September
1955, Turkey resembled a tinderbox of jingoism and anti-Greek sentiment which was being fanned by both the government and the opposition. The spark that started the anti-Greek riots was a bomb explosion at 12:10 a.m. on the morning of Tuesday, 6 September 1955, in
the yard of the Turkish Consulate in Thessaloniki, Greece. The consulate was adjacent to the house where Kemal Atatürk was born. The
explosion shattered some windows in both buildings but did not cause
any other damage.⁴⁶ It did not take long for Greek army experts to
determine that the bomb had not been thrown into the yard but had
been placed there from within. A few days later, following an investi-

gation, Greek authorities arrested two Turks, Hasan Uçar and Oktay Engin, and charged them with planting the bomb. Uçar was a guard at the Turkish Consulate, and Engin was a student from Komotini in western Thrace who was known to have had ties with the consulate.[47] It was not until 1957, however, that the two men were actually convicted of the crime by a Greek court.

Engin had returned from Turkey a few days before the incident, carrying three fuses with him. In his memoirs, Grivas-Digenis, who had been privy to the investigation of the case by Greek authorities, maintained that "Oktay Engin was an obedient instrument of *Kibris Türktür.*"[48] Engin escaped to Turkey in September 1956 and was hired by *Cumhuriyet.* Greek sources say that he was also employed by MIT, Turkey's secret service, and rose to a top position in the agency by the late 1980s.[49]

In the absence of concrete proof of who committed the bombing immediately following the incident, it was inevitable that the Greeks would be blamed for it. The bombing of Atatürk's birthplace was a provocation *in extremis.*[50] The day after the riots, Acting Turkish Foreign Minister Zorlu stated in London that these riots might be considered "a natural reaction of the Turkish people to the damage done to the birthplace of Kemal Atatürk."[51]

The bombing incident was first reported by Turkish state radio on 6 September. During its mid-day news program, it announced that a bomb had exploded outside the house where "beloved Atatürk was born."[52] That day, the pro-government afternoon newspaper *Istanbul Ekspres* came out with an extra edition to announce the incident. The headline, covering half of the front page, read "Atatürk House Damaged by Bomb."[53] It was the largest headline ever to have appeared in *Istanbul Ekspres.* Other headlines in the paper read "Bomb that Exploded in Salonica Damaged Seriously Beloved Atatürk's House," and "This Event Enraged the People." A subtitle said that Greek censorship was keeping news of the bombing from reaching the public.[54] In the photographs accompanying the report, Atatürk's house appeared to have been seriously damaged by the explosion. It was later proven that the photographs had been doctored.[55]

As soon as the extra edition of *Istanbul Ekspres* came out, Kâmil Önal coordinated the distribution of the newspaper along with thousands of *Kibris Türktür* placards which would be posted in windows of additional commercial establishments owned by Turks throughout Istanbul.[56]

Moreover, a highly inflammatory statement made by Önal was published in the extra edition of *Istanbul Ekspres*. He stated that *Kibris Türktür* was following developments very closely and, blaming the Greeks for the bombing of Atatürk's house, he said:

We do not see harm any more in proclaiming openly that we shall make those who laid hands on our Sacred Ata [Atatürk] pay very dearly.[57]

Throughout 6 September, *Kibris Türktür*'s propaganda mechanism was in high gear fomenting further agitation. The *Kibris Türktür* headquarters in the building housing the TNSF office served as the center of operations for planning the demonstrations scheduled for that night. All plans were being closely coordinated with student leaders and labor union leaders. Hikmet Bil was in charge of giving instructions concerning final preparations for the demonstrations to Kâmil Önal, Hüsamettin Ganoztürk, Nedim Üsdiken and Orhan Birgit, all members of the *Kibris Türktür* Central Executive Committee which was in continuous session in the organization's headquarters.

On the morning of 6 September, Hikmet Bil had met with Prime Minister Menderes to discuss the plans for the demonstrations.[58] According to Bil, Menderes told him that "Zorlu's job in London is to push the Turkish case and torpedo the [Tripartite] Conference. Zorlu wants us to be active in Turkey."[59] This statement was consistent with Hikmet Bil's secret circular of 16 August. It had said that, in view of the Tripartite Conference, *Kibris Türktür* should act in such a way as to intimidate London and Athens through the "manly voice" arising in Turkey. Indeed, the political objective of the anti-Greek demonstrations was to show the world, and especially Britain, Greece and the United States, that Turkey's concern over the Cyprus issue was so profound that no settlement was possible without Ankara's consent.

Kibris Türktür and TNSF each issued a proclamation on the bombing incident which blamed it on the Greeks. The *Kibris Türktür* proclamation was drafted by Hikmet Bil and Orhan Birgit, both journalists, and was approved by Hüsamettin Ganoztürk (TNSF president) and Nedim Üsdiken. They were all members of *Kibris Türktür*'s Central Executive Committee. The TNSF proclamation was written by Ganoztürk and Üsdiken and was approved by Hikmet Bil.[60] These proclamations were distributed by the thousands around Istanbul.[61] The *Kibris Türktür* proclamation is reprinted below in its entirety (emphasis added):

Proclamation of the Cyprus is Turkish Society

Following the bomb attack on the house of the great liberator Atatürk in Salonica, the presidency of the Cyprus is Turkish Society held an extraordinary meeting and decided to proclaim the following to Turkish public opinion and to the Greek people:

1. Every Turk continues to cherish with profound reverence in his heart and memory the city of Salonica, over which the Greek flag flies today, as a city which occupies a prominent place in our nation's struggle for freedom and as the birthplace of our immortal liberator Atatürk.

The "Atatürk House" which also comprises the Turkish Consulate, located in this historical city of western Thrace *which we regard as original Turkish soil*, is already Turkish territory under international law.

2. Considering, for this reason, the infamous attack as one directed against the Turkish fatherland as a whole, the Cyprus is Turkish Society proclaims that it regards the occurrence as *the drop which makes the cup overflow* and since the attack has been perpetrated on the eve of September 9—"the day of national warning to Greece"—it announces that *it is no longer possible for us to control our patience already strained to a point of breaking*.

3. The fact that the Greek authorities—instead of punishing the guilty in a manner setting a deterring example—have been endeavoring to explain things away by claiming that the perpetrators are not Greek citizens *proves in an irrefutable manner that the Greek authorities are directly implicated in the incident*.

4. If the Greek government and those who directly or indirectly support it in these incidents—regardless of which part of the world they may be in—should fail to come to their senses, they will find themselves faced with our hatred and strength in a manner which will completely overshadow the year 1922.

We now address you dear citizens: The Greek imperialists, who in our weakest moment treacherously came to invade our country, set fire to our homes, murder our mothers, brethren and wives in cruel fashion, and kill our fathers as martyrs, appear to have forgotten the fact that they were swept into the waters of the Mediterranean in September 1922, *so they are today directing their aggression at the house in which our beloved Atatürk was born in Salonica, an abode which forms part of the very heart of the fatherland*. Tighten your ranks! Be extremely watchful of the doings of *those among you who really do not belong to us* and repeat the national oath: *Cyprus is Turkish and shall remain Turkish!* Those who think otherwise or endeavor to undo this oath shall dearly pay for their actions regardless of where they may be.

The *Kibris Türktür* proclamation is an important document for two reasons. First, it was an incitement to anti-Greek violence. Understandably, for the Turkish people, the bombing of Atatürk's birthplace was a sacrilege against the Turkish nation. By blaming the Greeks for the bombing and by suggesting that the Greeks of Istanbul were acting as a fifth column, *Kibris Türktür* was inviting the Turkish masses to take action against the Greeks of Istanbul. As the proclama-

Figure 2: Demonstrators in Istanbul carrying the *Kibris Türktür* placard on the night of 6 September 1955. It shows a map of Cyprus cradled in the crescent of the Turkish flag. This photograph appeared in the Istanbul newspaper *Yeni Sabah* on 7 September 1955.

tion said, "Be extremely watchful of the doings of those among you who do not belong to us." In addition, the proclamation called the bombing of Atatürk's home "the drop which makes the cup overflow" and makes it impossible "to control our patience." The immediate effect of the proclamation was to add to the already powerful anti-Greek sentiment in Turkey and bring it to the point of hysteria. Second, the proclamation presents a clearer picture of the Pan-Turkish ideology of *Kibris Türktür*. In the document, not only was Cyprus considered a Turkish island, but western Thrace and Thessaloniki were considered Turkish as well.

On the afternoon of 6 September, some labor unions were actively assisting *Kibris Türktür* in the preparation of the riots. For instance, the offices of the Textile Union were used for the preparation and distribution of placards for the demonstrations.[62] On the night of the riots, the demonstrators were also equipped with special instruments of destruction that had apparently been distributed to them earlier. According to a U.S. Embassy report, some of these instruments "were especially designed for ripping corrugated iron shutters off store windows."[63] They included clubs, axes, hammers and iron bars, that is, equipment which was not readily available in the streets for demon-

Figure 3: Turkish youth in Istanbul are waving a Turkish flag on the night of 6 September 1955. They have added a *Kibris Türktür* slogan which reads, *Kibris Türktür Türk Kalacak* (Cyprus is Turkish and Turkish it Shall Remain). This photograph appeared in the Istanbul newspaper *Milliyet* on 7 September 1955.

strators to use. A U.S. Embassy report based on information received from the Istanbul police chief stated that the tools had been collected and distributed to the demonstrators by labor unions.[64] It also appears that certain army units were involved in their distribution. At 5:30 p.m. on 6 September, four army trucks were seen parked opposite Tophane Çeşmesi (Tophane Fountain) on Meclisi Mebusan Avenue. Soldiers in the trucks unloaded and distributed iron bars, clubs and axes to groups of individuals who then moved in two directions toward Galata and Beyoğlu where Greek shops were located.[65] Other trucks transported demonstrators to Greek neighborhoods in Istanbul that were several miles away from Taksim Square where the main demonstration was to take place.

The rally organized by *Kibris Türktür* in Taksim Square was to begin at 6:30 p.m. Tens of thousands of people quickly gathered in and around the square, while groups of demonstrators began appearing in other parts of the city. As the crowds moved through the streets of the city, they carried the following: Turkish flags, pictures of Kemal Atatürk, the *Kibris Türktür* placard (see figure 2) and flags bearing the slogan *Kibris Türktür Türk Kalacak* (Cyprus is Turkish and Turkish it Shall Remain) (see figure 3).[66] The demonstrators chanted this slogan along with the following slogans:

> *Yikin, Kirin Gâvur Mallidir*
>
> (Demolish and Break the Property of the Infidels)
>
> *Müslümanlarin Düşmanidir*
>
> (They are Enemies of Muslims)
>
> *Öldürmek Yoktur*
>
> (No Killing)

These slogans are indicative of two important characteristics of the demonstrations. First, the slogans added an element of religious fervor to the strong nationalist flavor of the anti-Greek agitation. A U.S. Embassy report on the riots referred to the use of the word "gâvur" by many demonstrators.[67] The Turkish term "gâvur," which means "infidel," was used in reference to the Greeks, and, as infidels, the Greeks were also regarded as "enemies of Muslims" by the mob. This partially explains the systematic attack and destruction of 90 percent of the Greek Orthodox churches in Istanbul. Certainly, besides referring to the Greeks, the term "gâvur" pertained to other "infidels"—the Armenians and Jews of Istanbul. The fact that Armenian churches and Jewish synagogues were spared from attack, however, indicates how well the riots were organized. In this respect, a U.S. Embassy report to the State Department stated:

There was, in fact, clear evidence that the attacks were deliberately directed against Greek Orthodox churches. It would appear that religious fanaticism, to the extent that it was present, was channelled primarily against the Greek Orthodox Church as part and parcel of a basically anti-Greek movement.[68]

The second important characteristic of the slogans is that they called only for the destruction of property and asked that the "infidels" not be killed. Although 16 Greeks did die and 32 were seriously injured as a result of the riots, the slogans indicate that the demonstrators were given previous instructions to avoid killing that night. This is confirmed by the indictment against *Kibris Türktür* members which said that Osman Tan, chairman of the *Kibris Türktür* branch in Sariyer, addressed demonstrators in Yenimahalle the night of the riots and told them: "Boys, strike and break but do not kill."[69]

Following brief but strongly anti-Greek speeches in Taksim Square, part of the crowd started splitting into smaller groups of 20 to 30 individuals.[70] Some of these groups included female students. The groups were led by *Kibris Türktür* branch leaders such as Aydin Konuralp, Oztürk Ganoztürk, Sarafim Saglamel, Mustafa Eroglu and Erol

Demiroğlu.[71] A U.S. Embassy report on the riots stated that "the rioting groups seemed to be operating under leaders who directed the rioters toward destroying Greek shops, homes, schools and Greek Orthodox churches."[72] According to the report:

It seemed that separate groups had started rioting in almost every section of the city, up and down the Bosporous clear to the Black Sea and out on the Prince's Islands in the Sea of Marmara. The Greek population was spread out all over Istanbul and, almost without exception, there was some rioting in every section of the city and its environs—that is, the spots of rioting were spread over an area fifteen miles long and ten miles wide.[73]

Thus, while demonstrators started attacking and looting Greek shops on fashionable Istiklal Avenue near Taksim Square, other groups were attacking Greek property, schools and churches in Büyükdere and Yenimahalle, both located on the outskirts of Istanbul, 15 miles away.

By 9 p.m., the city's *lumpenproletariat* had joined in the demonstrations. The *lumpenproletariat* included *hamals* (porters), unemployed urban workers, and villagers who had recently moved into the city and were living in conditions of utter poverty. Their participation indicates that socioeconomic discontent was mounting at the time.[74] This discontent, added to the anti-Greek hysteria, transformed the demonstrations into a mass riot where mob violence was directed overwhelmingly against the Greek community. A comparatively small number of Armenian and Jewish shops and homes were also attacked. The mob looted the famous Adler jewelry store which was owned by one of the most prominent Jewish families in Istanbul.

The Turks of Istanbul were becoming increasingly envious of the relative prosperity of the Greek, Armenian and Jewish minorities. These minorities, who enjoyed a higher standard of living than the Turks, were seen as controlling the city's commercial and financial life. This increased popular resentment against them. However, the main cause of the riots was not socioeconomic. The riots did not represent a spontaneous popular explosion of "haves" against "have-nots," as has been suggested.[75] Instead, it was a well-planned assault against the Greek minority. However, the mob did take the opportunity to vent its socioeconomic frustrations that night when the state's mechanisms of social control—the police and the army—allowed or even facilitated the attack against the Greek community. Hence, the day after the riots, the streets of Istanbul were strewn with worn-out shoes as impoverished city dwellers found new shoes to wear in the looted shops, perhaps for the first time in their lives.

In the end, it was nationalist emotions aroused by the Cyprus issue that were the driving force behind the well-organized riots. A U.S. consular report from Istanbul a week after the riots took place stated that "there have been many indications that the destruction was well-organized."[76] On 29 September 1955, the U.S. Consulate in Istanbul reported to the State Department that "there was elaborate advanced planning for widespread destruction of the property of the indigenous Greek community which plans involved many people and careful preparations."[77] The police stood by and watched the destruction. U.S. Consul General in Istanbul Arthur Richards was an eyewitness to the riots. That night, he reported to the secretary of state: "I personally witnessed looting of many shops while police stood idly by or cheered on the mob."[78]

It was not until after midnight, after a very long delay, that the army was ordered to move in and slowly begin to restore some order. By then, however, it was too late. Already, the Greek neighborhoods of Istanbul, which included some of the city's most famous boulevards and fashionable suburbs, looked—as a British journalist put it—like the bombed parts of London during the Second World War.[79] By the time the riots were over, 73 churches, eight burial places, 26 schools, 1,004 homes, 4,212 shops and stores, 21 factories, 12 hotels, 97 restaurants and 23 warehouses lay in ruins.[80] The Greek minority had been dealt a decisive blow and the riots marked the beginning of the end of its presence in Istanbul.

Contrary to what one might have expected, neither the governments of the Christian West, in general, nor the United States, in particular, took an openly critical stand against Turkey in the aftermath of the assault on Greek Orthodox institutions in Istanbul. The response of NATO governments was muted and Washington remained apathetic. U.S. Secretary of State John Foster Dulles, who had already received a detailed account of the riots from the U.S. Consulate in Istanbul and the U.S. Embassy in Ankara, was silent for 12 days. On 18 September, he sent the *identical* note to both the Turkish and Greek prime ministers. In his note, Dulles barely mentioned the anti-Greek riots. He only referred parenthetically and obliquely to the "unhappy events of the last two weeks" and urged both Turkey and Greece to show restraint and continue their cooperation for the sake of NATO unity.[81] In other words, Dulles, the quintessential cold warrior, apparently did not consider it morally or politically appropriate to take a position concerning the anti-Greek riots. Dulles's stand caused a wave of protest in Greece and laid the foundations of anti-American sentiment among a wide spectrum of Greek public opinion.

Following the riots, Istanbul police arrested 3,151 individuals. All but 17 of them were soon released. Nine of those detained were leading figures of *Kibris Türktür*. Five of the nine—Hikmet Bil, Kâmil Önal, Hüsamettin Ganoztürk, Orhan Birgit, and Nedim Üsdiken—were members of the *Kibris Türktür* Central Executive Committee. The other four—Aydin Konuralp, Sarafim Saglamel, Osman Tan and Erol Demiroglu—were branch leaders of *Kibris Türktür*. Two of the remaining defendants who were kept in jail, Vedat Pekgirgin and Göksin Sipahioğlu were editors of *Istanbul Ekspres*. The other six were students. After being incarcerated for four to six months, all 17 were released. However, they were all indicted under martial law regulations for their role in the 6 September riots. In addition, six leading figures of the Izmir branch of *Kibris Türktür* were indicted, bringing the total number of defendants to 23. Following the lifting of martial law, their case was transferred from the military court to an Istanbul criminal court and they all faced the following charges:

1. Perpetration of hostile acts against a foreign state [Greece] of a nature to involve the country [Turkey] in war or seriously impair Turkey's relations with the country in question.

2. Public provocation and instigation to criminal action.

3. Publication and dissemination of alarming reports.

4. Abetting criminal action, destruction of incriminating evidence and unauthorized removal of official seals.[82]

It is noteworthy that the first charge was of an extremely serious nature. The defendants were charged with hostile acts against Greece, acts that might have resulted in a Graeco-Turkish war. It is quite ironic that the Greek political and military leadership at the time did not react to the riots in a way that acknowledged the gravity of the situation and the possibility that it might have led to war with Turkey. It seems that Turkish leaders were expecting a much stronger and decisive reaction from Greece—not necessarily involving a military response—than the one adopted by the Greek government.

On 24 January 1957, the Istanbul criminal court announced its verdict. All 23 defendants were acquitted. In pronouncing the verdict, the court stated that the prosecution, in summing up its case on 14

January, had dropped all charges and requested acquittal of all accused. The grounds for acquittal as given by the prosecution were as follows:

Cyprus [is a] Turkish island forming part of [the] motherland. [Therefore, the] Turkish people could hardly remain indifferent to continuous provocations in Cyprus and in Greece. [As a consequence, the 6] September disturbances were in substance [a] result[ant] product of such provocations.[83]

The acquittal of the members of the *Kibris Türktür* Central Executive Committee and its branch leaders represented a moral and political victory for *Kibris Türktür* and for its ideology and activism. The grounds for acquittal make this apparent. In the final analysis, the court itself adopted the *Kibris Türktür* thesis that Cyprus *is* a Turkish island. The court also found that *Kibris Türktür*'s mobilization of the Turkish public was a justifiable response to "continuous provocations in Cyprus and Greece." The inclusion of the statement that "Cyprus is a Turkish island forming part of the motherland" in the court's opinion was an additional indication that Turkish irredentism with regard to Cyprus had been espoused by Turks of all social strata.

Following the acquittal of the *Kibris Türktür* officials, the organization continued its activism concerning the Cyprus issue for several more years. The Turkish foreign ministry appointed the organization's president, Hikmet Bil, to the position of press attache of the Turkish Embassy in Beirut. *Kibris Türktür*, however, had reached its zenith and had served its purpose. Its role in Turkey as an agit-prop organization regarding the Cyprus issue, its effectiveness in mobilizing Turkish public opinion around Turkish irredentist and Pan-Turkish slogans, and its instrumental role in the anti-Greek riots of 6 September 1955 have had a lasting impact on the situation in Cyprus and on Greek-Turkish relations.

The ideology of *Kibris Türktür* was avowedly Pan-Turkish. Though its irredentism was directed primarily toward Cyprus, it was also advocated with regard to Greece. The organization's irredentist agenda concerning Cyprus was clear and vocal. When the major political forces in Turkey offered their support to *Kibris Türktür*, they endorsed its irredentism toward Cyprus. Turkey's foreign policy has not changed in any meaningful way since *Kibris Türktür* was established in 1954 and Turkey's irredentism toward Cyprus took hold of Ankara's foreign policy. The *Kibris Türktür* line was also adopted by the Turkish-Cypriot leadership in 1954 and still marks its policies today. Two Turkish-Cypriot leaders who have personified the *Kibris Türktür* line are Dr. Fazil Küçük and Rauf Denktash, especially the latter.

NOTES

[1]See Frederick Sondern, Jr., "Istanbul's Night of Terror: An Eyewitness Account of One of the Most Destructive Riots of Our Times," *Reader's Digest* (May 1956): 185.

[2]Turkish newspaper *Sabah*, Istanbul, 1-5 October 1986, quoted in Alexandris, "To Meionotiko Zetema," 499.

[3]The statistics quoted are based on an account of the riots in *American Embassy, Ankara, Despatch 228* and on figures given in Alexandris, *The Greek Minority*, 259.

[4]Alexandris, "To Meionotiko Zetema," 499.

[5]For understandable reasons, it was difficult to establish exact figures on rapes. The estimate of the U.S. Embassy in Ankara was "40-50 cases of rape." Alexandris puts the number at 200. See *American Embassy, Ankara, Despatch 228* and ibid.

[6]Reported in the Greek newspaper *Macedonia*, Thessaloniki, 8 September 1955.

[7]Alexandris, "To Meionotiko Zetema," 499, 515.

[8]On the role played by the Menderes government in masterminding the riots and the trial and conviction of Menderes and Zorlu, see Walter Weiker, *The Turkish Revolution, 1960-1961* (Washington, D.C.: The Brookings Institution, 1963), 33-35; Alexandris, *The Greek Minority*, 252-266; Ferenc A. Váli, *Bridge Across the Bosporous: The Foreign Policy of Turkey* (Baltimore: The Johns Hopkins Press, 1971), 236-237; Crouzet, *Le Conflit de Chypre*, 708-726.

[9]See *Indictment 1150*.

[10]Foley, *Legacy of Strife*, 29.

[11]Ibid.

[12]*Indictment 1150*.

[13]Ibid.

[14]Ibid.

[15]On partisan strife in Turkey in the second week of August 1955, see *The Times*, London, 12, 15-16, 18-19 August 1955.

[16]Alexandris, *The Greek Minority*, 253-255.

[17]The anti-Greek campaign in the Turkish press was described in *American Consul General, Istanbul, Despatch 116.*

[18]On this rumor about a massacre on 28 August 1955, see *American Consul General, Istanbul, Despatch 306; American Embassy, Ankara, Despatch 153; American Embassy, Ankara, Despatch 228.*

[19]Reported in *The Times*, London, August 9, 1955.

[20]Ibid.

[21]*The Times*, London, August 29, 1955.

[22]*Indictment 1150.*

[23]Ibid.

[24]Ibid.

[25]Ibid.

[26]Crouzet, *Le Conflit de Chypre*, 689.

[27]*Indictment 1150.*

[28]Ibid.

[29]See *Turkey and Cyprus: A Survey of the Cyprus Question*, 49.

[30]As reported in *The Times*, London, August 26, 1955.

[31]See *Turkey and Cyprus: A Survey of the Cyprus Question*, 48.

[32]See *The Times*, London, August 27, 1955.

[33]Quoted in *American Embassy, Ankara, Despatch 153.*

[34]See *Keesings Contemporary Archives*, 27 August-3 September 1955, 1496.

[35]*American Consul General, Istanbul, Despatch 306.*

[36]See Alexandris, *The Greek Minority*, 253.

[37]Turkish newspaper *Cumhuriyet*, Istanbul, 28 August 1955, quoted in ibid., 253-254.

[38]Turkish newspaper *Hürriyet*, Istanbul, 28 August 1955, quoted in Alexandris, *The Greek Minority*, 256.

[39]*Observer*, London, 28 August 1955, quoted in Ierodiakonou, *To Kypriako Problema*, 126-127.

[40]"American Embassy in Ankara to Secretary of State," Despatch No. 344, Secret, 7 September 1955.

[41]*American Embassy, Ankara, Despatch 153.*

[42]*Indictment 1150.*

[43]Ibid.

[44]Ibid.

[45]Ibid.

[46]Alexandris, *The Greek Minority*, 256-257.

[47]Ibid.

[48]Grivas-Digenis, *Apomnemoneumata*, 58.

[49]Alexandris, "To Meionotiko Zetema", 543.

[50]The Greeks continued to be blamed for the bombing after the 6 September riots. On 14 September 1955, the famous Turkish journalist Hüseyin Cahit Yalçin wrote a long article in *Ulus*, the organ of the opposition RPP, about the riots. In the article, Yalçin referred to "the Greeks who threw the bomb into Atatürk's house . . ." Quoted in Alexandris, *The Greek Minority*, 258. On 25 February 1956, Turkish Deputy Prime Minister and Foreign Minister Fuat Köprülü, speaking in the Grand National Assembly, protested vigorously that Greece was acting in a provocative manner in the way it investigated the bombing of Atatürk's house. Köprülü stated that "Greek efforts to show that the Salonica [Thessaloniki] explosion was engineered by Turkey" were provocative because they constituted "a stone thrown at Turkey." See *Turkey and Cyprus: A Survey of the Cyprus Question*, 65.

[51]Reported in "American Consul General in Istanbul to Department of State," Despatch No. 159, 9 September 1955.

[52]*Indictment 1150.*

[53]Ibid.

[54]Ibid.

[55]In his memoirs, Grivas-Digenis provides detailed information on the Greek police investigation into the doctored photographs of Atatürk's house. See Grivas-Digenis, *Apomnemoneumata*, 57. See also Alexandris, *The Greek Minority*, 257.

[56]*Indictment 1150.*

[57]Ibid.

[58]Alexandris, "To Meionotiko Zetema", 501.

[59]Alexandris, *The Greek Minority*, 264.

[60]*Indictment 1150.*

[61]*American Embassy, Ankara, Despatch 228.*

[62]Ibid.

[63]Ibid.

[64]Ibid.

[65]Based on a personal and confidential interview in January 1991 with an eyewitness, a Greek from Istanbul, who happened to be passing by Tophane Çeşmesi on the afternoon of 6 September 1955. He saw soldiers unloading iron bars from military trucks. He was later expelled from Turkey and settled in Athens.

[66]*Indictment 1150.*

[67]*American Embassy, Ankara, Despatch 228.*

[68]*American Embassy, Ankara, Despatch 153.*

[69]*Indictment 1150.*

[70]*American Embassy, Ankara, Despatch 228.*

[71]*Indictment 1150.*

[72]*American Embassy, Ankara, Despatch 228.*

[73]Ibid.

[74]On the socioeconomic grievances at the time and their role in the riots, see Alexandris, *The Greek Minority,* 258.

[75]The socioeconomic interpretation of the riots was advanced by Professor Kemal Karpat. He cites the dean of Turkish journalists, Hüseyin Cahit Yalçin, in support of the thesis that the primary cause of the riots was socioeconomic. See Karpat, *Turkey's Politics,* 422.

[76]*American Consul General, Istanbul, Despatch 116.*

[77]"American Consul General in Istanbul to Department of State," Despatch No. 138, Confidential, 29 September 1955.

[78]"American Consul General in Istanbul to Secretary of State," Control No. 2678, 6 September 1955.

[79]*Daily Mail,* London, 14 September 1955.

[80]These figures are found in *American Embassy, Ankara, Despatch 228.*

[81]On John Foster Dulles's note to the Turkish and Greek governments, see Alexandris, *The Greek Minority,* 267.

[82]"American Consul General in Istanbul to Secretary of State," Despatch No. 633, 25 January 1957.

[83]Ibid.

7

Enter the Turkish Officers and TMT

A new Turkish organization made its appearance in Cyprus on 9 September 1955, the anniversary of the Greek defeat and evacuation of Smyrna [Izmir] in 1922 and the date *Kibris Türktür* had proclaimed, four days earlier, as the "day of national warning to Greeks." It was named *Volkan* (Volcano) and its objective was to counter EOKA. (*Volkan* had also been the name of a journal published in Istanbul in 1909 by an extremist Islamic group called the Muhammadan Union. Over the next decade, this organization came to be known as the *Volkan* group.[1]) According to Grivas-Digenis, EOKA's leader, the members of *Volkan* were trained by young Turkish officers who came to Cyprus clandestinely from Turkey and by British intelligence officers.[2] Compared to EOKA, *Volkan* was not a powerful organization. This factor, combined with the intercommunal violence which erupted in 1957, led to the establishment of another secret Turkish organization, *Türk Mukavemet Teşkilâti* (Turkish Resistance Organization, or TMT). By the fall of 1957, TMT superseded *Volkan* and took over the political activities formerly carried out by Dr. Küçük's CTP, which had begun to concentrate on propaganda activities. TMT soon emerged as a powerful and dynamic politico-military force which exercised critical influence over the affairs of the Turkish-Cypriot community. It adopted as its emblem the *bozkurt*, one of the main Pan-Turkish symbols. The *bozkurt* image (grey wolf), as used by TMT, was usually superimposed on a map of Cyprus and was accompanied by the crescent of the Turkish flag (see figure 4).

The exact nature of the ties between TMT and Pan-Turkish groups in Turkey remains unclear. Very little research has been done on this inherently difficult subject because of the clandestine character of TMT. Still, the fact that TMT's emblem was the *bozkurt* makes it apparent that the objectives of the organization were based on the precepts of Pan-Turkish ideology. The six declared principles of TMT were the following: (1) to ensure the safety of the lives and property of the Turkish Cypriots, (2) to stand up to the threat of terrorism from the *Enosis* movement, (3) to deter attacks against the Turks, (4) to ensure the security of the Turkish community and fight against communism, (5) to ensure that the rights of Turks are not threatened by the Greeks and the British, and (6) to consolidate the bonds between Turkish Cypriots and the motherland, and advance the unity of the Turkish community with the motherland.[3]

While details about the establishment of TMT are still not known, it appears that four persons played a role in founding the organization—Riza Vuruşkan, Kemal Tanrisevdi, Burhan Nalbantoğlu and Rauf Denktash. They probably held the founders' meeting in Cyprus at the end of July 1957. What is certain is that the key figure in the establishment of TMT was Riza Vuruşkan, a lieutenant colonel in the Turkish army who also became the first TMT commander, or *bayraktar*. It is believed that his wife, Jihan, was from the town of Lapithos in the Kyrenia district of Cyprus.

It appears that the decision to form TMT was made at the highest level of the Turkish government. Dr. Küçük said he first met Riza Vuruşkan when he was introduced to him by Prime Minister Menderes during a visit to Turkey in 1957. The two men probably met in the spring of that year. At the time, Menderes was faced with mounting domestic problems and the fact that he had a meeting with Vuruşkan and Dr. Küçük suggests that he wanted to involve the Turkish military even more deeply in the Cyprus issue. By then, the Turkish armed forces were growing restless because of the abuses of the Menderes regime. For his part, Menderes expected to create an external diversion for the military through the "grand national cause of Cyprus."[4] Dr. Küçük subsequently met with Vuruşkan at the office of a lieutenant general in the Turkish army. "During our meeting," Küçük wrote, "it was decided that Vuruşkan should come to Cyprus as 'civil adviser.' He arrived in Cyprus under an assumed name and started residing here."[5]

Vuruşkan came to Cyprus sometime in the summer of 1957. Using the name Ali Conan or Ali Bey, he posed as a banker who was going to be working for the *Iş Bankasi* (Business Bank). According to Dr. Küçük, "Vuruşkan was the founder of TMT and its first *bayraktar* and,

of the *bozkurt* (grey wolf) represent TMT emblems as they appeared in the official publication of the organization entitled *TMT Notlari* (TMT Notes) (Lefcoşa (Nicosia): Halkin Sesi, 1972). On the left, the *bozkurt* image is superimposed on a map of Cyprus. The ten arrows are rising from the points on the map where the ten command posts of the *Mücahit* force (military force) of TMT were located. All the arrows are linked to the central command post in Nicosia.

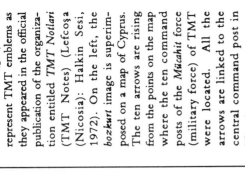

within a short time, he organized every village, and, thus, we were able to defend ourselves against EOKA . . ."[6] In his memoirs, General Grivas-Digenis states that he was informed of the arrival of a Turkish officer in Cyprus named Hasan Tahsin Ogerlat on 8 February 1957, before Vuruşkan arrived. Ogerlat had come to Cyprus to organize the Turkish-Cypriot underground. According to Grivas-Digenis, Ogerlat, who was born in Cyprus, arrived on the island disguised as a photographer.[7]

Several hundred members of TMT operated underground. They were Turkish-Cypriot nationalists who were trained and guided in Cyprus and Turkey by a small group of Turkish officers. TMT established cells in towns and villages and selected the cadres who were sent to Turkey for military training.[8] TMT was financed by Turkey which also provided most of its arms.[9] Thus, TMT emerged as the organized military arm of the Turkish Cypriots against EOKA and its campaign for *Enosis*. Simultaneously, it became the organization through which the geopolitical policy of Turkey was enforced in Cyprus. It was a policy which aimed at effecting the gradual segregation of the two communities. This would, in turn, make partition a logical solution and an impediment to *Enosis*. Still, partition was considered to be a concession by Turkey since Turkey maintained that it was entitled to the whole island. After 1956, however, *taksim* (partition) became the primary Turkish demand. It was considered the most realistic policy at the time, especially since Britain favored it as a way of increasing diplomatic pressure on the Greek side, in general, and on Archbishop Makarios, in particular.[10]

In 1957, Turkish Cypriots were urged to disengage from any cooperative ties they had with Greek Cypriots. As a consequence, that year, Turks stopped trading with Greeks, avoided shopping in Greek stores, stopped smoking Greek cigarettes, and deferred from visiting their Greek neighbors.[11] The Turkish separatist stance was best expressed by the TMT slogans *Taksim veya Ölüm* (Partition or Death) and *Vatandas Türklerden Mal Aliniz* ("Patriots, buy from Turks," or as it came to be known "From Turk to Turk"). This was a historic development as far as relations between the two communities were concerned. Indeed, up until the 1950s, Greek and Turkish Cypriots had coexisted peacefully and cooperation between them had been most evident and quite close in the economic field.[12]

In addition, TMT sought to purge the Turkish-Cypriot language from

Greek influence. Most Turkish-Cypriot merchants and shop owners spoke Greek in addition to their mother tongue. The 1960 census indicates that 38 percent of all Turkish Cypriots declared Greek as their second language.[13] In fact, most Turks could carry on a conversation with their Greek neighbors in Greek. As a consequence, Greek had become the language of communication between Greek and Turkish Cypriots, both in their business transactions and in their everyday contacts. The TMT policy of severing contact between Turks and Greeks was meant to remove the need as well as the opportunity for Turkish Cypriots to use the Greek language.

While TMT was enforcing the "From Turk to Turk" campaign in Cyprus in 1957, a similar campaign was being waged in Istanbul. The Istanbul campaign was organized by the Turkish National Student Federation which had worked closely with *Kibris Türktür* in its planning of the anti-Greek riots of September 1955. The objective of the TNSF campaign was to discourage Turks from patronizing Greek-owned shops in Turkey's largest city. Echoing TMT's separatist slogan in Cyprus, a TNSF leaflet stated:

Fellow Turk, think that every penny that is earned at your expense by those [the Greeks] who suck you financially is becoming a bullet against our brothers in Cyprus. It is a national duty that you enter into no transaction with them [the Greeks]. A Turk ought to buy from another Turk.

Signed: Turkish National Student Federation[14]

This campaign was another blow to the Greeks in Istanbul who had begun their exodus to Greece in the aftermath of the September 1955 riots.

In the meantime, TMT used force to implement the "From Turk to Turk" policy in Cyprus. It assassinated Turkish Cypriots in high profile positions, such as leftist union leaders and journalists, who persisted in advocating cooperation between Turks and Greeks.[15] The only Turkish-Cypriot political group to go against the TMT separatist policy was the small Turkish-Cypriot Communist Party (TCCP) whose members insisted on cooperating with Greek-Cypriot labor unions and with the Greek-Cypriot Communist Party, AKEL. TCCP was silenced very quickly through TMT's use of intimidation and violence. An additional reason for the targeting of Turkish-Cypriot communists by TMT was the fact that they were viewed as arch enemies of Pan-Turkism. Anti-communism had become one of the main credos of Pan-Turkish ideology.[16] TMT forced most TCCP members to publicly denounce their affiliation with the party. Two of TCCP's leaders were assassinated by TMT and its offices were set on fire.[17] Dr. Küçük sided with TMT from its inception. Rauf Denktash, who was already emerging as a dynamic leader in the Turkish-Cypriot community second only to Dr. Küçük, was a leading figure of TMT.[18] Thus, TMT's policy of separatism not only prevailed; it also became the political doctrine of the Turkish-Cypriot elite.

Since TMT was founded and led by Turkish officers, it may be concluded that these officers were the de facto military leaders of the Turkish Cypriots in their violent confrontation with the Greeks during the late 1950s. In political terms, the Turkish-Cypriot leadership under Dr. Küçük still appeared to be in a position to act as genuine spokesmen of the Turkish Cypriots in terms of decision-making. However, this leadership was actually subordinate to TMT officers and, by extension, to Turkey.[19] In the final analysis, the Turkish officers were enforcing the policy of the Turkish government in Cyprus.

FROM 1963 TO THE INVASION: RULE BY THE TURKISH MILITARY

TMT was not dissolved when Cypriot independence was achieved in 1960. In fact, the overall influence of Turkish officers in Turkish-Cypriot affairs became preponderant during the 1960s. Mutual suspicion stemming from the ethnic violence of 1957 and 1958 did not allow either the Greek-Cypriot or the Turkish-Cypriot community to let its guard down following independence. Instead, both sides armed themselves and retained some paramilitary units just in case violence started anew. Intercommunal fighting did break out again in Nicosia following the Christmas 1963 constitutional breakdown and it spread quickly throughout the island. This ethnic violence, which continued into 1964, was more intense and widespread than that occurring in 1957 and 1958, and it set the process in motion for the physical separation of the two communities.[20]

Civil strife was especially bloody between the last week of December 1963 and April 1964 when revenge killings of civilians were not uncommon. By the late spring of 1964, distinct territorial lines of ethnic separation were in place for the first time. The Turkish Cypriots set up a self-proclaimed autonomous civil administration to oversee the territory they controlled—about four percent of the republic—and left the Cypriot government in control of 96 percent of the country. Initially, this civil administration was led by a "General Committee." Following the declaration of the "Provisional Turkish-Cypriot Administration" (PTCA) on 28 December 1967, the "General Committee" was replaced by the eleven-member "Executive Committee," presided over by Dr. Küçük. Rauf Denktash, who was in Turkey at the time, became vice-president of the "Executive Committee."

The territory under Turkish-Cypriot control consisted of 39 enclaves of varying size scattered throughout the island. The largest and most important one was the Nicosia-Kyrenia enclave which included the Turkish quarter of Nicosia. The Turkish and Turkish-Cypriot politico-military command was based in the Turkish Embassy in the Turkish sector of the city. Twenty-two of the enclaves, mostly in the Paphos district, were very tiny and consisted of one or two villages. Approximately 60 percent of the Turkish-Cypriot population lived in the enclaves. The rest lived in towns and villages where the population was a mixture of Greek and Turkish Cypriots. While the Turkish Cypriots in the areas of mixed population were technically under the authority of the Cypriot government, their political allegiance was to the leadership in the Turkish sector of Nicosia whose orders they obeyed.

Turkish Cypriots lived in the enclaves for about ten years, until the Turkish invasion of 1974. During this period, their contact with Greeks varied from limited to non-existent. To the extent that there was contact, it often depended on the locality and the level of tension in that area. In the city of Kyrenia, where 700 Turkish Cypriots resided in a mixed neighborhood called *Pano Kerynia*, no Kyrenia Turk was harmed during the period of conflict from December 1963 to the end of 1967. However, overall Greek-Turkish contact was reduced to a minimum during this period. Mutual fear and mistrust accounted partially for this lack of contact, but another critical reason was the policy of self-imposed isolation the Turkish-Cypriot side was following. It called for severance of all transactions and contacts with the Greek Cypriots and refusal to acknowledge the authority of the Cypriot government. This policy of segregation and isolation was enforced by a security apparatus supervised by Turkish officers. Turkish Cypriots who violated the orders were subject to varying degrees of punishment, depending on the seriousness of the offense. The type of punishment was determined by the *sancaktar*, the district military commander.[21]

The relaxation of tension and the absence of any serious ethnic violence between 1968 and 1973 led to limited contact between the two communities. This was particularly the case in the economic field. By 1972, about 7,000 Turkish-Cypriot laborers, or 15.2 percent of the 46,000-strong Turkish-Cypriot labor force, worked for Greek-Cypriot enterprises outside the enclaves. Nonetheless, this economic relationship did not indicate any underlying trend toward a political rapprochement between the two communities.

The employment of Turkish Cypriots by Greek Cypriots was controlled by the *sancaktar*. Turkish Cypriots could work for Greek Cypriots only after he granted them special permission to do so. They were permitted to leave the enclave in the morning but were required to return by nightfall. The stagnant Turkish-Cypriot economy and rising unemployment in the enclaves were the primary reasons for the decision to allow Turkish Cypriots to work for Greek enterprises. However, the Turkish-Cypriot leadership remained as adamant as ever in its insistence that the government of President Makarios was illegitimate, and this leadership continued to act as the only legitimate authority for the Turkish Cypriots.

Beginning in 1968, signs of discontent among Turkish Cypriots gave rise to an effort to organize an opposition party. The main source of discontent appeared to be the economic conditions in the enclaves and the authoritarian spirit permeating the ruling circles of these enclaves. Unemployment was particularly high among Turkish-Cypriot graduates of Turkish universities who had returned to Cyprus after completing their studies. A considerable number of these students had been influenced by radical leftist ideologies while in Turkey. Upon their return to Cyprus, many of them were displeased by the lack of opportunity and the existence of a militarized society in the enclaves.

Opposition to the Turkish-Cypriot regime and to Rauf Denktash crystallized in December 1970 when Ahmed Berberoglu formed the Republican Turkish Party (RTP).[22] The extent of popular support at the time for this leftist-oriented opposition party remains unclear. After RTP was formed, Berberoglu was unable to pose any effective challenge to Denktash and the ruling circles. Their political control over the Turkish-Cypriot community continued to be overwhelming, and their policy, which was leading to partition, remained unchanged. The formation of the enclaves had provided the Turkish-Cypriot leadership with a very important weapon with which to pursue the policy of segregation and partition.

The Greek-Cypriot leadership concluded that time was working against the Turkish Cypriots because the enclaves constituted only a small fraction of Cypriot territory and there was a state of permanent economic stagnation in these enclaves. The government expected that it would only be a matter of time before Greek-Cypriot prosperity would lure the Turkish Cypriots into giving up their policy of segregation and self-imposed isolation, and agree to a *status quo ante* settlement. However, the course of events belied Greek-Cypriot expectations. The political significance of the enclaves far exceeded their miniscule size. Indeed, these enclaves represented a form of geographically-based ethnic segregation that was a prelude to the partition of Cyprus.

Despite the existence of a civil administration, Turkish-Cypriot society moved quickly toward militarization. This militarization was favored by circumstances. Security concerns and the need for military defense against the far superior government forces simply overwhelmed the Turkish Cypriots. They not only had to confront the Greek-Cypriot National Guard, but, by the fall of 1964, they were faced with a reinforced division of the Greek army under General George Grivas-Digenis's command as well. The primary mission of these Greek forces, which left Cyprus after the crisis of November 1967, was to deter a military invasion by Turkey. Without them, the National Guard was not able to defend Cyprus against a Turkish assault, as the 1974 invasion has shown.

From a regional perspective, the Greek Cypriots felt as if they were a minority vis-à-vis Turkey because they were living in the shadow of Turkey's military might. Since Christmas 1963, they had been terrified of the Turkish armed forces, and many of them had panicked whenever Turkey threatened to invade the island or sailed its warships near Cyprus. On the other hand, in Cyprus *per se*, Turkish Cypriots were the actual minority. They felt extremely threatened by the Greek Cypriots and their isolation contributed to reinforcing a siege mentality. Therefore, military defense dominated all the affairs—civil, social and economic—of this minority. It was inevitable that those who controlled the Turkish-Cypriot military structure would also be in a position to dominate the Turkish-Cypriot society politically. Indeed, in times of conflict and extraordinary crisis, such as the one faced by the Turkish Cypriots between 1963 and 1974, military and political affairs tended to become indistinguishable.

Between 1963 and 1974, Turkish-Cypriot defense was undertaken by the *Mücahit* force (Fighters of Islam), which was organized by TMT. Although it had some regular military units, it was primarily a paramilitary force. Turkish officers exercised complete control over it.[23] The commander of the force, the *bayraktar*, was a colonel attached to the Turkish Embassy in the Turkish sector of Nicosia. The *Mücahit* force was estimated to be about 10,000-strong and was deployed unevenly around the 39 Turkish-Cypriot enclaves.[24] The strength of deployment was contingent upon the size of the enclave, its population and its needs at any given time.

Administratively, the enclaves belonged to seven districts: Nicosia, Chatos, Famagusta, Larnaca, Limassol, Paphos and Lefka. Each district was commanded by a *sancaktar,* who usually carried the rank of lieutenant colonel. The seven districts were divided into 17 subdistricts. A subdistrict consisted of one or more enclaves, depending on the size of the enclave. Each of the subdistricts was under a commander known as a *serdar,* who usually carried the rank of major. The *serdars* came under the command of the *sancaktars,* who reported to the *bayraktar* and took orders from him. The Turkish commanders of districts and subdistricts, the *sancaktars* and *serdars,* came to be known under the generic name of pasha.

Although Riza Vuruşkan had been both the founder and first commander of TMT, Kenan Çoygün, a colonel in the Turkish army, became the first commander, or *bayraktar,* of the newly organized *Mücahit* force. Çoygün arrived in Cyprus on 3 October 1962 under the name Kemal Çoşkun. He arrived about a year before the Christmas 1963 crisis, perhaps anticipating the likelihood of such a crisis. Between Christmas 1963 and the invasion of July 1974, the *Mücahit* force came under the command of five colonels, including Çoygün. With the exception of Çoygün who served for more than four years, each of these colonels served in Cyprus for two years or less (see table 7).

The *sancaktars* who came to Cyprus *before* the crisis of Christmas 1963 arrived under various types of civilian cover. The first *sancaktar* to arrive was Orhan Ozatay who entered the country legally on 4 November 1962. At Nicosia Airport passport control, he declared that he was a tobacco expert. (Cyprus has a tobacco-producing region on the Karpasia peninsula where a number of Turkish villages were located.) In reality, Ozatay was a lieutenant colonel in the Turkish army and he served as *sancaktar* of the Lefka region from early 1964 until he left the country on 28 September 1966. He left Cyprus via the port of Famagusta, posing as one of the departing Turkish officers who had served in the Turkish contingent on the island. This contingent rotated every six months as stipulated under the 1959 Zurich-London agreements.

On 20 February 1963, a Turkish national, Remzi Güven, arrived at Nicosia Airport. At passport control, he declared that he was an official of a charitable organization and had come to Cyprus to assist *Evkaf*, the Muslim religious foundation for charity and education in Cyprus. Güven was actually a lieutenant colonel in the Turkish army who served as Nicosia's *sancaktar* until 1965 when he was succeeded by Lieutenant Colonel Derviş Sertaç Sevim. On 14 September 1965, Güven left Cyprus from the port of Famagusta as a member of the rotating Turkish contingent.

On 6 August 1963, six months after Güven's arrival, another lieutenant colonel in the Turkish army, Eftal Akça, arrived at Nicosia Airport declaring that he was a school inspector who would be working as an advisor to the Turkish-Cypriot school system. From Christmas 1963 until September 1966, he served as *sancaktar* of the Limassol region. On 28 September 1966, he sailed to Turkey from Famagusta, along with Ozatay.

On 10 August 1963, four days after Akça's arrival in Cyprus, yet another Turkish lieutenant colonel, Turgut Sokmen, came to Cyprus through Nicosia Airport. He also declared on the employment form he filled out at customs that he was a school inspector. Following the crisis of Christmas 1963, he became *sancaktar* of the Famagusta region. On March 3, 1966, Sokmen departed from the port of Famagusta with the rotating Turkish contingent.

Barely two months before the intercommunal fighting erupted in December 1963, another "school inspector" from Turkey came to Cyprus. Turgut Giray Budak, a lieutenant colonel in the Turkish army, arrived at Nicosia Airport on 26 October 1963. After Christmas 1963, he became *sancaktar* of the Larnaca region. On 28 September 1966, Budak departed for Turkey from the port of Famagusta with the Turkish contingent, along with Ozatay and Akça (see table 7).

The arrival of six Turkish officers under cover in the 15 months

TABLE 7: TURKISH OFFICERS WHO SERVED IN CYPRUS WITH
TMT AND THE MÜCAHIT FORCE: 1955-1974
(PARTIAL LIST)

NAME	RANK IN TURKISH ARMY	RANK IN TMT	ARRIVAL IN CYPRUS	DEPARTURE FROM CYPRUS
Riza Vuruşkan	Lt. Colonel	Commander	Summer 1957	1959 (?)
Kenan Çoygün	Colonel	Commander	3 Oct. 1962	25 Feb. 1967
Orhan Ozatay	Lt. Colonel	District Commander	4 Nov. 1962	28 Sept. 1966
Remzi Güven	Lt. Colonel	District Commander	20 Feb. 1963	14 Sept. 1965
Eftal Akça	Lt. Colonel	District Commander	6 Aug. 1963	28 Sept. 1966
Turgut Sokmen	Lt. Colonel	District Commander	10 Aug. 1963	3 Mar. 1966
Turgut Giray Budak	Lt. Colonel	District Commander	26 Oct. 1963	28 Sept. 1966
Derviş Sevim	Lt. Colonel	District Commander	Mar. 1965 (?)	Mar. 1967 (?)
Ferit Cengiz	Lt. Colonel	District Commander	18 (?) Oct. 1966	30 Mar. 1968
Mehmet Eris	Colonel	Commander	2 Dec. 1966	9 July 1968
Riza Vuruşkan	Colonel	District Commander	1 Aug. 1967	21 Sept. 1967
Akin Erkal	Colonel	Commander	3 July 1968	4 July 1970
Ömer Alper Suat	Colonel	Commander	19 June 1970	7 July 1972
Hakki Özkan	Colonel	Commander	25 June 1972	After July 1974

preceding the outbreak of fighting in late December 1963 raises the question of whether Turkey was planning to precipitate a crisis which would lead to the partition of Cyprus sometime in 1964. It is possible, however, that fighting started accidentally in Nicosia and spread throughout the island when things somehow got out of control. While Greek-Cypriot forces were able to take over some of the Turkish posts quickly, there was stiff organized resistance at other posts by well-armed Turkish-Cypriot forces. Indeed the government forces were surprised to find stockpiles of arms in the Turkish-Cypriot positions they captured. Commenting on Turkish-Cypriot fighting capabilities, TMT founder Riza Vuruşkan wrote that "it is most probable that the Greeks had launched their operation estimating our force weaker than what we were."[25] The organized state of the Turkish-Cypriot resistance indicated that the Turkish officers who had arrived in Cyprus earlier had been clandestinely arming and training the Turkish Cypriots.[26]

It can be argued that the Turkish officers who arrived in Cyprus under cover before the crisis of Christmas 1963 had come to reorganize TMT into the *Mücahit* force with the assistance of the officers in the Turkish contingent. With the existence of this force, the Turkish Cypriots would not be unprepared in the event fighting broke out between the Greek and Turkish Cypriots. Certainly by fall 1962, there had been clear signs that the Cypriot constitution was unworkable and that tension between Greek and Turkish Cypriots might lead to a violent confrontation.[27] Both communities were secretly preparing for such an eventuality. With regard to the Turkish side, it is inconceivable that the clandestine arrival of Turkish army officers in Cyprus could have taken place without the full knowledge and approval of the Turkish government. Greek army officers also started arriving in Cyprus surreptitiously after the intercommunal conflict started during the Christmas 1963 holidays.

The Turkish military command structure in Cyprus organized the *Mücahit* force, but several impediments faced by the Turkish military headquarters in Nicosia worked against developing it into a tightly controlled military force. Rather than developing into a regular army, it remained primarily a paramilitary force, even though some of its battalions in the Nicosia-Kyrenia enclave were well-trained and disciplined. There were two reasons for this. First, the Turkish-Cypriot enclaves were dispersed throughout Cyprus and most of them were too tiny to allow the tactical deployment of military units. Second, the Cypriot government was in a position to supervise entry into and exit from most of the enclaves through police checkpoints, especially at times of tension. These two factors hindered communications and logistical links among enclaves, district commands and the military headquarters in Nicosia. The emergency situation and the reliance of the villagers on the *Mücahit* force for their defense tended to favor the concentration of power in the hands of the district military commanders, the *sancaktars*. In fact, civil authority in the districts had shifted de facto to these commanders.[28] In the final analysis, the Turkish Cypriots were ruled by Turkish officers since military authority dominated or even absorbed civil authority at the district and local level.

Certainly, the representatives of local civil authority, the *muhtars*, were still present in the Turkish-Cypriot villages. In many villages, especially the smaller ones, the local commander was usually a Turkish Cypriot. All local commanders, however, came under the command of a *sancaktar*. Being officers of the Turkish army, the *sancaktars* embodied the historic traditions of the Turkish military and the glory of the Ottoman past. They were well-respected by the villagers and were obeyed by the local population, despite occasional misgivings concerning the condescending behavior of some officers.

In addition to their military role which rendered them the authority figures in the enclaves, the *sancaktars* performed another function which further enhanced their power and influence. Between 1964 and 1974, the Turkish-Cypriot economy and welfare system depended on financial aid from Turkey. Turkey provided an average of $15 million annually to pay the salaries of civil servants, finance public works projects and fund the welfare system. Because the *sancaktars* were representatives of Turkey and were in positions of authority, they became the agents who determined how aid from Turkey was to be distributed throughout each district. The distribution was carried out according to guidelines established by the *bayraktar*, who oversaw the general allocation of funds. By distributing welfare funds, the *Mücahit* force, in the end, became interwoven with the community's social structure.[29]

With the transfer of civil authority from the hands of Turkish-Cypriot officials into the hands of Turkish officers, the *sancaktar* emerged as the highest civil authority in each of the seven administrative districts. Each district was administered by the District Administration Council (DAC) which was presided over by the *sancaktar*. In his absence, the vice-president of the Council—the Turkish officer who was second in command in the district—chaired the DAC.

The jurisdiction of the DAC extended to most aspects of local civil administration. Since the Turkish enclaves were relatively isolated from one another and lacked a strong central authority, each district enjoyed substantial administrative autonomy. The DAC also had decision-making power over economic matters in each district and exercised some judicial authority.

The DAC in the Famagusta district had 14 members. In addition to the president and vice-president, it had 12 Turkish-Cypriot members—local officials, civil servants and professionals.[30] The mayor of the Turkish sector of Famagusta, Kemal Sariçi, was a DAC member and was clearly under the authority of the Famagusta *sancaktar*. From 1964 to 1966, Lieutenant Colonel Turgut Sokmen was the *sancaktar* and president of the Famagusta DAC.

The Famagusta DAC could discipline civil servants and assign duties to them. It could also issue exit permits, allocate funds for welfare projects, regulate prices, and impose import duties and taxes. In addition, it had the authority to confiscate movable and immovable property, and impose fines payable at the office of the *sancaktar*. For instance, on 16 June 1967, the Famagusta DAC decided that any Turkish Cypriot who purchased a car from a Greek Cypriot without the permission of the *sancaktar* would be fined 50 to 100 pounds ($75 to $150), and the car would be confiscated for a period of two to four months. On 7 July 1967, the DAC prohibited the sale of non-Turkish refreshments, such as Coca Cola, in Turkish-Cypriot shops, even if they were located outside the Famagusta enclave. On 22 August 1967, the DAC imposed a duty of 100 mils per *oke* (15 cents per pound) on what it called "foreign" cigarettes. This did not include cigarettes from Turkey which were duty-free. On the same date, the DAC fined Mustafa Mehmet Laptali 60 pounds ($90) for entering into a transaction involving Cypriot government officials. Laptali had bought a house from another Turkish Cypriot, but the deed of sale was executed at the Cypriot government Department for Land and Surveys. In other words, the DAC was responsible for all non-military matters except general policies affecting the welfare of the Turkish-Cypriot community as a whole, such as the budget and the salaries of civil servants. Such matters were handled by the leadership in the Turkish sector of Nicosia.

The existence of the DAC and the fact that the majority of its members were Turkish Cypriots had in no way diminished the power and authority of the *sancaktar* in civil affairs. In fact, the authority of the *sancaktar* over the DAC was absolute since its members were appointed by him and served at his discretion. The *sancaktar* had the power to make a decision on any civil matter without the knowledge or approval of the DAC. For instance, Lieutenant Colonel Ferit Cengiz, *sancaktar* of the Paphos district from October 1966 to March 1968, issued orders and regulations concerning all civil matters, including those pertaining to personal and family hygiene, sanitation, and neighborhood improvement. He also imposed fines, received financial contributions, distributed welfare funds, supervised food distribution, financed public works, and regulated car registration and insurance. More specifically, in an order issued on 19 November 1966, Cengiz announced that he was rewarding three "compatriots" for the spirit of voluntarism they had exhibited. Thus, Cengiz stated, "I have given five pounds (7.5 dollars) to the fighter Hüseyin Kâzim, three pounds (4.5 dollars) to the municipal employee Cemal Tezcan and three pounds to the construction worker Raif Mustafa." In the same order, Cengiz announced some of the monetary contributions he had received to finance public works. He announced that the following had been given to him for the construction of public restrooms and roads: 20 pounds from Ali Şefik and his wife, 60 pounds from Sitki Kadizade and 125 pounds from Kâzim Başit (see appendix A, document 2).

Cengiz also issued instructions on matters pertaining to the upbringing of children. On 15 August 1967, Cengiz issued the following order (see appendix A, document 7):

Following an inspection of the Çamlica area, it has been observed that Gülderen Izzet has not watered the tree that he has been assigned to look after.

Assigning your child to water the tree aims at teaching him good habits in order to benefit the community. By watering the tree, the child offers a service to the community.

It is important to teach your children to avoid laziness and stay away from bad habits. I would ask you to be careful so that your child carries out his duties.

> (Signed)
> Cengiz
> SANCAKTAR

In the order dated 19 November 1966, Cengiz also addressed the Turkish Cypriots as *Müslüman Kardeşlerin* (my Muslim Brothers) and asked them to behave in a manner befitting Turks and good Muslims in striving to achieve their goals (see appendix A, document 2). In an order dated 31 October 1966, Cengiz asked the Turks of the Paphos district to take good care of their mosque and to keep the town and villages in the district especially clean on Friday, the Muslim Sabbath, when they performed their ritual ablution (*abdest*) (see appendix A, document 1). The invocation of Islam by Cengiz, an officer of the Turkish army, is remarkable because the military has maintained a secular outlook in Turkey. It indicates that Turkish officers made use of Islam in Cyprus to win public support among Turkish Cypriots in the pursuit of political objectives. Following the Turkish invasion and occupation of northern Cyprus in 1974, the Turkish armed forces embarked upon the Islamization of the occupied territory. (This subject is discussed in chapter 10). Thus, it does not appear that the invocation of Islam by Lieutenant Colonel Cengiz in Paphos in the second half of the 1960s was an aberration as far as the attitude of Turkish officers toward Islam in Cyprus was concerned.

In the final analysis, the *sancaktars* set the policy guidelines for the local communities in each region and issued executive orders regulating social and economic life. (See appendix A for copies of Cengiz's orders on matters of civil administration, documents 1-3, 5, 7.) They enforced these orders through the *muhtars* and through the local bodies, such as the police and the municipal agencies, which came under the *sancaktar's* authority. Thus, in all the enclaves, the Turkish officers emerged as the absolute rulers of the Turkish Cypriots.

The situation was not very different at the center of power in the Nicosia district where the authority of the Turkish-Cypriot leadership was being further eroded by Turkish officers. The nominal leader of the Turkish Cypriots was still the veteran politician Dr. Fazil Küçük. Following the constitutional breakdown at the end of 1963, he became president of the "General Committee" of the self-proclaimed autonomous Turkish-Cypriot civil administration. He also presided over the "Executive Committee" which was established at the meeting on 28 December 1967 declaring the "Provisional Turkish-Cypriot Administration." Indicative of Turkey's involvement in Turkish-Cypriot affairs was the fact that this meeting was attended by Zeki Güneralp, secretary general of the Turkish foreign ministry and Suat Bilge, the ministry's chief legal adviser. As Dr. Küçük's authority and power gradually eroded and shifted to Turkish officers, he became more of a symbolic father figure to the Turkish Cypriots than the key decision-maker of his community.

The real power in Turkish-Cypriot affairs was exercised by the *bayraktar* stationed at the Turkish Embassy in Nicosia. He headed a regime which was a military one in all but name only. From the time intercommunal fighting erupted in December 1963 until 25 February 1967, the *bayraktar* was Colonel Kenan Çoygün, known under the *nom de guerre* "*Bozkurt*." Çoygün received his orders from the Turkish government. The fact that the *bayraktar* was stationed at the Turkish

Embassy indicated that he was in close and constant touch with the Turkish government.

Vital decisions affecting the Turkish-Cypriot community as a whole were made by the *bayraktar*. In addition to determining how economic aid from Turkey was to be allocated, he also issued executive orders on matters such as emigration, though emigration was discouraged. In order to enforce the regulations on Turkish-Cypriot emigration, Çoygün issued an order providing for the confiscation of the property—land, home, and car—of the Turkish Cypriots who either left Cyprus "illegally" or violated the terms of their "leave of absence" abroad. He was the de facto ruler of the Turkish Cypriots and he exercised despotic power in the sense that there was neither a Turkish-Cypriot leader—not even Dr. Küçük—nor an institutional mechanism to curtail his power. The only control over the *bayraktar's* power emanated from the Turkish government.

The Turkish-Cypriot center of civil administration in the Nicosia district came under the control of the *sancaktar* as it did in the other enclaves. The first *sancaktar* of the Nicosia region was Lieutenant Colonel Remzi Güven. He was succeeded by Lieutenant Colonel Derviş Sevim, the legendary "Kale Bey," who served as *sancaktar* in the mid-1960s.[31] Sevim initiated a series of public works, outlawed the carrying of arms in public, banned gambling, and fired several Turkish-Cypriot police officers for not adequately carrying out their duties in the campaign against gambling. Dr. Küçük's authority eroded even further when Sevim ordered the heads of all administrative services to report directly to the *sancaktar*. In short, Dr. Küçük was left out of the decision-making process concerning the most critical affairs of his community. It was men like Çoygün and Sevim who held the real power in the crucial Nicosia region, rather than any Turkish-Cypriot leader.

Dr. Küçük's authority grew even thinner as Rauf Denktash came to be regarded as more capable and dynamic than the senior Turkish-Cypriot leader. Denktash was elected president of the Turkish-Cypriot Communal Chamber (TCCC) in 1960. He could have been his community's spokesman for security affairs, given his experience in TMT, but he was living in Turkey from 1964 to 1968. In March 1964, Denktash found himself forced to stay in Turkey where he was in transit returning from a trip abroad. Greek-Cypriot press reports at the time indicated that, if he were to attempt to return to Cyprus, the

Cypriot government would either prevent him from returning or would arrest him upon his arrival and charge him with instigating armed rebellion against the state.

These were difficult times for Denktash. While he was in Turkey, there was a propaganda campaign being waged among the Turkish Cypriots to discredit him. Circles around Dr. Küçük accused Denktash of abandoning the Turkish-Cypriot community. These circles said that he could have returned to Cyprus but, instead, chose to stay in Turkey where they claimed he was living a comfortable life. In reality, Denktash lived modestly in a small Ankara apartment with his wife and sons. He was often visited by his friends from Cyprus, Naim Attiloğlu, Orhan Müderrisoğlu and Dr. Hasan Nihat. They were all prominent members of the Turkish-Cypriot community and they urged him to go back to Cyprus. They told him that the majority of the Turkish Cypriots wanted him to return.

It is still unclear what the relationship between Denktash and the Turkish government was at the time. It seems, however, that the government in Ankara was reluctant to allow or facilitate his return to Cyprus. Conceivably, the Turkish government was concerned that his return to Cyprus might arouse passions, precipitate a new round of fighting and drag Turkey into a military adventure at a time when the Turks were at a disadvantage militarily. The presence of a Greek division in Cyprus from 1964 to 1967 had rendered an invasion extremely problematic. An article published in September 1967 indicates that there might be some merit to the argument that Turkey was reluctant to allow Denktash to return to Cyprus. In the article, Riza Vuruşkan praised Denktash for being the leader of those who believed that the solution in Cyprus "lies in an armed struggle." "Because of this conviction," Vuruşkan wrote, "he [Denktash] is now living in exile in Turkey."32

Denktash attempted to return to Cyprus twice between 1964 and 1968. The first attempt was made during the crisis in the coastal villages of Kokkina and Mansura in July and August 1964. On 1 August 1964, Denktash came to Kokkina on a Turkish destroyer, along with Vuruşkan. Denktash returned to Turkey 12 days later, most likely because the Greek-Cypriot National Guard had been able to isolate the Kokkina enclave. The advance of the National Guard was thwarted only after the intervention of the Turkish Air Force. Vuruşkan stayed behind and served as commander of the Kokkina district until he returned to Turkey on 21 September 1967.

Denktash's second attempt to return to Cyprus was more dramatic. It is unclear what the exact role of the Turkish government in this attempt was, but it is inconceivable that Denktash left Turkey without the knowledge of at least some circles in the government. On 29 October 1967, Denktash sailed from the port of Alexandretta in a caique. His companions were two other Turkish Cypriots, Nedjat Konuk and Erol Ibrahim. Konuk was the president of the Turkish-Cypriot Student Association in Ankara. Off the coast of Cyprus, Denktash and his two companions boarded a speedboat and headed for a Turkish-controlled beach near Larnaca. The boat reached the Cypriot coast around midnight on 31 October, but, instead of landing on the beach near Larnaca, it landed 90 miles east of the city near the Greek village of Agios Theodoros on the Karpasia peninsula. Denktash, who was armed, was arrested almost immediately by a Greek-Cypriot army patrol, along with his two colleagues. He gave the patrol a false name, Arif Hasan, but he was recognized at once. Denktash probably thought that this was to be the end of him since he was stranded on an isolated beach in the middle of the night, surrounded by a Greek-Cypriot army unit that could have planned his disappearance through drowning or other means. But he was treated with dignity and was allowed to return to Turkey 12 days later.

A few days after this incident, on 15 November 1967, a new round of fighting erupted in the Kofinou area of the Larnaca district. The fighting led to a serious Graeco-Turkish crisis. At the time, Greece was ruled by a military junta whose policies toward Cyprus led from one disaster to another. The November 1967 crisis ended with outright Greek capitulation as the Greek division was withdrawn from Cyprus the following month, along with General Grivas-Digenis. From a military point of view, the withdrawal of the Greek division meant that a Turkish invasion was much more likely to succeed. In September 1955, the Greek military had adopted a passive role in the aftermath of the anti-Greek riots against the Greek minority in Turkey. Now, it was quickly retreating from Cyprus under Turkish pressure. Again, as in September 1955, the first national priority of the Greek military was to fight communism and build a "Hellas for Christian Hellenes" (*Ellas Ellinon Christianon*). Despite the junta's rhetoric to the contrary, it was apparent that it viewed Cyprus as a secondary issue.

The years of Denktash's absence from Cyprus, between 1964 and 1968, were very decisive as far as the political evolution of his community was concerned. By the time he returned to the island and rejoined his community, power was firmly in the hands of Turkish officers. Equally important was the fact that it was precisely between 1964 and 1968 that the Turkish-Cypriot enclaves were created, and, through them, the separation between Greek Cypriots and Turkish Cypriots was consolidated politically, administratively and geographically. These developments, which were momentous for the Turkish-Cypriot community, took place under the guiding hands of Turkish officers such as Kenan Çoygün, Mehmet Eris, Derviş Sevim and Ferit Cengiz—officers who acted in the venerable Turkish tradition of warrior rulers.

This does not mean that Denktash exercised no influence during the years he was living in Turkey. Following his lawful return to Cyprus in April 1968, he emerged as the undisputed leader of the Turkish Cypriots. It was he who represented his community in the intercommunal talks which lasted from June 1968 to July 1974. Given the dominant influence of Turkey in Turkish-Cypriot affairs, the question has often been whether Denktash has represented the wishes of the Turkish Cypriots or has merely been a puppet of Turkey. It can be argued that Denktash has been a dynamic leader in his own right who has represented his community's interests as they were *remolded* by Turkey. By 1968, the military, political, diplomatic and economic dependence of the Turkish-Cypriot community on Turkey was overwhelming and the rule of the Turkish officers over the community was well entrenched. Thus, during the 1960s, the interests of the dominant party—Turkey—converged with the interests of the subordinate party—the Turkish-Cypriot community. In such an asymmetrical relationship, the interests of the subordinate party were bound to be coopted by the interests of the dominant party. Consequently, any leader to emerge from within the ranks of the Turkish-Cypriot community, such as Rauf Denktash, Osman Örek, Derviş Eroğlu, Kenan Atakol or Asil Nadir, has represented the interests of his community as these interests have been *transformed* during the prolonged crisis. Certainly, there has been—and still is—political opposition to Denktash because there have always been political factions, class interests and ideological divisions within the Turkish-Cypriot community. After 1974, these factions became political parties which competed with Denktash's National Unity Party.

In the final analysis, the circumstances in the 1960s were abnormal politically and *sui generis* militarily. They were conducive to increased Turkish-Cypriot dependence on Turkey, in general, and on Turkish army officers, in particular. From the Turkish-Cypriot perspective, such dependence offered the minority community the optimum defense in its confrontation with the Greek-Cypriot majority. From Turkey's perspective, the Turkish officers in Cyprus not only "protected their brothers" and advanced Turkish strategic objectives, but they were also acting in the best tradition of the military's role in shaping the sociopolitical system in Turkey.

NOTES

[1]See Lewis, *The Emergence of Modern Turkey*, 215, 403.

[2]See Grivas-Digenis, *Apomnemoneumata*, 98. On the British role in Turkey's clandestine activities in Cyprus, see also Stephen Xydis, *Cyprus: Reluctant Republic* (The Hague: Mouton, 1973), 111; Foley, *Legacy of Strife*, 30.

[3]The objectives of TMT are found in the TRNC publication written by Sabahattin Ismail, *Kibris Sorunu* (The Cyprus Problem) (Istanbul: K.K.T.C. Turizm ve Kültür Bakanliği Yayinlari, 1986), 98.

[4]Crouzet, *Le Conflit de Chypre*, 947-948.

[5]Upon learning of Riza Vuruşkan's death, which took place in Ankara on 15 February 1979, Dr. Küçük made this statement concerning his meetings with Menderes and Vuruşkan in 1957. His statement was made as a tribute to Vuruşkan. See *Halkin Sesi*, 16 February 1979.

[6]Ibid.

[7]See Grivas-Digenis, *Apomnemoneumata*, 211

[8]Ismail, *Kibris Sorunu*, 98.

[9]See Halil Ibrahim Salih, *Cyprus: The Impact of Diverse Nationalism on a State*, (University of Alabama Press, 1978), 9-10. On Turkey's aid to TMT, see also Bahcheli, *Greek-Turkish Relations since 1955*, 40, Xydis, *Cyprus: Reluctant Republic*, 111.

[10]On the adoption of the idea of partition by Britain and Turkey in 1956, see Stephens, *Cyprus: A Place of Arms*, 148-150.

[11]On the TMT policy of partition and the measures taken to enforce the policy "From Turk to Turk," see Nancy Crawshaw, *The Cyprus Revolt:*

An Account of the Struggle for Union with Greece (London: George Allen, 1978), 285-288, 304; Salih, *Cyprus: An Analysis*, 63.

[12]Costas Kyrris, *Peaceful Coexistence in Cyprus under British Rule (1878-1959) and after Independence* (Nicosia: Government of Cyprus Public Information Office, 1977); Paschalis M. Kitromilides, "From Coexistence to Confrontation: The Dynamics of Ethnic Conflict in Cyprus," in *Cyprus Reviewed*, ed. Michael Attalides (Nicosia: The Juris Cypri Association, 1977), 35-70.

[13]On the subject of Greek as the second language of many Turkish Cypriots, see Patrick, *Political Geography and the Cyprus Conflict*, 13.

[14]Quoted in Alexandris, "To Meionotiko Zetema," 545.

[15]Among the Turkish Cypriots assassinated by TMT were: Fazil Onder, editor of the weekly Turkish newspaper *Inkilapci*, murdered on 24 May 1958; Ahmet Yahya, committee member of the Turkish-Cypriot Athletic Cultural Center, murdered on 29 May 1958; Ahmet Gurkan and Mustafa Hikmet, publishers of the newspaper *Cumhuriyet*, murdered on 23 April 1962; and Derviş Kavazoğlu, journalist, murdered on 11 April 1965. Kavazoğlu and his Greek-Cypriot friend Costas Michaoulis were on their way to Larnaca when they were both killed near the Turkish village of Lourougina.

[16]See note 35, chapter 4.

[17]Salih, *Cyprus: An Analysis*, 62-63.

[18]See the interview with Denktash in *The Times*, London, 20 January 1978.

[19]British author Stanley Mayes maintains that, by 1955, both Dr. Küçük and Rauf Denktash had become totally subservient to Turkey. According to Mayes, "When the situation became tense, they [Küçük and Denktash] turned to Ankara, and, from then on, they were its obedient servants." Stanley Mayes, *Cyprus and Makarios* (London: Putnam, 1960), 101.

[20]On developments in 1963 and 1964 and the military preparations by both Greek and Turkish Cypriots, see Glafkos Clerides, *Cyprus: My Deposition*, vol. 1 (Nicosia: Alithia Publishing, 1989) 195-233. On the continued role of TMT after 1960, see Salih, *Cyprus: An Analysis*, 92; Crawshaw, *The Cyprus Revolt*, 353-354; Clerides, *Cyprus: My Deposition*, 220.

[21]The penalties included imposition of a fine, whipping or imprisonment. For instance, Turkish Cypriots were fined 25 pounds if they visited a Greek-Cypriot hospital even for purposes of a medical examination. They also paid a fine if they spoke to a Greek Cypriot. They faced imprisonment or whipping if they entered a Greek sector. These penalties and a list of

corresponding offenses appeared in a "Report of the UN Secretary-General on the Operations of the UNFICYP," 12 December 1964, 19 UN SCOR Supplement, October–December 1964, 230–231. Concerning the self-imposed isolation of Turkish Cypriots, see two other UN documents: "Report of the UN Secretary-General on the UNFICYP," S/5764, Paragraph 113, New York, 16 June 1964; "Report of the UN Secretary-General on the UNFICYP," S/6426, Paragraph 106, New York, 10 June 1965.

[22]On Turkish-Cypriot discontent, the role of Turkish-Cypriot students returning from Turkey, and the formation of the opposition party, RTP, under Berberoğlu, see Patrick, *Political Geography and the Cyprus Conflict*, 160, 163–165.

[23]Ibid., 37, 69.

[24]Ibid., 69.

[25]See Riza Vuruşkan's article in the Turkish newspaper *Zafer*, Ankara, 29 September 1967. In his article, Vuruşkan criticizes Turkey for not providing adequate military assistance to the Turkish Cypriots.

[26]A substantial number of Turkish-Cypriot arms had been smuggled to Cyprus from Turkey between 1959 and 1963. On this subject, see Mayes, *Makarios: A Biography*, 61; Salih, *Cyprus: An Analysis*, 63, 92; Clerides, *Cyprus: My Deposition*, 220.

[27]On disagreements over the constitution and the rising tension by 1962, see Kyriakides, *Constitutionalism and Crisis Government*, 70–103.

[28]Patrick, *Political Geography and the Cyprus Conflict*, 84.

[29]Ibid., 160, 363, 369.

[30]In the spring of 1967, the Turkish-Cypriot members of the Famagusta District Administration Council were: Ali Atun, physician; Hasan Güvener, physician and member of the Cypriot House of Representatives; Ismail Karakiozlu, educator; Kemal Karateri, dentist and member of the Turkish-Cypriot Communal Chamber (TCCC); Ismet Kotak, head of the Turkish-Cypriot Cooperative Bank in Famagusta; Osman Mehmet, lawyer and member of the TCCC; Ismet Bessim, former clerk in the offices of the District Administration; Hasan Raif, member of the TCCC; Ahmed Sami, former head of the Famagusta District Administration; Kemal Sariçi, mayor of the Turkish sector of Famagusta; Ayhan Çifcioğlu, lawyer and member of the TCCC, and Orhan Zihni, former judge.

[31]Derviş Sevim, who had taken part in the 1974 invasion, was the most prominent retired Turkish officer to settle in Cyprus. He was one of the

first to be granted "citizenship" and given property in Kyrenia. He became involved in politics and, in May 1976, he ran unsuccessfully for mayor of the Turkish sector of Nicosia as a candidate of the Populist Party. Sevim died on 3 February 1990 in Turkey, and his death received wide publicity in the Turkish-Cypriot press. See, for instance, the Turkish-Cypriot newspaper *Kibris Postasi*, 4 February 1990.

[32] *Zafer*, 29 September 1967.

8
Cyprus, Pan-Turkism and Turkish Islam Since the 1960s

During the 1960s and 1970s, the Pan-Turkish group in Turkey that focused to the greatest extent on the Cyprus issue was *Kibris Türk Kültür Derneği* (Cyprus Turkish Cultural Association, or CTCA). This organization was founded in Istanbul in 1946 but was overshadowed by *Kibris Türktür* in the 1950s. In the 1960s, CTCA became more active and established branches in the major Turkish cities. One of its founders, Halil Fikret Alasya, a Turkish-Cypriot author and teacher living in Turkey, emerged as the most prominent Pan-Turkish theoretician on Cyprus in the 1960s.

In 1966, CTCA published a booklet on Cyprus entitled *Diş Politikamiz ve Kibris* (Our Foreign Policy and Cyprus). It contained a lecture that Alparslan Türkeş gave to the organization on 17 December 1965. Türkeş was an advocate of Pan-Turkism and the *Kibris Türktür* policy that Cyprus is an integral part of Turkey. In 1975, CTCA published another book on Cyprus under the auspices of its Istanbul district director, Professor Derviş Manizade. Rauf Denktash wrote an article in the book praising TMT.[1]

In 1985, CTCA published an 81-page manual in English under the title *Greece and Terror*. It asserts that the modern Greek nation-state has been a "terrorist state" since its inception in 1821 and continues to be one today. Athens, it says, is a mastermind of international terrorism that "threatens the free world."[2] It is significant that this Pan-Turkish publication dealing with the sensitive issue of terrorism was published in Turkey where book censorship has long been and still is strict.[3] A U.S. public relations firm under contract with the Turkish government assisted in the distribution of the book in the United States.

At the present time, circles of the Turkish foreign ministry elite do not hesitate to associate themselves with the activities of groups with Pan-Turkish tendencies, especially those addressing the Cyprus problem. One such example is a new nationalist association focusing on Cyprus called the Cyprus Turkish Research Promotion and Solidarity Foundation (CTRPSF), established in Ankara in July 1990. Halil Fikret Alasya was one of its founders, along with three other leaders of CTCA—Professor Derviş Manizade, Kaya Gülboy and Dr. Dogan Remzi. In addition to these advocates of the ideology that Cyprus is Turkish, the CTRPSF's founders include current and former officials of the Turkish foreign ministry—Ecmel Barütçü, ambassador to Brussels; Kormaz Haktanir, a high official in the foreign ministry; Ilter Türkmen and Osman Olçay, former ministers of foreign affairs; Ümit Halük Bayülken, retired ambassador and former minister; Kamuran Gürün, former foreign ministry director general; Ercumen Yavuzalp, former director general of the foreign minister's office; and Ertuğrul Kumcuoğlu, "ambassador" to the TRNC. Just as the editor of *Hürriyet,* Hikmet Bil, was among the founders of *Kibris Türktür* in the 1950s, the current editor of *Hürriyet,* Ertuğrul Özkuk, is a founding member of CTRPSF. Asil Nadir, a Turkish-Cypriot businessman and the chairman of Polly Peck, is also a founding member of the organization.[4] Polly Peck is a British-based conglomerate that has financial interests in occupied Cyprus (see chapter 10).

The objectives of CTRPSF include (1) establishing a research, information and publication center in order to propagate Turkish views on Cyprus abroad, (2) supporting the participation of Turkish Cypriots in art exhibitions and festivals outside Cyprus, and (3) inviting well-known politicians, scientists, writers and artists to visit Turkey and the TRNC to participate in conferences held by the organization. The objectives of CTRPSF reflect—on a smaller scale—the objectives of the *Türk Kültürünü Araştirma Enstitüsü* (Institute for Research of the Culture of the Turks). Since November 1962, this institute has published the scholarly Pan-Turkish periodical *Türk Kültürü* (Turkish Culture).[5] Jacob Landau characterizes *Türk Kültürü,* a widely-known periodical which is currently published annually, as probably "the best example of moderate Pan-Turkism and scholarship."[6] *Türk Kültürü* has always expressed an undoubtedly irredentist line as far as Cyprus is concerned.

The primary contributor to *Türk Kültürü* on the Cyprus issue has been Halil Fikret Alasya.[7] Born in Nicosia in 1912, he studied history and pedagogy at Istanbul University, graduating in 1937. He wrote his first book, *Kibris Tarihi* (History of Cyprus), in 1939 and became a prolific writer on the Cyprus issue. He was among the founders of the Institute for Research of the Culture of the Turks and president of its Cyprus section. After the 1974 invasion, Alasya founded the Association for Solidarity between the Turks of Cyprus and Western Thrace. At present, he is an adviser to the "president" of the TRNC, Rauf Denktash.

Given the scholarly character of *Türk Kültürü* and the wide scope of topics it has covered, the attention it has given to the Cyprus problem has been extraordinary indeed. It is another indication of the importance Pan-Turkists place on the Cyprus issue and the continuity of their interest in the subject. An overview of the articles published in *Türk Kültürü* from November 1962 to December 1973—when it regularly appeared as a monthly—indicates that, with the exception of the subject of Kemal Atatürk, Cyprus was the single topic receiving the most attention. During this eleven-year period, *Türk Kültürü* published at least 150 articles about Kemal Atatürk and 93 articles and news editorials about Cyprus.[8] The February 1964 issue was dedicated to Cyprus.[9] In 1970, 14 articles and news editorials about Cyprus appeared in the publication.[10] Certainly, from November 1962 to December 1973, *Türk Kültürü* covered many other topics. It dealt extensively with the ideology and life of Ziya Gökalp, the most prominent theorist on the subject of Turkish nationalism, and focused heavily on the topic of the Turkic-speaking populations in Soviet Azerbaijan and Turkestan, and in Iraq and Bulgaria. It also published at least 15 articles about Greek-Turkish relations, focusing on the "plight of the Turks of western Thrace." Greek Thrace has always been high on the agenda of Pan-Turkish groups, and it is emerging as a major issue in Greek-Turkish relations.[11]

In addition to the special attention paid to Cyprus throughout the 1960s by scholarly publications such as *Türk Kültürü*, Turkish politicians continued their interest in the Cyprus issue and there was intense political party activism concerning the subject in Turkey. Among Turkey's contemporary political leaders who have been associated with Pan-Turkism and the Cyprus issue, Alparslan Türkeş is perhaps the most important, as well as the most controversial. Türkeş, who was born in Cyprus in 1917, had an adventurous career in the military and was a prominent figure in Turkish politics during the 1960s and 1970s. He was one of the leaders of the 1960 military coup in Turkey. In

1963, he resigned his commission and entered politics. In 1965, he became the leader of the Republican Peasants and Nation Party, a medium-sized conservative party. In 1969, the name of the party was changed to Nationalist Action Party (NAP) and it became a movement with fascist tendencies. One of the party's symbols was the *bozkurt* (grey wolf) and NAP's youth groups were called *bozkurtlar* (grey wolves).[12] Their emblem, a grey wolf and the crescent of the Turkish flag, resembled the emblem adopted in the late 1950s by TMT. The *bozkurtlar* were paramilitary operatives who were also known as "commandos," and they carried out their activities through organizations which called themselves "Idealist" *(Ülkücü)*.[13] Idealist groups proliferated in Turkey throughout the 1970s. Their members were extreme nationalists who advocated Pan-Turkism and were vehemently anti-communist. The most important of the Idealist groups was the *Ülkü Ocakları Derneği* (Association for the Hearths of Ideals) which reportedly had 100,000 members.[14] The *bozkurtlar* became "the *force de frappe* of the strongest right-wing mass movement in Europe, namely the NAP."[15]

NAP never won more than 17 seats in the 450-member Turkish Grand National Assembly. Still, it left its mark on Turkish politics. It received close to one million votes in the 1977 election, or 6.4 percent, almost double the 3.4 percent it received in the 1973 election. In addition to having a disciplined organization and special appeal among the discontented youth, it engaged in militant activism and was able to influence national policies by participating in the Nationalist Front coalition governments formed in 1975 and 1977 under Süleyman Demirel. In 1975, NAP was given two ministries and its leader, Alparslan Türkeş, served as deputy prime minister of Turkey from March 1975 to July 1977. In 1977, the party was given five ministries. During the years the party participated in the government, "NAP militants flooded civil service and took up sensitive posts in the state apparatus."[16] Opposition leader Bülent Ecevit also feared that what he called the "fascist-oriented" NAP was penetrating the armed forces. In 1977, four of the party's deputies were retired army officers and Ecevit was concerned about the ties between the *bozkurtlar* and some officers of the armed forces.[17]

The elevation of Türkeş to the position of deputy prime minister put him in charge of internal security and the secret service.[18] It is not clear what role these government departments have played in planning and executing the transfer of settlers to occupied Cyprus, but it should be noted that the largest wave of settlers—about 28,000, or 38 percent of the overall total—was transferred to occupied Cyprus while Türkeş was deputy prime minister.

Given the role NAP has played in Turkish government and politics, it is important to be aware of the position taken by the party and its leader with regard to Cyprus. Throughout the 1960s and 1970s, Türkeş campaigned tirelessly to advance the Pan-Turkish ideology that Cyprus is Turkish. He proclaimed publicly and passionately that Cyprus had always been and still was part of "Greater Turkey" and that the same held true for Greek Thrace.[19]

The National Salvation Party (NSP), another right-wing extremist party, played a key role in Turkish politics under the coalition governments formed in 1974, 1975 and 1977. Under Nekmettin Erbakan, NSP emerged as the major Islamic party of the 1970s, one advocating "Islamic solutions" to Turkey's problems.[20] Although the NSP slogan, "A Great Turkey Once Again," had a Pan-Turkish ring to it, Erbakan proclaimed that Turkey would have to return to its Islamic roots if it were to become a great power again. As far as the Cyprus issue was concerned, Erbakan's stand was similar to that of Türkeş's, namely that Cyprus belongs to Turkey. It is significant that NSP received 11.8 percent of the popular vote in the 1973 election and emerged as the third largest party in Turkey. In January 1974, NSP became the junior partner of the left-leaning Republican People's Party in the coalition government under Prime Minister Bülent Ecevit. The RPP-NSP coalition lasted until September 1974, thus the invasion of Cyprus took place while it was governing Turkey. Following Ecevit's fall from power in September 1974, NSP participated in Demirel's Nationalist Front coalition governments formed in 1975 and 1977, as did Türkeş's NAP. Thus, while Türkeş's militants were flooding the civil service, "Islamic militants of the National Salvation Party" were taking over trade and industry.[21]

As it turned out, Turkey made critical decisions concerning Cyprus—the 1974 invasion of the island, the consolidation of the occupation and the mass transfer of settlers between 1975 and 1977—during a period when Turkey was ruled by coalition governments. In these coalitions, it was remarkable that the political extremists—the ultra-nationalists of NAP and the religious right-wingers of NSP—exercised considerable influence on Turkish government policies. The influence of these two parties rendered irredentism a very powerful force which became further entrenched in Turkish foreign policy during the 1970s.

Ankara's policy toward Cyprus has, of course, exhibited extraordinary continuity since 1955. Irrespective of the regime in power—whether civilian or military, or conservative or socialist—the *minimum* objective of the Turkish policy toward Cyprus has consistently been *taksim* (partition). Since 1974, the spirit of irredentism has permeated Turkish policy, not only toward Cyprus, but toward Greece and the Aegean as well. Since then, Turkey has been pursuing a policy of territorial revisionism in the Aegean by demanding that Greece accept drastic changes in the existing legal status of the Aegean islands, and the Aegean sea and airspace. No current Turkish political leader—the left-leaning Bülent Ecevit, the centrist Erdal İnönü, the conservative Süleyman Demirel or the conservative advocate of modernization Turgut Özal—has expressed any fundamental disagreement with the basic thesis that Cyprus belongs to Turkey or that, at the very least, Cyprus should be under the hegemonic control of Turkey.[22] All of these Turkish politicians are generally in agreement that the status quo in the Aegean must be revised so that "the Aegean ceases to be a Greek lake." In December 1990, the Turkish foreign ministry issued an announcement in which it accused Greece of having an "expansionist policy in the Aegean."[23]

Since 1955, Turkey's political forces, including the army, have exhibited a remarkable consensus regarding the country's policy toward Cyprus and Greece. The emergence of extremist parties such as Türkeş's NAP and Erbakan's NSP, and their inclusion in this consensus, does not indicate that these parties moderated their irredentist and aggressive stand on important policy issues concerning Cyprus and Greece in order to be part of the consensus. In fact, an irredentist line on the Cyprus issue and the Aegean seems to have become an axis around which Turkey's political forces share a consensus. As a consequence, Turkish military pressure and coercive diplomacy toward Cyprus and Greece has continued since 1974, and the Turkish government's policy toward its two western neighbors has not changed in any fundamental way since then.

While Pan-Turkism has been the critical factor in the development of Turkish policy on the Cyprus issue, Islamic sentiments have become increasingly more important in the effort to rally support for the

Turkish Cypriots among Arab and Islamic countries. These sentiments have played a major role in the development of Turkey's policy toward Cyprus. Many Pan-Turkists have been dubious as to whether Islam is the force that can unify all Turks.[24] At the same time, in appealing to people outside Turkey who speak Turkic languages—the "Outside Turks"—Pan-Turkists *are* appealing to Muslims.

There are two reasons why the Turkish government and the Denktash regime have been emphasizing the Islamic dimension of the Cyprus issue even more since the beginning of the 1980s. First, despite Atatürk's secular reforms, Turkey is still a Muslim society par excellence, and the Islamic ethos is very deeply rooted among the overwhelming majority of the population. Second, Turkey and the rest of the Middle East have been experiencing an Islamic resurgence.

Shortly before the establishment of the "Turkish Republic of Northern Cyprus" in November 1983, then-TFSC "President" Rauf Denktash made what he called "An Appeal to the Muslim World" to grant recognition to the new "state" that was to be formed. In the appeal, which he made on behalf of the "Muslim Turkish People of Cyprus," he denounced the Greek Cypriots for seeking the "ultimate destruction of the Islamic people" of Cyprus. Denktash concluded his appeal as follows:

In conclusion, we, the Muslim Turkish people of Cyprus, call on the Islamic countries to develop and increase their solidarity with us, in the face of the crusader-like support being accorded to Greek-Cypriot people by the Christian world.[25]

When visiting Arab and Muslim countries to participate in various Islamic fora, Turkish officials and TRNC "President" Rauf Denktash have been soliciting support for their stance on the Cyprus issue. In these fora, the Turkish Cypriots have been referred to as the "Muslim Turks in Cyprus" and their cause has been presented as an Islamic cause, not unlike that of the Palestinians. Speaking at the Islamic Foreign Ministers Conference in Morocco from 6 to 10 January 1986, Vahıt Haletoğlu, who was Turkish foreign minister at the time, stated that the Christian world was supporting the Greek Cypriots and defending their cause. "The time has come for the Muslim world to support the Turkish Cypriots and defend their cause in the same manner," he added.[26] Six weeks later, in a message to countries belonging to the Islamic Conference Organization, Denktash stated: "I invite all Islamic countries to see all the realities in Cyprus and not to help the

Greek Cypriots who have wanted to possess the whole of Cyprus for the last 23 years. The Greek Cypriot-Greek duo in Cyprus is trying to *eliminate the roots of Islam* and usurp the rights of Turks [in order] to Hellenize Cyprus (emphasis added)."[27] Speaking in the same vein at the Islamic Foreign Ministers Conference in Riyadh, Saudi Arabia, on 15 March 1989, Turkish Foreign Minister Mesut Yilmaz stated that "the Muslim Turkish people of Cyprus, in their struggle, also count on the support of their Muslim brethren." He also criticized Israel for its treatment of Palestinians in the occupied territories.[28] By using Islam in order to give the Cyprus question an Islamic dimension, Turkey and the TRNC are being consistent with the policy of the systematic Islamization of occupied Cyprus which began with the 1974 invasion.

Another significant factor affecting Turkish behavior toward Cyprus has been Turkey's perception that Greece lacks the political will to risk a confrontation over the Cyprus question and the problems facing the Greek minority in Turkey. Turkey reached this conclusion by the end of 1955 after the Cyprus crisis had already erupted and after Greece had reacted timidly to the anti-Greek riots in Istanbul and Izmir in September of that year. In the early 1950s, Greece was preoccupied with the process of reconstruction following the devastation of the Nazi occupation and the ravages of the civil war. The Turkish perception of Greek weakness, combined with a series of subsequent Greek and Greek-Cypriot political blunders, rendered Turkey an even more aggressive player in Cyprus. In addition, there is the reality that Turkey is a stronger military power than Greece. In comparison to Turkey, Cyprus is a dwarf in terms of territory, manpower, economic resources and overall military capability.

Other important factors shaping Ankara's policy toward Cyprus have been domestic politics in Turkey, the British policy of encouraging Turkey to become actively involved in Cyprus, and strategic consider-ations. Turkey regards Cyprus as vital to its defense, especially with regard to the protection of sea lanes leading to Turkish ports.

Within this complex picture of historical antagonisms, religious fervor, geopolitics, the Cold War climate and the Turkish perception of Greek weakness, Cyprus and Greece have appeared, in Turkish eyes, to be the weak link in the chain of territories around Turkey. The Turkish elite has had no desire to antagonize its superpower neighbor to the north or neighboring countries to the east by officially advanc-ing irredentist claims concerning Turkic-speaking peoples—the

Azerbaijanis in the Soviet Union, the Azeris in Iran and the ethnic Turks in the Kirkuk region of Iraq. Cyprus and Greece have been a very different story, however, for they have offered Turkey an opportunity to pursue a low-risk policy of irredentism. On one hand, Turkey's overall policy vis-à-vis its Soviet, Iranian and Arab neighbors has been consistent with the Kemalist doctrine of a territorially content Turkey. Cold War considerations have been balanced with the rapprochement between Turkey and the Soviet Union. The Turkish policy toward Cyprus, and increasingly toward Greece, has been driven, not by adventurism, however, but by opportunity resulting from successive Greek and Greek-Cypriot blunders in 1955, 1959, 1963, 1967 and 1974. What Pan-Turkism did was to inject aggressiveness into the Turkish policy regarding Cyprus. This factor has rendered Ankara's Cyprus policy much more action-oriented—through the activism of pan-Turkish groups such as *Kibris Türktür* and TMT—than otherwise would be have been the case.

The Turkish government has treated the Cyprus issue as both a nationalist and an Islamic issue. The conversion of Christian churches into mosques in occupied Cyprus demonstrates to the Turkish public that Cyprus represents, not only a victory over the Greeks, but a Turkish Muslim conquest as well. Most foreign policy crises in Turkey since the mid-1950s have stemmed from disputes with the country's only Christian neighbors, the Greeks and Greek Cypriots. The Soviets and Bulgarians, linked through the mighty Warsaw Pact, have been regarded as "atheist communists." The rest of Turkey's neighbors—the Iranians, Iraqis and Syrians—are Muslims. By reviving memories of past conflicts between Muslim Turks and Christian Greeks, the protracted disputes between Turkey and its Christian Greek neighbors have taken on religious overtones. By stressing the religious aspects of these disputes, the Turkish elite can direct the rising Islamic sentiments among the masses toward an external enemy—the perennial Christian Greek infidel. Turkey's campaign in the Arab and Islamic world on behalf of the "Muslim Turks of Cyprus" has somewhat diffused pressures coming from the Turkish masses that are increasingly calling for a more important role for Islam in Turkish society.

Overall, the weak link construct concerning Cyprus and Greece offers the Turkish political elite the only external focus toward which it can direct domestic pressures emanating, not only from Pan-Turkish and Islamic fundamentalist sentiments, but from the economic and social problems accompanying the modernization of Turkish society since the 1950s as well. Precisely because Cyprus and Greece constitute the only weak link in the countries bordering Turkey, they offer a target for a militaristic policy. This policy, however, does not place Turkish territorial integrity under serious threat or jeopardize Turkey's alliances. Rather, it serves to enhance Turkey's internal cohesion.

Contrary to the widespread Greek belief that Turkish policy toward Cyprus and Greece has been dictated above all by American and British desires, this policy has exhibited considerable autonomy and dynamism in the pursuit of Turkey's national objectives. The irredentist goals of Pan-Turkism have been pursued in Cyprus, and successive Turkish governments have utilized Pan-Turkism unobtrusively, but to the maximum extent possible, without putting other more important priorities at risk. Pan-Turkish objectives have been increasingly interwoven with Turkish Islam to shape Ankara's policies toward Cyprus and Greece. Thus, the policy of surreptitiously pursuing Pan-Turkism has become a landmark—albeit a hidden one—of Turkey's skillful diplomacy with regard to Cyprus since the beginning of the Second World War.

NOTES

[1] See Derviş Manizade, *Kıbrıs: Dün, Bugün, Yarın*, 160-161.

[2] See *Greece and Terror* (Ankara: The Cyprus Turkish Cultural Association, Head Office, 1985), 5-6, 8, 11, 25, 31, 41.

[3] On the state of censorship in Turkey, see the report by Helsinki Watch, *Paying the Price: Freedom of Expression in Turkey* (New York: International Freedom to Publish Committee of the Association of American Publishers, 1989). The report lists 1,394 books and other publications in Turkish and other languages that have been banned by Turkish authorities. The Turkish government has been extremely sensitive about publications dealing with the issue of terrorism. See p. 68.

[4] The names of the founding members of the Cyprus Turkish Research Promotion and Solidarity Foundation were published on 1 August 1990 in *Kıbrıs*, a Turkish Cypriot newspaper owned by Asil Nadir.

[5] On the Pan-Turkish character and activities of the Institute for Research of the Culture of the Turks, and on the periodical *Türk Kültürü*, see Landau, *Pan-Turkism in Turkey*, 129, 158-159.

[6] Ibid., 158.

[7]For a sample of articles on Cyprus in *Türk Kültürü*, see Halil Fikret Alasya, "Kibris'i Tehdit Eden en Büyük Tehlike: Komünistlik" (The Biggest Danger Threatening Cyprus: Communism), *Türk Kültürü* 3 (January 1963): 56-58; Fahir Armaoğlu, "Kibris'ta Türk Haklari" (Turkish Rights in Cyprus), *Türk Kültürü* 14 (December 1963): 7-11; Beria Remzi Özoran, "Kibris Türkü ve Rum Tahrikleri" (The Cypriot Turks and Greek Provocations), *Türk Kültürü* 89 (March 1970): 332-341.

[8]These figures represent an incomplete count based on a review of the *Türk Kültürü* monthly issues in the volumes available at the Princeton University Library. Eleven monthly issues were missing in the series dating from November 1962 to December 1973.

[9]*Türk Kültürü* 2, no. 16 (February 1964).

[10]*Türk Kültürü* 8, no. 87 (January 1970); no. 88 (February 1970); no. 89 (March 1970); no. 92 (June 1970); no. 94 (August 1970); no. 96 (October 1970).

[11]On Pan-Turkish activities vis-à-vis Greek Thrace and the Muslim minority residing there, see Alexandris, "To Meionotiko Zetema," 523-552. See also Landau, *Pan-Turkism in Turkey*, 91, 150-151, 155-156, 159, 162-163, 165, 186.

[12]Landau, ibid., 149-150.

[13]Birand, *The Generals' Coup in Turkey*, 50.

[14]Landau, *Pan-Turkism in Turkey*, 148-149.

[15]Birand, *The Generals' Coup in Turkey*, 50.

[16]Ibid.

[17]Ibid., for information on Ecevit's fears about penetration of the armed forces by NAP. See also Ağaoğullari, "The Ultranationalist Right," 205-206.

[18]See Birand, *The Generals' Coup in Turkey*, 19.

[19]Alparslan Türkeş, *Diş Politikamiz ve Kibris* (Our Foreign Policy and Cyprus)(Istanbul: Kibris Türk Kültür Derneği, 1966).

[20]On the ideology of the National Salvation Party and its emergence as a potent political force in Turkish politics, see Binnaz Toprak, "The Religious Right," in Schick and Tonak, eds., *Turkey in Transition*, 218-235.

[21]Birand, *The Generals' Coup in Turkey*, 50.

[22]For Turgut Özal's views, see note 56, chapter 4.

[23]See *Newspot*, 20 December 1990.

[24]See Landau, *Pan-Turkism in Turkey*, 45-47, 145-148, 154, 180-181.

[25]See "President" Rauf R. Denktash, "An Appeal to the Muslim World: Why a Northern State?" 15-19, and "President" Rauf R. Denktash, "Turkish Federated State of *Kibris*: A Case for International Recognition," 20-21, *The Muslim World League Journal* 2, no. 2, Mecca, Saudi Arabia (November/December 1983).

[26]"Turkey Carries Weight in Islamic Conferences," *Newspot*, 17 January 1986.

[27]"Denktash Urges Islamic Countries Not To Be Influenced by Greek-Greek Cypriot Tricks," *Newspot*, 28 February 1986.

[28]For Yilmaz's speech at the Riyadh conference, see *Newspot*, 24 March 1989. While Turkey has repeatedly criticized Israel in international fora, Turkish-Israeli relations have remained positive. Turkey also strengthened its ties with the Arab and Islamic world throughout the 1980s.

9

Politics in the TRNC

THE SUPREMACY OF THE TURKISH MILITARY

When the Turkish armed forces effected the de facto partition of Cyprus in 1974, Turkish-Cypriot dependence on the Turkish military became even more pronounced than it had been during the previous decade. Since 1974, the TRNC has been totally integrated militarily with Turkey. The Turkish occupation forces in Cyprus are part of the Second Turkish Army Corps. These forces are deployed offensively and participate routinely in land, sea and air maneuvers involving occupied Cyprus, southern Turkey and the eastern Aegean. The Turkish army is responsible for both the external and internal security of the TRNC. While there is a 1,450-member police force in the TRNC, the police chief is under the jurisdiction of the Turkish army command.

The political role of the Turkish military in the TRNC is enhanced, not only by the military integration of the TRNC with Turkey, but by two other factors as well. One is the extraordinary concentration of military forces on such a tiny piece of land amidst such a small Turkish-Cypriot population. The presence of a large number of Turkish soldiers gives the Turkish-Cypriot society a unique character which is bound to affect the political process and the political outlook of Turkish Cypriots, both as individuals and as an organized entity. This is especially true because the Turkish military is politically conscious and experienced in governing a country. The commander of the Turkish invasion forces in 1974, General Bedrettin Demirel, was a military man with definite ideas on how Turkey—and by extension "liberated Turkish Cyprus"—should be ruled.[1] Demirel was a close friend and classmate of Kenan Evren, the general who led the military coup of 12 September 1980 in Turkey and proceeded to rule Turkey for the next nine years. Demirel was a strong supporter of military intervention in government and he had urged Evren to take such a step in Turkey as early as September 1978.[2] Demirel had also envisioned a specific plan for reorganizing the Turkish administrative, political and economic structures following the coup. In the final analysis, the Turkish military in Cyprus carries with it the tradition of political activism which is bound to affect the politics as well as the organization of the "state" in northern Cyprus.

The second factor enhancing the political role of the Turkish military in the TRNC is the emotional and psychological attachment of the Turkish Cypriots to the armed forces of Turkey. It has already been shown that Turkish army officers became the authority figures in the Turkish-Cypriot enclaves after 1963. Yet, despite the dominant role of these officers, Turkish Cypriots were not convinced that Turkey would intervene militarily to "liberate" them. As time went by and they continued to live in enclaves, their doubts increased.[3] From 1963 on, they prayed and dreamed that the Turkish army would arrive one day as their savior. When Turkey finally invaded in 1974 and partitioned Cyprus, they felt redeemed and they still regard the Turkish army as their permanent guardian angel.[4] The Turkish Cypriots celebrated for months after the invasion. The main symbol of their veneration—and a tangible one—was the Turkish army. More than anything, this army was the embodiment of the Turkish nation and its values. Certainly, with the passage of time, the glory surrounding these armed forces is fading. As for the army's omnipresence in the TRNC, it is not inconsistent with the values of a culture that has long been and still remains authoritarian in character.

Since the politicization of the Turkish-Cypriot community in the 1950s, the Turkish military has left its mark on the political development of this community. The protracted intercommunal conflict and the dynamics inherent in a majority-minority confrontation have combined with the ideologies of Turkish nationalism and Pan-Turkism to draw Turkish Cypriots closer to Turkey and its military. In turn, army officers advancing Turkey's geopolitical objectives in Cyprus have played a crucial role in charting the political course of the Turkish-Cypriot community. Turkish officers founded and guided TMT, the dominant politico-military organization of the Turkish Cypriots in the 1950s. Turkish officers became the de facto rulers of a community in crisis in the 1960s, the period when the foundations of partition were laid. And finally, through the 1974 invasion, the Turkish military became the "redeemer" of the Turkish Cypriots, effecting the de facto partition of Cyprus. In every sense of the word, the TRNC—the entity where the Turkish Cypriots live and conduct their political, social and economic affairs—is a child of the Turkish military. It is this military which became a nation-builder under Kemal Atatürk. It is this military which ruled Turkey on three occasions—in 1960, 1971, and 1980—and is still considered the custodian of the country's political and social system. And it is this military which is politically nurturing its own child, the "Turkish Republic of Northern Cyprus."

AN AMALGAMATED BODY POLITIC: SETTLERS AND TURKISH CYPRIOTS

Another dimension of Turkish-Cypriot ties to Turkey concerns the legal and political incorporation of Anatolian settlers into the TRNC. These two aspects of integration into Turkish-Cypriot society are interrelated since settlers from Turkey are entitled to full political rights in the occupied zone of Cyprus by virtue of becoming "citizens" of the TRNC. The fact that a Turkish citizen has settled in occupied Cyprus does not automatically entitle him or her to TRNC "citizenship," however. The authorities of the TRNC have the right to grant "citizenship" to some settlers and deny it to others.[5] This renders the settlers, who are already indebted to the Denktash regime for giving them a home and a piece of land, even more dependent on the regime for political patronage. As an illegal entity under international law, the TRNC has no authority to issue internationally recognized citizenship documents or passports, however.

There are three ways to apply for a "naturalization certificate" which entitles a settler to become a "citizen." One way is to submit an application to the "minister of interior" who is authorized to issue the document after the applicant takes an oath of allegiance to the "state." (A copy of a "naturalization certificate" appears in appendix B.) A second way is to apply to the director of the "immigration department" which sends its recommendation for "citizenship" to the "Council of Ministers" for approval. The third procedure is also administered by the "immigration department." Officials of this department are authorized to issue a document which is equivalent to a "naturalization certificate" at the settlers' homes. Accordingly, officials of the "immigration department" go to the villages and towns in the occupied area, enter the settlers' personal data in a special registry, and issue an ad hoc certificate after approving the application on the spot. This certificate is called "Passport and Identification Information of Citizens of the Turkish Republic" and is equivalent to a "naturalization certificate" since it bestows on the owner the full rights of a "citizen" of the TRNC.[6]

The third method of granting TRNC "citizenship" to settlers has been employed frequently in the occupied zone for two main reasons. First, the Anatolian peasants are illiterate and, therefore, they are not in a position to fill out applications for "citizenship." Someone has to do it for them. Second, this method allows a large number of settlers to become "citizens" in a short period of time. For instance, the Turkish press reported that in five days, just prior to the spring 1980 elections in the TRNC, 14,149 settlers were registered as "citizens." Reportedly, the total number of settlers granted "citizenship" by 26 March 1980, was 31,290.[7] The fact that settlers can become "citizens" and acquire voting rights overnight can be manipulated by the regime to influence the outcome of elections and referenda.

The shrinking Turkish-Cypriot population is an even more important reason for increasing the number of "citizens" that vote. Turkey and the TRNC consider voting in elections to be very important. The elements of political pluralism in the TRNC, including regular elections, are considered essential to enhancing the image of the TRNC in the West and bestowing upon it the legitimacy it is seeking. The settlers and the Turkish Cypriots are registered as voters in a single registry and both cast their votes by secret ballot as "citizens" of the TRNC. Electoral results are based on counting valid ballots cast by TRNC "citizens." Thus, there is no distinction between the ballots of the settlers and those of the Turkish Cypriots, and no way of knowing the precise distribution of votes between the two groups.

The TRNC's voting population accounts for about 65 percent of the total population and is comprised of "citizens" over 18 years of age. This percentage is consistent with the TRNC population distribution by age.[8] Thus, in the 1985 "presidential" election, 105,065 of a total population of 160,287 were eligible voters. There were 91,810 registered voters, comprising 87 percent of the eligible voters. Certain TRNC officials are the only ones who know how many of these voters were settlers and how many were Turkish Cypriots.

The TRNC conducted a census on 14 January 1990 in view of the "presidential" election on 22 April 1990 and the "parliamentary" election on 6 May 1990. However, before the elections were held, the only census figure that was announced was the number of registered voters which was 101,069. It is highly unusual to release only the number of registered voters during an election while withholding information on the number of eligible voters and the total population figure.[9] The TRNC has exhibited great efficiency in producing very detailed statistics on other aspects of its society, as the *TRNC Statistical Yearbook, 1987* demonstrates.[10] (As noted, however, emigration statistics are not revealed in the *TRNC Statistical Yearbook, 1987*.)

The TRNC electoral process and the merging of the settler and Turkish-Cypriot vote have created an amalgamated body politic linked closely with Turkey. The settlers provide another organic bond between occupied Cyprus and Turkey, in addition to that created by the army. The legal mechanism which expedites this political amalgamation is "citizenship." Thus, Turkish-Cypriot political autonomy, which has been eroding steadily since the 1950s, has diminished even further with the legal and political incorporation of the settlers into the TRNC. The consequence of this process has been to eliminate the vestiges of an autonomous Turkish-Cypriot collective will. Indeed, Turkish Cypriots have ceased to have an *identifiable* political will of their own. It is literally impossible to define legally and politically the existence of such a will under the TRNC constitution and laws, and the political process derived from them.

Under the TRNC electoral process, the "citizens" can express their political preferences by voting for the party of their liking and thus voting for or against Rauf Denktash, or by approving or rejecting a proposition in a referendum. These elements of political pluralism, however, in and of themselves, do not amount to the expression of Turkish-Cypriot political will, as such, as an examination of voting patterns in TRNC elections and referenda indicates. For instance, the most important election held in the TRNC up until now has been the "Constitutional Referendum" of 5 May 1985, in which voters approved the fundamental charter upon which the TRNC's "legality" rests. Out of 91,810 registered voters, 70,423 (76.7 percent) cast a vote, while 23.3 percent abstained. Of those voting, 49,411 (70.1 percent) voted for the constitution and 21,012 (29.8 percent) voted against it. Nobody, however, can state with a reasonable degree of certainty whether the majority of the Turkish Cypriots approved or rejected the constitution of their own "state" since their vote is legally and politically indistinguishable from that of the settlers.

The same principle of amalgamated voting holds true for the "presidential" and "parliamentary" elections. In the April 1990 "presidential election," Denktash received 66.7 percent of the vote compared to the 32 percent cast in favor of his main opponent, Ismail Bozkurt. In the May 1990 "parliamentary" election, the ruling National Unity Party (NUP) received 54.5 percent of the vote, while the opposition coalition called the Democratic Struggle Party (DSP) garnered 44.3 percent. Again, the amalgamated vote of settlers and Turkish Cypriots makes it impossible, with any reasonable degree of certainty, to determine the political preferences of the latter concerning these candidates. In short, Turkish-Cypriot political will, as a reflection of the collective will of a distinct political community, has been marginalized to the point of extinction.

The lack of an identifiable Turkish-Cypriot political will assumes special significance in view of the Turkish-Cypriot claim to the right of separate self-determination, an idea that was promoted in the TRNC throughout 1989.[11] By early 1990, it became an official TRNC position, and Rauf Denktash made it a key condition in the 26 February 1990 summit meeting he had with the president of Cyprus, George Vassiliou, at the UN headquarters in New York. The issue was one of the major causes of the collapse of the UN-sponsored intercommunal talks a few days later.

There are two primary problems associated with the idea of separate self-determination as advanced by the Turkish-Cypriot side. The first problem is a general one involving the criteria which make ethnic and religious minorities in the Middle East eligible for self-determination within the boundaries of established nation-states, including Turkey. The second problem pertains to the identification of the Turkish Cypriots themselves. The principle of self-determination rests on the fundamental premise that, within a given territory, a distinct and identifiable group exists which desires to determine its political future freely. As noted, in legal terms, Turkish Cypriots do not constitute a group that is identifiable and distinct from the settler "citizens" of the TRNC. Politically, it is impossible to define the Turkish-Cypriot collective will through the electoral process. In the final analysis, the political amalgamation of settlers and Turkish Cypriots renders the concept of self-determination for Turkish Cypriots meaningless, at least as far as international legal principles are concerned. Furthermore, as the Turkish-Cypriot population declines due to emigration and the settler population continues to increase, the Turkish Cypriots are in the process of becoming a minority vis-à-vis the settlers. Thus, Turkish nationals who settle in occupied Cyprus and become "citizens" of the TRNC will be in a position to determine the TRNC's political future in elections or referenda. This is yet another factor which renders self-determination for Turkish Cypriots a dubious proposition.

In the absence of an identifiable Turkish-Cypriot collective will, the question arises as to exactly who is represented by "President" Denktash and the TRNC "government." It can be argued that they represent the political will of an amalgamated body politic in the TRNC. This, however, is not the legal equivalent of the will of the Turkish Cypriots.

SETTLERS IN PARTY POLITICS

Under the conditions created by the transformation of the TRNC into a Turkish province and the absence of an identifiable Turkish-Cypriot collective will, the political process in the occupied zone takes place within the parameters set by Turkey and the custodian of the Turkish polity—the armed forces. Although the influence of the Turkish armed forces is dominant in the civil administration and security apparatus of the TRNC, the existence of a multiparty system in the occupied zone is consistent with the *sui generis* role of the military in Turkey. After all, it was the military which put Turkey on the path of a "guided democracy." Sociopolitical conditions in the TRNC are much more conducive than those in Turkey to the application of the "Turkish model of democracy." The TRNC is much more amenable to the military's control of its political system than Turkey is because of its location, small size, small population and relatively high degree of social cohesion. The politics of the TRNC can, therefore, be called the *sui generis* politics of a de facto province of Turkey. Consequently, the role of political parties, and especially the role of the settlers' party, is examined here in the context of transforming the TRNC into a Turkish province.

The establishment of the "Turkish Federated State of Cyprus" in 1975 led to a proliferation of political parties in the occupied zone, a process that accelerated with the Unilateral Declaration of Independence in 1983. By 1985, there were about a dozen political parties in the TRNC. There are four worth mentioning. The most important party is the one that has been in power since its establishment in 1975,

Usulal Birlik Partisi (National Unity Party, or NUP). It was founded by Rauf Denktash and serves as his electoral power base. Following his ascendancy to the "presidency" of the TRNC in 1983, Denktash stepped down from his position as leader of NUP. Its present leader is Derviş Eroğlu who is also the "prime minister" of the TRNC. NUP is a right-wing party espousing an ideology similar to that of Turgut Özal's party in Turkey, the Motherland Party. According to the NUP charter, "the party puts above everything the serving of the communal and national interests of the Turkish-Cypriot people and the Turkish nation, of which the Turkish-Cypriot people are an inalienable part." A similar declaration is contained in the preamble of the TRNC constitution.

There are two major opposition parties in the TRNC. One is the center-right *Toplumcu Kurtuluş Partisi* (Communal Liberation Party, or CLP). It has been led by Mustafa Akinci, the former mayor of the Turkish sector of Nicosia, since it was formed in 1976. CLP is critical of Denktash, mainly with respect to his domestic policies, but since 1989 it has been increasingly critical of his foreign policy as well. During the June 1985 election, CLP received 16 percent of the vote. A political figure associated with the party, Ismael Bozkurt, ran unsuccessfully for "president" of the TRNC in the April 1990 election. He ran, however, not as the CLP candidate, but as an independent.

The second major opposition party is the left-leaning *Cumhuriyeti Türk Partisi* (Republican Turkish Party, or RTP). RTP is the oldest Turkish-Cypriot opposition party. It was founded in 1970 by Ahmed Berberoğlu who opposed Denktash's domination of the Turkish-Cypriot political arena. In 1976, RTP elected Özker Özgür as its new president. Since then, Özgur has emerged as the most forceful opposition figure in the TRNC. In the May 1985 "presidential" election, Özgur ran against Denktash and received 18 percent of the vote to Denktash's 70 percent. Advocating socialist policies, the RTP aspires to be the workers' party. Hence, it is critical of the free market economic policies of the Denktash administration and the highly uneven distribution of wealth in the TRNC. Özgur has also criticized Denktash for being intransigent on the Cyprus issue. In addition, Özgur has appeared to be concerned about the absorption of the TRNC by Turkey and the erosion of Turkish-Cypriot political autonomy. In this regard, he has been critical of the settlers' presence in the TRNC. Özgur seems to support the principle he refers to as "the political equality of the two peoples" in Cyprus, as well as the necessity for Turkey's military guarantees in any solution to the Cyprus problem.[12] During the spring 1990 election, Özgur and his party formed an alliance with the settler party, *Yeni Doğuş Partisi* (the New Birth Party, or NBP), against the ruling party, NUP. Özgur campaigned as a champion of the downtrodden who deplored the poverty and living conditions of the settlers, and he charged that the settlers had been abandoned by the Denktash regime. He also suggested, however, that the settlers are not necessarily an obstacle to the resolution of the Cyprus issue. After the spring 1990 election, he renewed his criticism of the influx of new settlers.

The New Birth Party was founded in 1984 as an umbrella party which absorbed the smaller, previously established settler parties in an effort to put an end to their political fragmentation. These smaller settler parties had been short-lived. The first attempt to form a settler party had been initiated by a retired air force officer, Selâhattin Oztokatli. In December 1978, Oztokatli persuaded a group of settlers who belonged to NUP, Denktash's party, to leave the party and form the Democratic Party under Oztokatli's leadership. This party was quickly replaced by a new settler party, the Reform and Progress Party, founded in 1979 by a retired army officer, Özer Ergene. This party, too, was short-lived because, in 1980, another retired air force officer, Ismael Tezer, founded the Turkish Unity Party. In the 1981 election, Tezer was elected deputy in the TFSC "parliament" and became "minister of social services."

By 1981, two more settler parties had been formed. One was the National Target Party, led by a retired army officer, Faiz Başaran, and the other was the Social Justice Party under Oztokatli, who had in the meantime disbanded his Democratic Party. Toward the end of 1982, there was a split in the Turkish Unity Party. Its leader, Ismail Tezer, was replaced by Bakki Topaloğlu. Tezer then formed yet another settler party, the Nationalist Turkish Party. Finally, in February 1984, the existing settler parties merged and formed the New Birth Party. Reportedly, Turkish "Ambassador" to the TRNC Inal Batu played an important role in bringing about this merger.[13] The leader of NBP was retired army officer Aytac Besessler. In the 1985 election, the party received nine percent of the vote and elected four deputies. It then became a junior partner in a NUP-NBP "coalition government," and Besessler became "minister of agriculture." In 1988, he was succeeded as NBP leader by Orhan Üçok. Besessler then joined Denktash's NUP.

In the spring 1990 election, NBP, under Üçok's leadership, broke away from the coalition it had entered into with Denktash's ruling NUP. It joined the two main opposition parties, CLP and RTP, in a coalition called the Democratic Struggle Party (DSP). The DSP coalition against NUP did rather well in terms of the popular vote, even though NUP won twice as many seats in" parliament."[14] The coalition received a clear majority of the votes in most villages known to be inhabited exclusively by settlers. For example, it received a majority in 14 of the 17 settler villages in the Famagusta district. In the Kyrenia district, DSP won a majority in four out of seven settler villages, while in the Nicosia district it won in one of the two settler villages.[15] This is additional evidence that we are indeed dealing with an amalgamated electoral body in the TRNC and that political differentiations and formulas which might have been relevant 15 or even 10 years ago are no longer applicable in the occupied zone.

The existence of an opposition in the TRNC has led to the tendency, especially among Greek Cypriots, to identify the political stance of Turkish Cypriots with that of the opposition parties, while the settlers are presumed to support Denktash. There might be some merit to this argument, especially with regard to Özgur's party, RTP. However, identifying the political preference of the Turkish Cypriots with those of the opposition is based on the assumption that there is a political dichotomy in the TRNC. Judging from the spring 1990 general election, and to the extent that it is possible to identify the political preference of the settlers, it appears that politics in the TRNC cannot be adequately explained through a Turkish Cypriot-settler dichotomy.

Although the settler parties which were founded by retired officers of the Turkish army were supposed to represent the more specific interests of the settlers, there are no significant differences between NBP and the ruling NUP in ideological terms. As far as the Cyprus issue is concerned, both parties favor even closer integration of the island with Turkey and they are against giving concessions to the Greek Cypriots.

In the final analysis, the existence and behavior of NBP should be seen in the context of transforming the TRNC into a Turkish province. In the amalgamated body politic of the TRNC, this settler party resembles other Turkish-Cypriot parties in the sense that they all operate within the political parameters set by the Turkish military in the occupied zone. In other words, what is important is not the existence of a settler party, as such, but the position of the settlers as a whole in the TRNC legal and political structures. By virtue of being "citizens" and voters, the settlers have contributed to marginalizing Turkish-Cypriot political autonomy even further.

NOTES

[1] General Bedrettin Demirel died on 10 November 1988 at the age of 71. Eight months after his death, the Turkish newspaper *Cumhuriyet* published Demirel's memoirs under the title "The Roads Leading to War." They were published in a series of 11 articles commencing 17 July 1989 and were edited by Erbil Tusalp. There has been speculation as to whether the memoirs were subjected to changes, given the fact that Demirel died eight months before they were published. The main subject of the memoirs is the 1974 invasion of Cyprus. Other topics are discussed as well, including the restructuring and reorganization of the Turkish state.

[2] See Birand, *The Generals' Coup in Turkey*, 39.

[3] See Volkan, *Cyprus—War and Adaptation*, 115.

[4] Ibid., 111-119, for insight into the psychology of the Turkish-Cypriot longing to be "redeemed."

[5] According to reports in the Turkish and Turkish-Cypriot press, there were settlers who had been in the TRNC for over five years but still had not been given "citizenship." See *Güneş*, March 3, 1990, and *Halkin Sesi*, 3 March 1990.

[6] See the document issued to Yusuf Donmez, a settler living in Lapithos in the Kyrenia district, in *Soz*, 11 April 1980. He was born on 2 March 1933 in the Sivas district of Turkey. Turkish Passport No. 292955 was issued to him in this district. TFSC Naturalization Document No. 17141 was issued on 21 March 1980. The document was signed by an official of the "immigration department."

[7] A report entitled "New Citizens from Turkey" written by Erdogan Özbalikki in the Turkish newspaper *Aydinlik*, Istanbul, says: "According to our findings on 21 March 1980, the number of Cyprus citizenship documents given to Turkish Republic citizens was 17,741; this number exceeded 31,290 on 26 March 1980. That is, within 5 days, 14,149 Turkish Republic citizens were registered as citizens of the Turkish-Cypriot Administration." See *Aydinlik*, 18 April 1980. A similar report was published in *Soz*, 16 April 1980.

[8] *TRNC Statistical Yearbook, 1987,* 12.

[9] For a report written on the TRNC census three days before it was conducted, see *Newspot,* 11 January 1990. On the secrecy surrounding the census
results, see *Ortam,* 17 August 1990.

[10] The *TRNC Statistical Yearbook, 1987* provides detailed information pertaining to various social and economic phenomena. For example, in the section
entitled "Vital Statistics," analytical tables include data on births which have
been broken down into the following categories: frequency of births in
urban and rural areas, age group of mother, literacy of mother and father,
location of birth and age group of mother combined, and the combined
factors of region, age group of mother and other living children at time of
birth. In the section entitled "Health," there are tables on "Persons
Vaccinated against Selected Infectious Diseases in the State Hospitals and
Health Centers" and on "the Number of X-Rays per Patient in State
Hospitals." In the section entitled "Social Security and Welfare," there are
tables on "Government Pension Gratuities by Scale" and "Widows of
Government Pensioners." In the section entitled "Agriculture," under the
table "Fruit Trees: Number of Trees and Production (1982-1987),"
detailed statistical data show that in 1987 there were 30,272 walnut trees
that produced 376 tons of walnuts, 64,235 almond trees that produced 155
tons of almonds, 455,600 carob trees that produced 3,029 tons of carob and
640,313 olive trees that produced 1,879 tons of olives. The total number of
trees in 1987 was 1,278,343 and they produced 11,425 tons of fruit. See
TRNC Statistical Yearbook, 1987, 17-21, 60-61, 108, 110, 124.

[11] See the declaration of the "Turkish-Cypriot Intellectuals' Self-
Determination Movement" and their letter to the UN secretary-general in
Newspot, 4 January 1990.

[12] On Özker Özgür's views on the settlers and other statements related to the
Cyprus issue, see *Güneş,* 3 March 1990; *Halkin Sesi,* 30 March 1990;
Ortam, 4 April 1990; *Yenidüzen,* 26 March and 12 April 1990.

[13] *Yenidüzen,* 3 March 1989.

[14] Because of the new electoral law of spring 1990, NUP won 55.5 percent of
the popular vote and secured 34 seats in the "parliament." DSP won 44.3
percent of the votes but gained only 16 seats. In this respect, the TRNC's
latest electoral law resembles the one in Turkey. Accordingly, in the 1987
elections, Özal's Motherland Party won 36 percent of the popular vote and
still secured 290 seats (about 65 percent) of the 450 in the Grand National
Assembly.

[15] According to official TRNC results of the 6 May 1990 general election

published in *Kibris,* 7 May 1990, the opposition Democratic Struggle Party won the majority of the votes in the following villages known to be inhabited exclusively by settlers: Famagusta district: Acheritou, Agios Elias, Agia Trias, Flamoudi, Gaidouras, Koilanemos, Leonarissos, Mousoulita, Neta, Patriki, Prasteio, Stylloi, Vathylakas, Voukolida. Kyrenia district: Agios Ambrosios, Larnakas Lapithou, Livera, Orka. Nicosia district: Katokopia.

10
Turning the TRNC into a Turkish Province

The study of the political dynamics in occupied northern Cyprus is meaningless if looked upon in isolation from the TRNC's relationship with Turkey. One of the most profound and visible consequences of the Turkish invasion has been the cultural transformation of the occupied territory of Cyprus into a province of Turkey. The massive influx of settlers, especially during the first three years after the invasion, has expedited the process of the Islamization-Turkification of the occupied zone since village life has been organized around Muslim customs.

The Islamization process started as soon as the Turkish army began occupying northern Cyprus. One of the army's first gestures was to convert the Church of *Panagia Glykiotissa* (Church of the Virgin Mary, Healer of Pain) in Kyrenia into a mosque so that the troops who had landed at a nearby beach during the invasion could pray (see figure 5). There were two mosques in Kyrenia where these troops could have prayed. But this church was apparently converted into a mosque at that time for the following reasons: First, from the Turkish point of view, the conversion symbolized the victory of the Turkish armed forces over the *gâvurlar*, the "unbelievers"—the Christian Greeks. Second, it signified the beginning of the Islamization process which subsequently took place throughout the newly occupied territory as church after church was converted into a mosque.

This process was given religious justification in the aftermath of the invasion when, in October 1974, a prominent Islamic figure in Istanbul, Mufti A. Seref, stated the following:

According to our religion, if needed, prayers can be held in a church but only under this condition: It is imperative that in the church there should be no

Figure 5: The Church of *Panagia Glykiotissa* in occupied Kyrenia, after it has been converted into a mosque. The cross and the belfry at the top of the church have been removed. This photograph appeared in the Turkish newspaper *Günaydin* on 12 October 1974.

religious objects of the infidels [Christians] or these objects should be covered. There should be nothing over the head that has any relationship with these objects. Then prayer can take place.[1]

The Mufti's statement was published in the Turkish press next to a picture of officers and soldiers praying in the Church of *Panagia Glykiotissa* after it had been converted into a mosque.[2] The statement indicated that, in converting the churches, the Turkish Muslims were asked to follow the guidelines of the Mufti. This required removing all "religious objects of the infidels," such as sacramental vessels, liturgical objects, iconostases, icons, frescoes and mosaics, from the interior of the church, or covering them. Some of the icons and other religious objects dated back to the sixth century, and several of them were believed by the Christian faithful to possess miraculous qualities. All religious symbols, such as crosses, were removed from the outside of the churches as well (see figure 6). The belfries were replaced by minarets (see figure 7).

Since 1974, at least 59 Christian Orthodox churches in occupied Cyprus have been converted into mosques (see table 8). The conver-

Figure 6: The church in the village of Agios Ambrosios in the occupied Kyrenia district, after it has been converted into a mosque. All crosses have been removed and loudspeakers have been installed in the center of the roof. Next to the church, there is a statue of Kemal Atatürk. On the base of the statue is the inscription YURTTA BARIŞ DÜNYADA BARIŞ (Peace at Home, Peace in the World)—a dictum of Atatürk's. The flags of Turkey and the TRNC are flying next to the statue.

sion of so many churches into mosques has no precedent anywhere in the Islamic world in recent history. Christian churches are generally respected in Islamic countries. In Iran, the churches of Christian minorities were respected and left unharmed during the Islamic revolution of 1979, and these churches have been protected since then. What is most remarkable is that the conversion of churches into mosques in occupied Cyprus has been carried out under the auspices of the Turkish armed forces, the professed guardians of secularism in Turkey. Indeed, Turkish officers have presided over the conversion of these churches and have led their soldiers in prayer inside them (see figure 8).

Turkification, which has been interwoven into the Islamization process, has involved changing the Greek names of all localities—villages, towns, cities and districts—into Turkish names. By 1975, the TFSC had issued maps of Cyprus on which all place names in the occupied zone were in Turkish. It is noteworthy that the names of localities were not changed back to the names given them by the Ottoman

Figure 7: The church in the village of Yenagra in the occupied Famagusta district, after it has been converted into a mosque. The belfry has been removed and replaced by a minaret with three loudspeakers.

administration; the localities were given new Turkish names. The distinction is important because, under Ottoman rule, most Cypriot villages and towns retained their Greek names, which had been recorded as such in Ottoman registries.[3] (A partial list of renamed villages appears in table 6.)

The changing of Greek place names in Cyprus into Turkish names had actually started by 1969, at least five years before the 1974 invasion. That year, the *Kibris Türk Maarif Müdürlügü* (Cypriot Turkish Directorate of Education) of the "Provisional Turkish-Cypriot Administration" produced demographic data on the Turkish-Cypriot population indicating that the names of villages, towns and cities had been changed.[4] The changing of these names by the PTCA was arbitrary and unlawful. For the sake of argument, one could put aside the question of legality and assert that the PTCA possessed the de facto political power to change the names of villages which were within the enclaves and were inhabited exclusively by Turkish Cypriots. However, the renaming of villages was not confined to the villages in the enclaves.

The PTCA took an additional step. It gave Turkish names to 39 villages where Greeks were the majority population and one village

Figure 8: Turkish officers, non-commissioned officers and soldiers are praying inside the Church of *Panagia Glykiotissa* in occupied Kyrenia, after it has been converted into a mosque. The walls of the church are bare since all icons and other symbols of Christianity have been removed. This photograph appeared in the Turkish newspaper *Günaydin* on 12 October 1974.

where the majority was Maronite (see table 9). The renaming of these villages with mixed populations acquires special significance, not only because the majority population in them was not Turkish, but also because the villages were under the jurisdiction and control of the internationally recognized government of Cyprus. In 18 villages, Greeks constituted over 75 percent of the population. In seven of them, Greeks represented over 90 percent of the inhabitants. However, in the Turkish view, even if only one Turkish family lived in a village where up to several thousand Greeks lived, this village was still considered Turkish and was renamed accordingly.

What is even more remarkable is the fact that many of these villages were renamed after the few Turkish families living in them had already moved away. Such was the case when the PTCA gave the following four towns and villages their Turkish names in 1969: (1) The town of Kythrea in the Nicosia district became Değirmenlik. According to the 1960 census, there had been just one Turkish family of four among 2,951 Greeks in Kythrea. (2) The village of Agios Epiktitos in the Kyrenia district became Çatalköy. There had been two Turkish fami-

TABLE 8: TOWNS AND VILLAGES WHERE CHRISTIAN CHURCHES HAVE BEEN CONVERTED INTO MOSQUES

DISTRICTS

NICOSIA

City of Nicosia
(Church of Saint Andrew)
Gerolakkos
(Church of the Annunciation)
Katokopia
(Church of the Virgin Mary
Chryseleousa)
Skylloura
Kythrea
(two churches)
Mia Milia
Morphou
(Church of Saint Paraskevi)
Prasteio Morphou
(Church of the Archangel
Michael)
Zodia (Kato)
(Church of the Holy Cross)

FAMAGUSTA

City of Famagusta
(Church of Chrysospiliotissa)
(Church of Saint Luke)
(Church of Saint Nicholas)
(Church of Saint George)
(Church of Saint John)
Agios Andronikos
(Church of Saint Photios)
Agios Elias
Akanthou
Aphania
Ardana
Ashia
Engomi
Eptakomi
Gaiduras
Gialousa
(Church of Saint George)
(Church of the Archangel Michael)
(Church of the Holy Trinity)
Gypsou
(Church of Saint John Prodromos)
Koma Gialou
(Church of the Archangel Michael)
Kyra
Lefkoniko
(Church of the Archangel Michael)
Leonarissos
(Church of Saint Dimitrios)
Limnia
(Church of Saint Nicholas)
Lysi
(Church of the Virgin Mary)
Makrasyka
(Church of Saint Luke)
(Church of the Virgin Mary)
Mandres
Palekythros
Patriki
Prasteio
Tavrou
Vasili
Vathylakas
Voukolida
Yenagra

KYRENIA

City of Kyrenia
(Church of Saint George)
(Church of Saint Barbara)
(Church of Panagia Glykiotis)
(Church of Saint Irene)
Agios Ambrosios
Bellapais
(Church of Saint George)
Dikomo
Kalogrea
Lapithos
(Church of Saint Paraskevi)
Larnakas Lapithou
(Church of Saint Dimitrios)
Livera
(Church of Saint Helen)
Orka
Panagra
Vasilia

NOTE: In towns and villages where no church is listed, it is known that at least one church in that town or village has been converted into a mosque, but information is not available as to the name of the church.

lies representing a total of eight Turks among 1,181 Greeks in this village. (3) The village of Agios Theodoros in the Famagusta district became Otluk. There had been 23 Turks from five families among 805 Greeks in this village. (4) The village of Perivolia in the Larnaca district, where 45 Turks had lived among 686 Greeks, became Bahçalar (see table 9). Following the intercommunal fighting of 1963 and 1964, the few Turks remaining in each of these villages sought refuge in the Turkish-controlled enclaves.[5]

In other words, the PTCA renamed villages that (1) were not under the de facto control of the PTCA, (2) had a clear Greek majority (in some cases, 99 percent were Greek), and (3) had no Turkish inhabitants at all. These three factors demonstrate that the renaming of localities went beyond the desire to gain control over the Turkish Cypriots who lived within the territory defined by the enclaves. The PTCA apparently renamed localities to demonstrate that villages and towns throughout Cyprus that were overwhelmingly Greek were considered Turkish.

By 1969, the cultural and administrative Turkification of Cyprus was already in progress. The Greek Cypriots barely took notice of the renaming of the villages, a process which began at least five years before the invasion and was completed by 1975. They thought the name changes to be of no consequence. Still, the PTCA regarded the renaming of villages and towns as "official." This factor and the appearance of the new names on documents and maps were indications of how Turkey looked at Cyprus, where de facto ethnic segregation had existed since the end of 1963. By the time these place names were changed in 1969, the Turkish-Cypriot enclaves were under the firm control of Turkish officers.

This policy of renaming Cypriot villages was a reflection of the inner logic of Pan-Turkism. According to Pan-Turkish ideology, Cyprus is a Turkish island. It was, therefore, no coincidence that the new Turkish names of Cypriot villages, towns and cities were published in the preeminent Pan-Turkish journal *Türk Kültürü* in August 1970. A map of Cyprus with renamed villages on it accompanied the publication.[6] An additional indication of Pan-Turkish influence in the renaming of Cypriot villages is that several of them were given names that are popular among Pan-Turkists. For example, in the Famagusta district in 1969, the Turkish-Cypriot village with the Greek name Agios Chariton was renamed Ergenekon. The name Ergenekon has a particular meaning in Pan-Turkish lore since it denotes the central Asian location where the Turks originated. Ergenekon was also the name of a well-known Pan-Turkish journal in the 1940s. In addition, the village of Tochni in the Larnaca district, which had both Greek- and Turkish-Cypriot inhabitants, was renamed Taşkent in 1969. Taşkent is the capital of the Soviet Republic of Uzbekistan where there is a large concentration of Turkic-speaking people. In its September 1969 edition, *Türk Kültürü* published a news commentary on the Turkic-speaking population of Taşkent. Accompanying the Taşkent commentary, there was another news commentary on the "Cypriot Turks."[7] Following the invasion, the "Turkish Federated State of Cyprus" changed the name of the Greek village of Vouno in the Kyrenia district to Taşkent.

The cultural transformation of occupied Cyprus was complemented by the Unilateral Declaration of Independence establishing the "Turkish Republic of Northern Cyprus" in 1983. In Turkish eyes, this "state" was established through the expression of popular will as the Turkish Cypriots exercised their "inalienable right to self-determination," and it legitimized the Turkish identity of the area. Rauf Denktash stated that the UDI demonstrated to the world that "we [Turkish Cypriots] have the right to self-determination and have used it."[8] The "official" name of the "state" established in occupied Cyprus in the image of Turkey is *Kuzey Kibris Türk Cumhuriyeti* ("Turkish Republic of Northern Cyprus"). The official name of Turkey is *Türkiye Cumhuriyeti* (Turkish Republic).

The Turkification of occupied Cyprus has also meant eradicating all evidence of the history and culture of the Greek Cypriots who inhabited the area before the invasion. Greek monuments and symbols have been replaced with structures and symbols of the Turkish culture. Statues of Kemal Atatürk and Turkish nationalist slogans, such as the Atatürk dictum *Ne Mutlu Türküm Diyene!* (What a Joy to be a Turk!), have become ubiquitous in occupied Cyprus. Enormous Turkish flags are also seen throughout the area. They are even carved and painted on hillsides.

However, the Islamization-Turkification process in the occupied zone would not have been complete without the transfer of settlers from Turkey to the empty Greek towns and villages. These towns and villages had churches and other physical evidence of the Christian Greek character of the people who had lived in them for centuries. With

TABLE 9: VILLAGES WITH A GREEK MAJORITY RENAMED BY THE
"PROVISIONAL TURKISH-CYPRIOT ADMINISTRATION" IN 1969

ORIGINAL NAME	RENAMED IN 1969	POPULATION IN 1960			
		GREEK	%	TURK	%
NICOSIA					
Agia Marina*	Gürpinar	375	85.3	65	14.7
Karavostasi	Gemikonagi	1,111	70.9	333	29.1
Kythrea	Değirmenlik	2,951	99.9	4	0.1
Neo Chorio	Minareliköy	1,157	83.5	230	16.5
Nisou	Dizardköy	366	77.2	108	22.8
Palekythro	Balikesir	862	77.5	251	22.5
Petra	Dereli	966	93.9	63	6.1
Skylloura	Yilmazköy	504	65.5	289	34.5
FAMAGUSTA					
Aphania	Gaziköy	498	62.2	303	37.8
Agios Andronikos	Yeşilkoy	771	64.0	434	36.0
Agios Theodoros	Otluk	805	97.2	23	2.8
Arnadi	Kuzucuk	308	75.5	100	24.5
Eptakomi	Yedikonuk	738	72.3	283	27.7
Komikepir	Büyükkonuk	645	69.4	289	30.6
Lapathos	Boğazici	375	64.8	204	35.2
Lithrangomi	Boltaşli	170	61.8	105	38.2
Syngrasi	Sinirüstü	175	63.2	102	36.8
Yenagra	Nergisli	301	52.1	277	47.9
LIMASSOL					
Kato Polemidia	Aş. Binatli	982	90.3	106	9.7
Koilani	Ceylan	999	96.6	35	3.4
Kolossi	Yunus	643	85.6	108	14.4
Moniatis	Elmali	262	74.4	90	25.6
Prasteio	Celiktas	227	66.4	115	33.6
Silikou	Silifke	261	61.1	166	38.9
LARNAKA					
Meneou	Menevi	148	87.1	22	12.9
Anaphotia	Akkor	559	85.6	94	14.4
Anglisides	Aksu	440	78.0	124	22.0
Dromalaxia	Mormenekşe	334	56.3	259	43.7
Perivolia	Bahçalar	686	93.8	45	6.2
Pyrga	Camlibek	273	71.7	108	28.3
Tremetousha	Tremese	346	55.3	280	44.7
Zygi	Terazi	86	50.6	84	49.4
PAPHOS					
Asprogia	Aktepe	149	59.6	101	38.4
Ano Arodes	Yu. Kalkani	391	78.2	101	21.8
Galataria	Yogurtcular	250	79.9	58	20.1
Kuklia	Sakarya	622	59.8	419	40.2
Timi	Ovalik	413	65.8	215	34.2
KYRENIA					
Agios Epiktitos	Çatalköy	1,181	99.3	8	0.7
Diorios	Yorgoz	514	58.9	359	41.1
Klepini	Arapköy	206	88.4	27	11.6

* This village had a Maronite majority.

their Anatolian inhabitants, the transformation of these villages into Muslim Turkish communities was ensured in a short period of time. Thus, the settler activity was a convenient yet efficient means of concluding the process of rapidly transforming the occupied zone from Christian Greek into Muslim Turkish. It was a transformation that the Turkish Cypriots could not have accomplished by themselves.

ECONOMIC DEPENDENCE

In the economic realm, Turkey dictates the policy to be followed by the TRNC and the TRNC is critically dependent on Turkey. In general, it is following the Turkish model of development which, throughout the 1980s, favored more free market economics and less state intervention in running the economy. The architect of this economic policy was the former prime minister and current president of Turkey, Turgut Özal. As prime minister, Özal visited occupied Cyprus in July 1986 and advised the Denktash regime on its economic policy while seeking to advance economic cooperation between Turkey and the TRNC. This cooperation was formalized in Ankara on 5 December 1986 when Özal and Derviş Eroğlu, the "prime minister" of the TRNC, signed a "Protocol of Economic Cooperation." The protocol, consisting of 34 articles, links the economies of the TRNC and Turkey in all spheres of economic activity. It also regulates monetary relations (currency, banking, foreign exchange and foreign capital), trade, investments, offshore companies, public companies, infrastructure projects and tourism. Its primary objective is to attract foreign capital to the TRNC. For this purpose, the protocol provides for a "Free Trade Zone and a Free Port Area" in Famagusta. It also provides incentives for the development of tourism, banking and communications systems in the occupied zone. As far as tourism is concerned, most visitors to the TRNC are Turks. Of the 274,000 tourists who visited the TRNC in 1989, 214,000 (78 percent) came from Turkey.[9] Foreign exchange earnings from Turkish tourists have been mediocre, however, especially since the TRNC adopted the Turkish lira as its currency.

The protocol and a series of "Workforce Agreements" also facilitate the movement of labor from Turkey to the TRNC. Accordingly, Turkish companies are free to take workers from Turkey to Cyprus. There were about 13,000 Turkish workers in the TRNC in 1990.[10] The workers, who come mainly from southern Turkey and are mostly unskilled, provide the TRNC with a pool of cheap labor, as do the settlers. Many of these laborers work more than 12 hours daily, primarily in construction and road building. They are paid wages which are below the minimum wage acceptable to Turkish Cypriots. They enjoy no benefits and live in crowded and unhealthy conditions, mostly in the old sector of occupied Nicosia.[11] Whatever the economic benefits of cheap labor from Turkey might be, they have been offset by rising unemployment among Turkish Cypriots who eventually emigrate.

Despite the free market guidelines of Turkey's economic package for the TRNC, the latter remains a stagnant economy dependent on the Turkish state and subsidized by it. Approximately half of the annual budget of the TRNC is financed by Turkey. Most of the TRNC's investment capital and 78 percent of its foreign aid are also provided by Turkey.[12] In addition, the TRNC receives 43 percent of its imports from Turkey. However, the occupied zone sends only 13 percent of its exports to Turkey primarily because most of its main export, citrus fruit, is sent to Britain. Overall, next to Turkey, Britain is the TRNC's major trading partner.[13]

Most of the export of the TRNC's citrus fruit to Britain has been carried out by the British-based conglomerate Polly Peck. The firm's chairman and main shareholder is the Turkish-Cypriot multimillionaire Asil Nadir, who is a friend and political supporter of both Rauf Denktash and Turgut Özal. Following the Turkish invasion, Nadir started building his financial fortune by making special arrangements with the Denktash regime to export citrus fruit from the groves left behind by Greek-Cypriot growers in the Morphou, Lapithos and Famagusta regions. In addition, Nadir signed special agreements with the regime which allowed him to operate hotels and other tourist facilities built by Greek-Cypriot entrepreneurs in Kyrenia and Famagusta and abandoned by them during the invasion. Thus, Nadir, through what became Polly Peck subsidiaries, gained control of 75 percent of TRNC exports. By the mid-1980s, he emerged as the largest single employer in the TRNC next to the "state." Nadir also became the largest owner of the print media in the TRNC. He owns the Turkish-Cypriot newspapers *Kibris*, *Bozkurt*, *Yeni Gün* and the *Cyprus Times*. He also owns the newspaper *Günaydin* in Turkey. In addition to its financial interests in the TRNC, Polly Peck has considerable agricultural and industrial holdings in Turkey, Japan and the United States. At the end of 1989, Nadir bought the Florida-based PPI Del Monte Fresh Produce BV Company.

Since August 1990, however, Polly Peck has been experiencing serious financial difficulties. By September 1990, the company's shares had suffered a precipitous drop on the London Stock Exchange. Trading of these shares was halted on 20 September 1990 while British and Turkish banks struggled to save the company.[14] Subsequently, the British Office for Serious Fraud started an investigation of Polly Peck. On 25 October 1990, a British court appointed three administrators to oversee the company's affairs. On 16 December 1990, Asil Nadir was arrested at Heathrow Airport in London upon his return from Turkey. He was charged with 18 counts of fraud and false accounting.[15] Nadir was released on 6.8 million dollars' bail, the highest ever set by a British court.

As a consequence of Nadir's financial misfortunes, Polly Peck's subsidiary companies in occupied Cyprus have experienced very serious hardship and have started laying off workers. In the final analysis, however, with or without Polly Peck, the survival of the TRNC economy is in the hands of the government in Ankara and its well-being is at the mercy of the forces which determine the course of the Turkish economy.

The total economic dependence of the TRNC on Turkey, the cultural absorption of the occupied zone by Turkey, and the political amalgamation of Turkish Cypriots and Anatolian colonizers have transformed the occupied part of Cyprus into a de facto province of Turkey. From the Turkish viewpoint, this transformation is irreversible, even though it is still incomprehensible to most Greek Cypriots that such a transformation has taken place.

NOTES

[1]See *Günaydin*, 12 October 1974.

[2]Ibid.

[3]See note at bottom of table 4, chapter 3.

[4]On the renaming of villages by the "Provisional Turkish-Cypriot Administration," see Patrick, *Political Geography and the Cyprus Conflict*, 278-323. Patrick presents a list of villages, towns and cities with their original Greek names and the new Turkish names given to them "officially" by the PTCA.

[5]According to the 1960 census, there were 623 population centers in Cyprus. Six hundred of them were villages, 17 were towns and six were cities. Three hundred ninety-two population centers were Greek, 117 were Turkish and 114 had a mixture of Greek and Turkish inhabitants. All six cities had a mixed population. As a consequence of the intercommunal conflict between December 1963 and August 1964, about 25,000 Turkish Cypriots fled 72 villages of mixed population and 24 Turkish villages, and sought refuge in the enclaves. By 1971, 2,000 Turkish Cypriots had returned to 22 villages. During the conflict of 1963 and 1964, about 2,400 Greek Cypriots and 900 Armenians fled their homes. Several thousand more fled during the fighting in Nicosia, Larnaca and Ktima, but they were able to return to their homes in a matter of weeks.

[6]See Halil Fikret Alasya, "Kibris'ta Türk Nüfusu ve Nüfusun Dağilişi" (Turkish-Cypriot Population and Population Distribution), *Türk Kültürü* 94 (August 1970): 663–669.

[7]See *Türk Kültürü* 8, no. 83 (September 1969): 871–872.

[8]See Denktash's statement in *Newspot*, 14 June 1990.

[9]*Birlik*, 7 April 1990.

[10]*Cumhuriyet*, 5 April 1990.

[11]The issue of cheap labor from Turkey and the conditions under which imported laborers work and live in the TRNC has been widely reported in the Turkish-Cypriot press. Reports on this subject include those in *Yenidüzen*, 23 January, 2 February, 17, 19, and 24 April, and 30 December 1989; 4 April 1990; and *Ortam*, 4 February 1989 and 5 April 1990.

[12]The TRNC economic dependence on Turkey can be inferred from statistics appearing in the *TRNC Statistical Yearbook, 1987*, 235–237. See also Nicos Vasiliou, *The Widening Economic Gap Between Greek and Turkish Cypriots and Consequences for a Federal Solution* (Nicosia, 1984), 5; Bahcheli, *Greek-Turkish Relations since 1955*, 111.

[13]*TRNC Statistical Yearbook, 1987*, 212–213; 218–219.

[14]For the financial troubles of Polly Peck, see *Financial Times*, London, 3 October 1990; *The Economist*, London (27 October 1980): 89. For a critical view of Polly Peck's activities in the TRNC, see *Ortam*, 2 February and 22 September 1990; *Yenidüzen*, 29 March, 26 April, 14 May, 28 June and 24 September 1990; *Cumhuriyet*, 19 October 1990.

[15]BBC, *News About Britain*, 4:00 GMT, 16 and 17 December 1990.

11
Conclusion

S ince the early 1950s, Turkey's policy on the Cyprus issue has been
inspired by the fundamental belief that Cyprus is a Turkish island
(*Kibris Türktür*). This belief has been sustained by historic and
ideological rationalization.

The historic argument rests upon the principle of the imperial
possession of territories. Ankara argues that Cyprus rightfully belongs
to Turkey since it was once part of the Ottoman Empire (1571-1878).
The ethnic and religious make-up of the population of Cyprus,
however, complicates the Turkish territorial claim to the island
because the overwhelming majority of the inhabitants is not Turkish
Muslim. Indeed, over 80 percent of the population is Greek Christian.
The Turkish-Cypriot Muslim component of the population at the
time of the 1974 Turkish invasion of Cyprus comprised 18 percent of
the population, a figure which had remained fairly steady since the
beginning of the twentieth century. Since the Turkish invasion, the
number of Turkish Cypriots has fallen to under 15 percent of the total
population.

The ethnodemographic statistics on the population of Cyprus do not
favor Turkey's claims to the island. Therefore, the Turkish
government and Turkish-Cypriot officials have been engaged in a
systematic effort to artificially alter these figures. They have produced
and disseminated demographic data that have been contrived.
Demographic statistics on Turkish-Cypriot population, emigration and
immigration have been manipulated in order to accommodate
Turkey's geopolitical objectives in Cyprus.

More importantly, Turkey has been altering the actual demographic
composition of Cyprus since the Turkish invasion. Since 1974, Turkey

has followed a policy of systematically colonizing Cyprus. By 1990, about 74,000 Anatolian settlers had been transferred to occupied Cyprus. Since the population estimate for Turkish Cypriots in 1990 was about 98,000, the ratio between settlers and Turkish Cypriots by that year was about three to four.

The manipulation of demographic data in Cyprus and the alteration of the ethnodemographic structure of the island by Turkey is not an uncommon phenomenon, especially with regard to the Middle East. When Iraq invaded and occupied Kuwait on 2 August 1990, one of the first actions of the Iraqi occupation forces was to confiscate the demographic statistics maintained by the Kuwaiti government. The apparent purpose of this action was to manipulate Kuwait's demographic data in such a way as to strengthen Iraqi territorial claims over the country.

The ideological justification for Turkey's belief that Cyprus is a Turkish island is seen through the lens of Pan-Turkism. In its extreme form, Pan-Turkism aspires to somehow bring under one roof the *Diş Türkler*, or "Outside Turks"—the Turkic-speaking populations living in an area extending from the Mediterranean to Central Asia. This extreme form of Pan-Turkism, which is not consistent with Kemal Atatürk's ideology, has been resisted by the Turkish political elite. Espousing Atatürk's ideas, or claiming to espouse them, continues to be a critical factor for any Turkish government seeking to legitimize its foreign policy. Turkey's rulers have, therefore, opted for a pragmatic form of Pan-Turkism which has coexisted with the ideology of Turkish nationalism as it was defined by Atatürk. Pragmatic Pan-Turkism is reflected in Turkish irredentist nationalism as it is applied to Cyprus and Greece, both viewed by Turkey as the weakest link in the chain of countries surrounding Turkey.

Islam has been used by Turkey to win support for its Cyprus policy among Arab and Islamic countries and to diffuse domestic pressures from Islamic groups to a certain degree. The systematic conversion of the Christian churches in the occupied zone of Cyprus into mosques, under the auspices of the Turkish armed forces, is indicative of Turkey's determination to make use of Islam in transforming the occupied zone into a Muslim Turkish province.

As far as diplomacy *per se* is concerned, Turkish diplomacy, with few exceptions, has outmaneuvered that of Cyprus and Greece over the last 40 years. A key instrument at play in Turkish diplomacy has been

Turkey's superior military might. In essence, Ankara has followed a policy of coercive diplomacy with regard to Cyprus and Greece, and they have not been able to come up with an effective response.

At the military level, Turkey has employed force against Cyprus twice, in 1964 and 1974. It also created *Türk Mukavemet Teşkilâti*, or TMT, a paramilitary organization, and utilized it in a key role to carry out Turkey's policies on Cypriot soil. In the process, TMT took full control of the Turkish-Cypriot community. In Turkey itself, *Kibris Türktür* (Cyprus is Turkish), an organization which was aided by the government and supported by the opposition, was instrumental in mobilizing public opinion to support the cause of a "Turkish Cyprus." *Kibris Türktür* was also instrumental in organizing the anti-Greek riots of 6 September 1955 in Istanbul and Izmir.

Overall, Turkey's policy toward Cyprus has exhibited remarkable continuity and consistency since the 1950s. In contrast, since that time, the Cyprus policy followed by the Greek Cypriots and the Greek government has been characterized by ideological inconsistencies, sloganeering, partisan bickering, continuous scapegoating and the lack of a common objective. This, in turn, has led to successive political, diplomatic and military blunders on the part of Greece and the Greek Cypriots. These include the London Tripartite Conference in 1955; the lack of a determined response by Greece to the anti-Greek riots of 1955 in Turkey; the Zurich-London agreements of 1959; the untimely proposals by Cypriot President Makarios to amend the constitution of Cyprus in November 1963; the lack of a Greek response to the Turkish bombing of northwest Cyprus in August 1964; the withdrawal of the Greek military division from Cyprus in December 1967; and above all, the military coup staged by the Greek junta against Makarios in July 1974.

Cyprus has also been caught in the middle of the conflicting interests of the superpowers in the region, a situation which has injected an element of superpower rivalry into an already intractable conflict. To a considerable degree, however, it has been the combined blunders of Nicosia and Athens that have contributed to the fact that Cyprus and Greece have become the weakest link in the chain of territories comprising Turkey's neighbors. Indeed, Cyprus is not only Turkey's smallest neighbor; it is also the weakest militarily. As a consequence, Cyprus has rendered itself an attractive target for the implementation of Turkish irredentism. Turkish policy toward Cyprus and Greece has not been adventurist in nature. Instead, it has been one that has taken full advantage of the opportunities offered by the other side. Following the inner logic of pragmatic Pan-Turkism, which has maintained its irredentist proclivities, the Turkish elite ordered the invasion of Cyprus in 1974 and occupied 38 percent of its territory only when it was convinced that such action would not lead Turkey into a prolonged military adventure. It is in this sense that pragmatic Pan-Turkism, while irredentist in character, does not advocate adventurism.

In 1983, the occupied territory became a self-proclaimed "state" called the "Turkish Republic of Northern Cyprus." The relationship between Turkey and the TRNC is not one of interdependence, which characterizes the emerging new world order; it is, rather, one of absolute dependency. By any standards, the cultural, military, political, diplomatic and economic dependence of the TRNC on Turkey is extraordinary. Indeed, it is unlikely that another example can be found in the world today where an entity claiming to be an "independent state" is so overwhelmingly dependent on another state. As a corporate entity, the TRNC has been incorporated into Turkey to become, de facto, its 68th province, thus joining the other Turkish provinces in the Mediterranean region—Adana, Antalya, Gaziantep, Hatay, Icel and Maras. The process of incorporating the Turkish-Cypriot community into Turkey has been characterized by gradualism since it has been taking place for nearly a quarter of a century. The political subordination of the Turkish-Cypriot community to Turkey began in the mid-1950s and continued throughout the 1960s. Following the invasion, the Turkish-Cypriot "state" that was established became a de facto province of Turkey.

The gradualism and patience which has characterized Turkey's irredentist policy toward Cyprus contrasts sharply with Iraqi leader Saddam Hussein's behavior following the invasion of Kuwait. By the last week of August 1990, Hussein had announced that Kuwait had been annexed by Iraq and had become its nineteenth province, a factor which intensified international reaction to Iraqi aggression and expansionism. However, the Turkish invasion of Cyprus and the Iraqi invasion of Kuwait shared the same fundamental objective. Each aggressor nation aimed at eliminating the identity of the conquered territory to facilitate its absorption into the occupier's respective domain.

Even though Turkey has avoided the temptation to annex occupied Cyprus outright, it has been able to use the "Turkish Republic of Northern Cyprus" to pursue its interests in the region. These interests emanate from Turkey's geopolitical position and its objectives in the eastern Mediterranean and the Middle East. By establishing an "independent" TRNC, Turkey has created a mini-Turkey in its own image in the heart of the eastern Mediterranean. Strategic control of Cyprus by Turkey through the TRNC renders Turkey an even more influential actor in Middle Eastern affairs, given Cyprus's proximity to Syria, Lebanon, Israel and the Suez Canal. Such control, combined with the increased dominance Turkey is seeking over the air and sea lanes in the eastern Aegean, will consolidate its position as the dominant power in the region—a power performing the dual role of the West's "bridge" to the Middle East and the region's "bastion of stability." Being the most powerful Muslim country in the region, Turkey aspires to radiating this "stability" into the inherently unstable Middle East. The Kuwait crisis might render Cyprus even more important strategically from the Turkish viewpoint.

One of the effects of the Turkish invasion of Cyprus was to transform the Cyprus conflict from an intercommunal dispute between Greek and Turkish Cypriots within Cyprus into an international conflict. The parties to this conflict are the Republic of Cyprus and the Greek Cypriots on one side, and the TRNC and Turkey on the other. The Turkish occupation army, the settlers, and the cultural and economic integration of the TRNC with Turkey are the main links which tie Turkey to the Cyprus conflict today.

Since 1976, the Cypriot government has opted to follow the path of a negotiated settlement to the Cyprus issue through what have been called "intercommunal" talks under UN auspices. Such a settlement would presumably be based on the establishment of a federal system of government. Nonetheless, the whole concept of "intercommunal" negotiations has been rendered obsolete by developments which have transformed the political landscape of Cyprus. In order to reflect the true meaning of the concept "intercommunal," it would be necessary for the Greek and Turkish Cypriots to conduct negotiations *as communities*. However, the transformation of the TRNC into a Turkish province has undermined the concept of "community" and rendered it irrelevant with respect to the Turkish Cypriots who have lost their political autonomy as a community. While TRNC

"President" Rauf Denktash represents the TRNC, he does not represent the Turkish-Cypriot political will because the existence of such a will, in legal or political terms, cannot be distinguished from that of the settlers. As a consequence, the intercommunal negotiations are "intercommunal" no more. Rather, they reflect the existing power relationship in Cyprus, which has shifted decisively to favor the Turkish side since 1974. It is no surprise, then, that the "intercommunal" negotiations have been going on for 15 years with no prospect for a solution. In the final analysis, these negotiations constitute a hopelessly outdated framework for resolving the Cyprus conflict.

A federal arrangement under the prevailing conditions in Cyprus today, with the TRNC being a de facto province of Turkey, would lead to the absorption of *all* of Cyprus into Turkey's geopolitical orbit. If legal, administrative and security arrangements between the Republic of Cyprus and the TRNC were made under the guise of federalism *before* the Turkish occupation ended, the settlers were withdrawn and Ankara renounced its territorial claims over Cyprus, the island would be linked organically to Turkey. Such arrangements would inevitably lead to the transformation of the entire island into a satellite of a regional superpower—Turkey. The vision of a Turkish Cyprus—*Kibris Türktür*—would then be closer than ever before to becoming a reality.

The Iraqi invasion and occupation of Kuwait and the allied military campaign under U.S. leadership, which led to Iraq's humiliating defeat and the liberation of Kuwait, is a watershed in the history of the Middle East. It has resulted in the unhinging of existing power balances in the region. Iraq has been eliminated as a major regional power, while Turkey has emerged as the closest ally of the United States in the area.

For its part, the United States heralded a new world order in the wake of Iraq's invasion of Kuwait. As U.S. President George Bush proclaimed in his address to a joint session of Congress on 11 September 1990, "no peaceful international order is possible if larger states can devour their smaller neighbors." It is very doubtful that Turkey, a regional power of the first magnitude, is willing to subscribe to this new world order. In all likelihood, Turkey's post-Ottoman imperial vision of the eastern Mediterranean will continue to guide its policies toward Greece and, especially, toward the weakest of its neighbors, Cyprus.

Appendix A
Documents Issued by the Sancaktar *of the Paphos District*

The documents reproduced below in Turkish consist of five orders and one balance sheet issued by Lieutenant Colonel Ferit Cengiz, *sancaktar* of the Paphos District from October 1966 to August 1967, and one order issued by Cengiz's second-in-command, Serdar Essat Fellah. They deal exclusively with affairs of civil administration and demonstrate clearly that the *sancaktar* was the highest civil authority in the district, in addition to being the military commander.

The documents are presented in chronological order and are accompanied by an English translation or summary.

SANCAKTABLIK KE
AYDIN.
31 Ekin, 1966.

A Y D I N   S A N C A G I

SIHHATİ KORUMA, TEMİZLİK, DUZEN, GUZELLEŞTİRME İŞLERİ
TALİMATI.

Baf Kazamız iç ve etrafı yaptığın iki günlük müşahedemde
sıhhatı koruma ve temizlik bakımından her an sari bir hastalık salgını ile
karşılanılacak durumda.Bu bakımdan mücahit,Türk Cemaatının her yaşta insanı
ve hatta çocuklarımızda aşağıda yazılı hususlara uyması gerekmektedir.Aşağı-
daki hususların Oba Beyleri,Petek Beyleri, her aile ferdi ile aile reisleri
tarafından dikkatle takip edilmesi,bu yapılması gereken işlerin talim, terbi-
yenin bir parçası olarak kabul edilmesini, her çalışmanın Türk Cemaatı için
"BİRİMİZ HEPİMİZ,HEPİMİZ BİRİMİZ İÇİN"prensibinin her fert tarafından birlik,
beraberliğin temeli olduğunun daima hatırlanmasını rica ederim:

1. Her hane ve müessese bir ağzı kapaklı çöp kabı bulundu-
racak.Bu çöp kapları inkânı olan hane ve müessesaelerde yan tAraflara konacak,
inkânı olmıyan durumlarda ise hanelerin ön tarafına düz bir şekilde, temiz
olarak konulacaktır.

2. Çöp kapları Belediye vazifelileri tarafından her gün
mutlaka toplanıp umumi çöp mahalline dökülecek, zaman zaman yakılacaktır.

3. Umumi yerler ve satış yerleri hiç bir surette cadde ve
yollara çöp atmıyacaktır.Kendileri tarafından bu gibi yerler ön ve etraflarl-
nın günde bir kaç defa süpürülmesini sağlanacaktır.

4. Bazı hane ve dükkânlar önü ve civarında yığıntı toprak,
taşlar vardır.Bu gibi Kasabamızı,köy ve mahallemizi çirkin gösteren maddeler
kaldırılacak,luzumlu olan toprak ve taşlar cadde,yollardan görünmiyecek
şekilde hane ve dükkânların iç taraflarına,bahçelere taşınacak,inkânı olmaya
durumlarda çukur yerlere taşınarak yollarLı düzeltilmesi temin edilecektir.

5. Cadde ve sokaklara bakan ev,müesseselerin ön ve yan
kenarları inkânı olduğu nisbette çiçeklendirilerek güzelleştirilecektir.

6. Açıkta hiç bir bulaşık suyu ve daha pis maddeler bulundurulmıyacak,dökülmiyecektir.Bu gibi pis su ve daha pis maddeler için çukurlar kazılıp üzeri örtülecek,bu çukurların dolması halinde toprakla doldurularak
yeni çukurlar açılacaktır.

7. Bilhassa terkedilmiş boş hane,irtibat hendekleri,mevziler
içi çocuklarınız tarafından insan pisliği ile kirletilmiştir.Bu gibi yerler,her
Petek Bölgesi Mücahitler tarafından temizlenecek;yakılabilen her türlü pislik-
ler toplanıp yakılacak,külleri toprakla örtülecek,yanmayan pislik ve luzumsuz
çirkin maddeler gömülecektir.Aile reislerinin çocuklarına bu gibi pislikleri
yapmaması için öğütlenmesi,terbiye etmesi gerektir.

8. Müesseselerin içleri de yeter derecede temiz değildir.
Her müessese amiri vazifeye başlamadan önce müesseselerin iç,ön ve etrafının
temiz olmasını sağlıyacaktır.Müesseseler içinde küçük çöp kutuları ve içi kum,
toprak dolu sigara atma kutuları bulundurulacaktır.

9. En ulvi bir ibadet yeriniz olan tek camimizin bahçesine
zaman zaman çocuklar,hayvanlar girmekte ve ibadetgâhımızı kirletmektedir.
Camimizin bahçesine çocukların girmesi sağlanacak,otlama ve diğer sebebler
için hayvan salınmıyacaktır.

10. Her cuma günü 0800 - 1100 saatleri arası Kasaba ve
köyleriniz için temizlik,güzelleştirme günü olarak kabul edilecek,bu mukaddes
gününüzde ferdin abdest alması gibi Kasaba, köyleriniz elbirliği ile temiz-
lenip güzelleştirilecektir.

11. Cadde,sokak ve meydanları daraltacak,çirkin gösterecek
şekilde hiç bir inşaat yapılmıyacak,inşaat yapmak ihtiyacında olan kimseler
Belediye Başkanlığından mutlaka inşaat müsaadesi alacaklardır.

...../2

ENGLISH SUMMARY OF DOCUMENT NO. 1

Order by Sancaktar Ferit Cengiz

Date: 31 October 1966

District: Paphos Regional Command

Subject: Instructions for hygiene, cleanliness and area improvement

Following a two-day inspection of the area with regard to conditions of hygiene, in order to prevent the outbreak of epidemics, we should act in unison for the sake of our children. Therefore, I call on the citizens to follow the instructions below:

1. Every home should have a garbage bin.

2. The garbage bins should be emptied daily by municipal employees.

3. Littering is not allowed in public places.

4. All debris in front of homes and shops should be removed.

5. People should plant flowers in their yards.

6. There should be no sewage running in the streets.

7. The dirt should be cleaned off of all abandoned homes.

8. Municipal places are not well cleaned. Those responsible should make sure they are kept clean.

9. Our most sacred place for prayer is our mosque. Children and animals enter and litter its yard. It should be ensured that the yard is kept clean.

10. Every Friday [Muslim Sabbath] from 8–11 a.m., there should be a period of cleaning in the towns and villages. On this sacred day when we engage in our ritual ablution (*abdest*), there should be general cleaning in the town and villages.

11. A municipal permit is required before any construction can commence.

-2-

12. Her nuessesece yangın vukuunda ilk söndürme gayreti
olarak uygun yer ve niktarda dolu şu, kum, toprak kovaları bulundurulacaktır.

13. Motorlu araçlar yollarda diğer araçların ve halkın
geçişine engel olacak gibi park etmiyecek, yolu boş bırakmak için
kaldırınlarda 15 cm.ye, kaldırınsız yerlerde de duvara değecek gibi
yanaşacaktır. Motorlu araç sürücüleri " YOL DAİMA YAYANINDIR"
kaidesini unutmamalıdır. Keza meydanlardada laâlettâyin yere park
edilmiyecektir.

14. Başı boş, sahipsiz köpekler bulundurulmıyacak,sahipli
köpekler mutlaka, tasmalı olacaktır.Sahipli tasmalı köpekler geceleyin
sahipleri tarafından bir yere bağlı olarak bulundurulacaktır.Sahipsiz
köpekler Belediye Başkanlığınca toplattırılarak itlâf edilecektir.

15. Kasaba dahilinde davar sahipleri hayvanlarını başı boş
bulundurdurmıyacak,başkasının bahçe ve ekinine zarar verdirmiyecektir.
Bilhassa tavuklar her hanenin kendi hudutları içinde bulundurulacaktır.
Keza hayvan dışkıları etrafa saçılmıyacaktır.Gübreleme için biriktirilen
fışkılar zaman zaman Kasaba dışındaki gübrelenecek tarlalara nakledi-
lerek orada bekletilecektir.

16. Cadde ve sokaklar Belediye görevlileri tarafından her gün
sabah saat 0500 : 0600 da süpürülecektir.

17. Hane ve müesseselerin bahçeleri boş,bakımsız bırakıl-
mıştır.Bu gibi yerler mutlaka çiçeklendirilmeli yahut bazı istifade
edilecek sebzeler dikilmelidir.Keza bahçecilik,ekine önem verilerek
boş tarla ve bahçeler sürülmeli,hane sahiplerinin refahının gelişmesi
sağlanmalıdır.

18. Bahçe ve hanelerin hudut çitleri de güzel değildir.
Bu gibi çitler düzeltilerek göze hoş görünecek bir şekle sokulmalıdır.

        Cemaat menfaatına uyulması gereken yukarıdaki hususlar
kendilerini ilgilendiren mevzularda Belediye Başkanlığı ve Polis
Müdürlüğü tarafından dikkatle takip edilerek her hafta Cumartesi
günleri yazılı olarak bir raporla her madde ayrı ayrı olarak Sancak-
tarlık ilgili kademelerine bildirilecektir. Önemli hadise ve bilerek
yapılacak olan ihmaller zuhurunda durum ivedilikle bildirilecektir.

        Türk Cemaat Kardeşlerinin yukarıdaki kaidelere tamamıyle
uymasını,birbirlerine ve Sancaktarlığa yardımcı olmalarını diler,
şimdiden ferden kendilerine teşekkür ederim.
        Gereğinin yapılmasını ivedilikle rica ederim.

                                        SANCAKTAR

12. Every citizen should have adequate water in storage so as to assist in case of fire.

13. Parking is allowed only in designated places.

14. Stray dogs will be caught by the municipal authority and put to death.

15. Those who have goats should make sure that the goats do not enter the gardens of other people and eat their plants and flowers.

16. Streets should be swept between five and six o'clock in the morning.

17. Empty lots should be planted with vegetables and flowers.

18. Many fences around homes and gardens are not well maintained. They should all be repaired to look more beautiful.

The municipal authority and the police will be checking every Saturday to ensure that every citizen complies with these instructions. In case of violations, a report to the *sancaktar* will be submitted for each individual case.

I would like to thank the brotherly Turkish community in advance for complying with the orders of the *sancaktar*.

(Signed)

Cengiz

SANCAKTAR

ı: D-VIII -/66.

SANCAKTARLIK KARARGAHI
A Y D I N.

19 Kasım, 1966.

Sayın Gazi Baf Sancağı, Müslüman Kardeşlerim;

Göreve başladığım günden beri el birliği ile Milli Birlik, beraberliği sağlamlaştırmak, Kasaba, Köylerimizi onarmak, bir Türk Cemaat ferdine yaraşır şekilde güzelleştirmek amacı ile gece gündüz çalışmaktayız. Fakat ben şahsen bu çalışma temposunun bizlere   uygun bir süratte olmadığı kanaatindeyim. Daha medeni ırklar ve milletler, kâinatın keşfedilmesi yolunda maddi, manevi bütün varlıkları ile çalışırken biz Türk Cemaatının bilhassa, çalışma zamanlarında kahve köşelerinde zaman öldürmesi benim vicdani kanaatime göre çok büyük bir zafiyettir.

Vatandaşlarıma aşağıdaki hususları tavsiye ediyorum;

1. Her rütbe ve makamdaki şahsın (Öğretmen, Polis, Hususi iş Sahipleri) genç, ihtiyar ve yetişmiş çocukların birbirine yardımcı olmaları, gerektiğinde rütbe, makam, tahsil, zenginlik, fakirlik derecelerine aldırmadan, kazma, kürek işlerinde dahi çalışarak kasabamız ve köylerimize faydalı olmaları, bilhassa tahsilli, varlıklıların bu işlerde önayak olarak örnek olmaları,

2. Çalışma zamanlarında, çalışan kişilere kötü örnek olacak şekilde kahvehanelerde tavla, oyun oynanması,

3. Toplum menfaatine yararlı olacak bir iş bulunamazsa, her vatandaşın kendi ev, dükkân, bahçe, yolunun onarımı ile meşgul olması,

4. İcra Heyetince verilecek toplum çalışması görevlerine her an gönüllü olarak hazır olunması,

5. Boş arsa, bahçelerinin sürülüp ekilmesi, temizlenmesi,

6. Badana işlerinin tamamlanması,

7. Fakir ve maddi gücü olmıyan ihtiyar vatandaşlara bu gibi işlerde yardımcı olması, onların işlerinin görülmesi,

8. Her şahsın, ailenin mazisi iyi ve hatalı tarafları ile geride kalmıştır. Mazi ile övünmek yerinmek, bir şey kazandırmaz. Bu gün için Cemaatimize hal ve istikbal lâzımdır. Ben şahsen hiç bir kimsenin mazisine fikir yürütmüyorum, yürütmüyeceğim. Aile fertlerinde biribirleri arasındaki menfaat düşkünlüğünden doğmuş niza, kavgaların unutulması gerekir. "İşte adû,arş Gazi Baflılar, Vatan İmdadına".

9. Ahlâki gelişme olarak geçlerimizin çalışmaya alıştırılması bakımından aile reislerince ve öğretmenlerimizce çocuklarımızın terbiye edilmesi.

10. Gençlerimize, yeni neslimize, örnek olacak onları, doğacak yeni aydınlık günlerimize güvenilir, övünülür bir şekilde sağlam yetiştirebilmek için, şahsi menfaatler yüzünden geçimsizlikler, aile kavgaları, partileşmeler gibi bütünlüğü bozucu hareketlerden kaçınarak "Her şey Vatan İçin", "Hepimiz birimiz Birimiz hepimiz için" temel kuralları yolunda yetişmelerinin sağlanması amacı ile var gücümüzle çalışmaya yönelmek,

11. İş zamanında mutlaka, iş kıyafetine girilmeli, tatil, bayram günleri ile Camiye gidildiğinde çok temiz olarak giyinmelidir,

12.Çalışan grupları seyretmek maksadı ile onların civarında dikilmek, onları işten alıkoymaktır. Seyretmeğe vakti olan bir kimsenin çalışmaya da vakti vardır. Bu gibi şahıslar hemen iş kıyafetine girip çalışanlara yardımcı olmalıdır.

13. Vatandaşlarımız büyük himmet göstererek idareye zaman, zaman para bağışında bulunmaları gerekecektir. Bu gibi yardımlar istendiği zaman, vatandaşlarımızın canıgönülden bu bağış görevine uymaları gerekir. Meselâ; Belediye Helâsı yapmak için Ali Şefik Bey £10., Eşi Denziye Ali Şefik £10. ve Mehmet Bey Ebu ekir vakfı mütevellisi Sıtkı Hadızade £60.,
Yol işlerinde kullanmak üzere eski bir kamyon almak için Yâzım A. Raşit £125. bağışta bulunmuşlardır. Kendilerine vatandaşlarım ve idare adına ,eşkkür ederim.

ENGLISH SUMMARY OF DOCUMENT NO. 2

Order by Sancaktar Ferit Cengiz

Date: 19 November 1966

District: Paphos Regional Command

Subject: How to work together to benefit the community

My Esteemed *Muslim* brothers of the heroic Paphos District:

Since I took over the post, we have been working day and night to improve living conditions in our district to a level that befits the Turks. I am not satisfied, however, with what I have seen. While they work hard for this purpose in other nations, the Turks waste their time in coffee shops instead of working. This is a great weakness. I, therefore, advise my compatriots to do the following:

1. Irrespective of social position, each individual should work, if necessary even with a shovel, to benefit our community.

2. During work hours, people should not play backgammon and cards in coffee shops.

3. If there is no need to work for the benefit of the public at a particular time, everybody should work to improve his home or shop.

4. Every individual should be willing and ready to follow the orders of the Executive Committee regarding public works.

5. Empty lots should be cleaned and orchards should be taken care of.

6. The whitewashing of homes should be completed.

7. The poor and the senior citizens should be assisted when they need help.

8. The past of each family, good or bad, should be set aside. Today, we are working for the present and the future. The family feuds of the past should be forgotten in the name of the heroes of Paphos.

9. In order for our youth to learn to work, it is necessary that they be instructed properly by the head of the family and by teachers.

10. Our youth should become a model of the new direction we are pursuing and should have faith in the bright future ahead. They should avoid partisan politics and family feuds. All together we shall build a future based on the ideal "One for the other and all for the motherland."

11. During work hours, you should dress in work clothes. When you go to the mosque, you should be very clean.

12. Do not loiter around people who are working.

13. Our compatriots offer a national service when they contribute financially for the needs of the community. For example, Ali Şefik Bey gave 10 pounds for the construction of public restrooms. His wife Remzi gave 10 pounds. Sitki Kadizade gave 60 pounds. For the construction of roads, Kâzim A. Başit gave 125 pounds. On behalf of the administration, I thank all these compatriots.

........2 ...

14. Vatandaşlarım arasında canıgönülden olağanüstü çalışanlar da vardır.
Bu gibi arkadaşlar takdire lâyıktırlar. Mücahit taşçı Bay Hüseyin Hâzım'ı
£5., Mücahit Belediye işçisi Bay Camal Tezcan'ı £3. ile Duvarcı usta
Raif Mustafayı £3. ile mükâfatlandırdım.

15. Yapılacak bir çok işler vardır. El ve gönül birliği ile, bütün imkân-
larımızı seferber ederek eksikliklerimizi tamamlıyacağız. Gazi Bafımızı
daha güzel yapacağımıza inanıyorum. Boş yere sarfedecek vaktiniz yoktur.
İmzasız yazılar, önemsiz şikâyetler ile kıymetli vaktinizi maalesef faz-
lasıyle işgal eden kardeşlerinin bundan böyle bu gibi yazı ve dilekleri-
nin dikkate alınmıyacağını bilmelerini isterim.

       Yukarıdaki temel fikirler, her Türk'ün, Müslüman'ın yapabileceği,
inandığı kurallardır. Bu gibi toplum yararına olan kuralları fedakârlıla
yaptıkça Türk Cemaatiniz için varılamıyacak hedef yoktur.

       Hepinizi saygı ile selâmlar, bu tavsiyelerime uyulmaya çalışılma-
sını rica ediyorum.

                                        (imza)

                                S A N C A K T A R.

14. Those of our compatriots who have done volunteer work deserve praise. For this reason, I have rewarded them and have given five pounds to the fighter Hüseyin Kâzim, three pounds to the municipal employee Cemal Tezcan, and three pounds to the construction worker Raif Mustafa.

15. There is a lot to be done and, working together, we shall further improve our heroic Paphos. I want my dear compatriots to know that, in the future, I will disregard letters that are not signed.

Every *Turkish Muslim* acting according to the faith should see that the above objectives are achieved. With such united spirit and self-sacrifice there is no task that the Turkish community cannot accomplish.

(Signed)

Cengiz
SANCAKTAR

SAYI: D.VIII -3A/66.

SANCAKTARLIK KARARGAHI
AYDIN.

21 Kasım, 1966.

SAYIN GAZİ BAF VATANDAŞLARIMIZ,

Kasabamızın güzellik ve onarımı için gece gündüz çalışmamızın meyvalarını almak ve biz Türk kardeşlerimizin birlik, beraberlik içinde daha medeni şartlar için yaşamamızı sağlamak ve bu günkü maddi inkânsızlıklarımızı yenmek amacı ile yardımlaşmaya ihtiyacımız olduğunu takdir edersiniz.

Başlamış olduğumuz imar, iskân işlerinden olan Fakir Yurdu, Park, Umumi Helâlar, Yollar, Spor Tesisleri gibi zaruri olan tesisleri yapabilmek için maddi yardımlarınıza ihtiyaç olduğu kanaatına vararak ve bu yardımı her vatandaşın maddi gücünde uygun bir miktarda yapacağına emin olarak hamiyetinize baş vuruyoruz.

Sizleri saygı ile selâmlar, bağışta bulunmanızı rica ederiz.

Belediye
Başkanı.

II.Serdar.

I,Serdar,

SANCAKTAR.

ENGLISH SUMMARY OF DOCUMENT NO. 3

Order by Sancaktar Ferit Cengiz

Date: 21 November 1966

District: Paphos Regional Command

Subject: Appeal for help to complete public works projects

ESTEEMED COMPATRIOTS OF HEROIC PAPHOS

In order to improve your city, it is necessary to work hard. We, along with our Turkish brothers, will also work so that you can live in more civilized conditions. In this effort, you need our assistance. We have initiated a series of public works, parks, public restrooms, streets, playgrounds, and, for all these, we need your sense of duty. We salute you with respect and urge you to carry out your obligation.

(Signed)

The mayor   Serdar I   Serdar II   Cengiz
                                         SANCAKTAR

KASABA TOPLUM KALKINMASI IÇIN

T E B E R R Ü   H E S A B I

1.12.1906'da elde mevcut	£ 246.000
7.12.1966 Uymak 3 Mücahitleri	20.800
" 2 "	23.250
" 4 "	23.075
" 5 "	20.875
" 1 "	19.675
" 6 "	29.375
" Karargâh	5.775
8.12.1966 Cemal D. Ali	25.000
9.12.1966 Hüseyin Kâzım	7.000
	£ 421.625
	=========

1.12.1966	Çarşı için 7 künk	£ 11.000
"	Helâ inşasında çalışan usta-ların 17 gündeliği	8.150
"	161 çinko, 16 okka çivi, 2 torba alçı, 81 tahta (Tribün)	135.000
9.12.1966	Elde Mevcut	267.475
		£ 421.625
		=========

Teşekkür Ederim.

S A N C A K T A R.

Baf, 9 Aralık, 1906.

ENGLISH TRANSLATION OF DOCUMENT NO. 4

Balance Sheet prepared by Sancaktar Ferit Cengiz

Date: 9 December 1966

District: Paphos Regional Command

Subject: MUNICIPAL DEVELOPMENT ACCOUNT

1 December 1966: Balance	246.000	1 December 1966: 7 pipes — 11.000
7 December 1966: Contribution by 3 fighters	20.800	" Daily Salaries for 17 workers building lavatories — 8.150
" 2 "	23.250	" 161 sheets of corrugated iron, 16 *okes* of nails, 2 sacks of gypsum, 81 wooden beams — 135.000
" 4 "	23.875	
" 5 "	20.875	9 December 1966: Balance — 267.475
" 1 "	19.675	
" 6 "	29.375	
Command	5.775	
8 December 1966: Cemal D. Ali	25.000	
9 December 1966: Hüseyin Kâzim	7.000	
	421.625	421.625

Thank You
(Signed)
Cengiz
SANCAKTAR

Paphos,
9 December 1966

Sayı: D.IV -6/67
Konu: İaşe Yardımı Hakkında

SANCAKTARLIK KARARGAHI
AYDIN.
19 Ocak,1967

     Vatandaşlara yapılan iaşe yardımlarından bazılarının beğenilmediği,yenmediği,atıldığı ve hayvanlara verildiği öğrenilmiştir. Bu düpedüz nankörlük,Tanrımızın nimetine karşı saygısızlık,günahtır.Hiç bir kimsenin bu çok çirkin,uygunsuz hareketi yapmıya hak ve hukuku yoktur.Unutulmamalıdır ki bu yiyecekler,paralar Anavatandan henüz tüyü bitmemiş yetim, öksüz çocukların haklarından kesilerek bizlere gönderilmektedir.Bu nankörlüğü tenzih ederim.

     Meselâ;buzlu et,bu gün medeni memleketlerin hepsi ve ordular buzlu et ile iaşe edilmektedir.Anavatanda da böyledir.Müteahhitlerimiz normal eti çok pahalıya satmaktadırlar,Kasabada 490 milse müteahhitten alınabilen et bazı köylerde 650 milse kadar yükseltilmiştir.Müteahhitlerin anlayışsızlığından İdare bu israf yolunu kapamış, buzlu et iaşesine başlamıştır.Zaman vatandaşların ağzının tadını düşüneceği zaman değildir,Ağzının tadını düşünen bu gibi vatandaşlara bundan sonra et istihkakı verilmiyecektir. Bu eti almak,ziyan etmek günah ve suçtur.Bu gibi vatandaşlar istemediklerini bildirecekler,eksik iaşe edileceklerdir.Keza normal iaşe ve Kızılay yardımından verilen,verilecek olan gıdalardan nohut,bulgur da ayni şekilde ziyan edilmekte, hayvanlara verilmektedir.Anavatan hayvanları değil,Türk Cemaatını beslemek için iaşe,para gönderiyor.

     Yeni Kızılay eşya ve iaşe yardımı gelmiştir.Hemen dağıtımına başlanacak,iaşe 3 aylık olarak verilecek ve vatandaşlar tarafından bu 3 aylık iaşe haftalara bölünecek 3 ay idare edilecektir.

     Bu iaşe maddelerini atmak,hayvanlara vermek,satmak kat'i olarak yasaktır.Bu nankörce işleri yapanlar İdareye bildirilecek ve bundan sonra iaşeleri kesilecektir.Bu durumun kontrolundan Polis,Belediye Görevlileri, İdareci,Muhtar ve her vatandaş sorumludur.Bu iaşeyi satın almak da yasaktır.

     Vatandaşları acı ve ağır bir dille söz ettiğim için özür dilerim.

     Bir tarafta ihtiyaç içinde olduğunu ifade edip,iaşe yardımı isteyipte yukarıdan verilen emir ve talimatlara göre yardım yapamadığımız vatandaşlarımız varken,bir kısım vatandaşlarımızın da verilen iaşeyi beğenmemesi,atması,hayvanlara vermesi,satması birlik ve beraberliğin bozulması, kemirilmesi demektir.Öyle olmalıdır ki İdarenin talimat,emirlerden ötürü iaşe edemediği vatandaşlar,iaşe edilen vatandaşlar tarafından yardımlaşma ile beslenebilmeli,İdarenin yardıma muhtaç olupta yardım yapamadığı vatandaşlar için duyduğu üzüntü giderilmelidir.

     Vatandaşlarımdan ziyankâr olmamalarını,biribirlerine yardımcı olmalarını,"IHTİYAÇ İÇİNDE OLAN U.DUGUNU DEGİL,BULDUGUNU YER" atasözünü unutmamalarını dilerim.

     Bu emir her vatandaşa mutlaka okunacaktır.

     Gereğine göre çok dikkatle hareket edilmesini rica ederim.

SANCAKTAR.

DAĞITIM:
    Oba ve Uymaklara
    İcra Dairesine
    Müesseselere
    Emniyet Müdürlüğü
    Belediye Başkanlığına
    Refah ve Göçmen Dairesine.

ENGLISH SUMMARY OF DOCUMENT NO. 5

Order by Sancaktar Ferit Cengiz

Date: 19 January 1967

District: Paphos

Subject: Food assistance provided by the Motherland

Food supplies provided to us by our motherland [Turkey] are being sold, thrown away or given to animals. I have been informed that frozen meat is being thrown away. In the civilized world and in our army, frozen meat is consumed daily. It is a sin to throw frozen meat away. I have also been informed that chick peas and cracked wheat are being given to animals. All this demonstrates great ingratitude. Our motherland provides us with money and food for the Turkish community, not for animals. The deprivation and sacrifice of children and orphans in the motherland has made it possible for this money and food to be sent to us. Food and other assistance has been provided through the Red Crescent. It will be distributed to last for three months. Accordingly, this assistance should be allocated in such a way every week so it can last for three months. It is strictly prohibited to sell or throw away food, or give it to animals. The police department and the municipal authorities should see that this does not happen. I'm sorry that I have to use such language for my compatriots.

(Signed)

Cengiz
SANCAKTAR

Distributed to:

Refugee Installations
Legal Services
Institutions
Police Directorate
Municipality
Refugee Solidarity Service

Sayı: D.VII1-14/67   SANCAKTARLIK KARARGÂHI
Konu: Motorlu Araçlara Sigorta   AYDIN.
yapılması.   20 Mayıs, 1967.

1. Yollarda kullanılan bütün motorlu araçlara sigorta
   yapılması kanuni bir mecburiyettir.Bununla kaza
   yapanların tazminat hususunun sigortalar tarafından
   karşılanması sağlanmış olmaktadır.

2. Yapılan kazanın Türk Polisi tarafından araştırılmasını
   kolaylaştırmak ve mümkün kılmak maksadıyle Türklere
   ait araçların Türk Sigorta Acentelerinde sigorta
   ettirmelerinin mutlaka sağlanması gerekmektedir.Bu
   maksatla en kısa zamanda bütün motorlu araç sahiplerine
   bu husus duyurulmalıdır.

3. Kasaba ve köylerdeki Türk Polis memurları Türk araç
   sahiplerinin araçlarını Türk sigortalarında sigorta edip
   etmediklerini devamlı surette kontrol edecekler ve bu
   hususa riayet etmiyenlerin hakkında kovuşturma yapılması
   için gereken kanuni işlem yapılacaktır.

4. Bölgenizde bulunan bütün motorlu araçların numaralarını,
   kime ait olduklarını ve hangi sigorta şirketinde sigorta
   edildiklerini en geç 1 Haziran,1967 gününe kadar tesbit
   edip bildirilmesini.

5. Gereğine göre hareket edilmesini önemle rica ederim.

                                          SERDAI)I.

Dağıtım: Otağ,Oba ve Oymaklar,
         Emniyet Müdürü
         Köy Emniyet Personeli.

ENGLISH SUMMARY OF DOCUMENT NO. 6

Order by Serdar Essat Fellah

Date: 20 May 1967

District: Paphos Regional Command

Subject: Motor vehicle insurance

1. Motor vehicle insurance is required by law.

2. In order to expedite the work of the Turkish police in case of an accident, all motor vehicle owners are required to insure their vehicles through Turkish insurance agents.

3. Police officers will make sure to check whether drivers carry insurance documents with them and will prosecute violators.

4. A registry should be prepared in which all motor vehicles are listed along with the names of their owners and their insurance.

5. Please see that this order is executed.

(Signed)

Essat Fellah
SERDAR I

Distributed to:

Refugee Installations
Police Directorate
Village Security Personnel

Sayı: D.VIII-17/67.   SANCAKTARLIK KARARGÂHI
                                                      .UŞAK.
                                                  ..15/8./.6.7.......

Sayın....................../........,
                    ..15./8./.67.......,...tarihinde ÇAMLICA bölgesinde yapılan
ağaç denetlemesinde çocuğunuz.GÜLDEREN..İZZET.'in..ağacının
sulanmamış olduğu görülmüştür.

        Ağaç sulama vazifesi çocuğunuza verilirken, onun iyi
yetişmesi, sorumluluk duygusunun, toplum yararına çalışma sevgisinin
gelişmesi hedef tutuluyordu. Sorumluluğu altında bulunan bir ağaca
bakmak, sulamak, çocuğu toplum yararına çalışmayı ve böyle bir çalışmanın
faydalarını öğretir.

        Çocuğunuzun bu sahadaki terbiyesi ile şahsen ilgilenip,
ihmalkârlık, tembellik, sorumsuzluk gibi kötü itiyatlara düşmemelerini
sağlamanızı ve kendilerine verilen vazifeyi hiç ihmal etmeden yapmaları
için daima ikazda bulunmanızı rica ederim.

                                              SANCAKTAR.

ENGLISH TRANSLATION OF DOCUMENT NO. 7

Order by Sancaktar Ferit Cengiz

Date: 15 August 1967

District: Paphos Regional Command

Subject: Teaching children good habits

Following an inspection of the Çamlica area, it has been observed that Gülderen Izzet has not watered the tree that he has been assigned to look after.

Assigning your child to water the tree aims at teaching him good habits in order to benefit the community. By watering the tree, the child offers a service to the community.

It is important to teach your children to avoid laziness and stay away from bad habits. I would ask you to be careful so that your child carries out his duties.

(Signed)

Cengiz
SANCAKTAR

Appendix B
"Naturalization Certificate"
of Abdullah Ayhan, a Settler from Turkey

The following document in Turkish is the "naturalization certificate" of Abdullah Ayhan, a settler from Turkey. The "certificate" was issued to Ayhan by the "Turkish Federated State of Cyprus" on 14 March 1980. The "naturalization certificate" is followed by an English translation.

YURTTAŞLIĞA KABUL BELGESİ

Belge No. ..1B422........

3/1975 Sayılı Kıbrıs Türk Federe Devleti Yurttaşlık Kanunu

Madde 6 (Tüzük Madde 12)

Aşağıdaki bilginin kendisine ait olduğunu bildiren ve kendisine bir yurttaşlık belgesi verilmesi için 3/1975 Kıbrıs Türk Federe Devleti yurttaşlık kanununda gösterilen şartları yerine getirdiği hakkında İçişleri Bakanını tatmin eden ....

ABDULLAH AYEAN .... (İsim) bir yurttaşlık belgesi almak için Kıbrıs Türk Federe Devleti İçişleri Bakanına müracaat ettiğinden ;

İçişleri Bakanı Söz konusu kanunun kendisine verdiği yetkiyi kullanarak adı geçen ABDULLAE AYEAN .... 'a

bu yurttaşlık belgesini verir ve kanun ile onun altında yapılan Tüzüğün gerektirdiği şekilde ve belli bir mühlet içinde Kıbrıs Türk Federe Devleti'ne sadakat yemini vermesi üzerine bu belgeyle .... 14.3.1930 .... tarihinden itibaren Türk Federe Devleti'nin bir yurttaşı olacağını ilân eder.

Bu dilekçeyi bugün .... 14.3.1980 .... tarihinde onaylayarak imza ettim.

(İmza) _[signature]_

İçişleri Bakanı veya
Muhaceret Müdürü.

İçişleri Bakanlığı,
Lefkoşa.

_____

DİLEKÇE SAHİBİ İLE İLGİLİ BİLGİ

Adı ve Soyadı   ABDULLAH AYEAN

Adres   DEREBOYU SOKAK NO.50 ALSANCAK

İş veya Meslek   GARSON

Doğum yeri ve tarihi   SERBAN   26.9.1950 (Bin dokuzyüz elli)

Cinsiyeti   E.

Bekâr/*Evli/*Dul/*Boşanmış   EVLI

Karı veya kocanın Adı ve Soyadı   RAHME AYEAN

Babanın Adı ve Soyadı ve Yurttaşlığı   HUSEYİN AYEAN   T.C.

Ananın Adı ve Soyadı ve Yurttaşlığı   ŞERİFE AYEAN   T.C.

K.T.F.D Kimlik Kartı No.   081268

(Lütfen çeviriniz)

Date: 14 March 1980
Subject: Naturalization Certificate of Abdullah Ayhan
Title of Document: CITIZENSHIP ACCEPTANCE DOCUMENT
Document No. 18422/Naturalization Law 3-1975, Turkish Federated
State of Cyprus/Article 6, Paragraph 12

In order to be issued a certificate of naturalization, the provisions of
Naturalization Law 3/1975 of the Turkish Federated State of Cyprus
should be fulfilled and an application should be filed with the minister
of interior.

(Name): ABDULLAH AYHAN
The minister of interior, through the authority vested in him by the
law, issues to ABDULLAH AYHAN this certificate of naturalization.
According to the law, and provided that he will take an oath of
allegiance within the given deadline, he is hereby declared a citizen of
the Turkish Federated State of Cyprus as of 14 March 1980.

Having approved this application today, 14 March 1980, I hereby
sign,

(Signed)
Minister of Interior
Director of Immigration

Ministry of Interior
Nicosia

VITAL STATISTICS
Name: Abdullah Ayhan
Address: Dereboyu Sokak No. 50, Alsancak [Karavas]
Profession: Waiter
Place and date of birth: Serban [Turkey], 29 September 1950
Sex: Male
Married/single/widowed/divorced: Married
Name of spouse: Rahme Ayhan
Name and citizenship of father: Hüseyin Ayhan, Republic of Turkey
Name and citizenship of mother: Şerife Ayhan, Republic of Turkey
Identity card number of the TFSC: 081268

(stamped photograph)

II KISIM

Kıbrıs Türk Federe Devletine Sadakat Yemini

Ben (tam isim) ..... ABDULLAH AYHAN T.6 A: /5207
Kıbrıs Türk Federe Devletine sadık olacağıma ve kanunlarına saygı ve riayet göstere-
ceğime söz veririm.

(İmza) ....

14/3/1980 ..... tarihinde önümde imza edilmiştir.

(İmza) ....
Hakim, Mukayyit veya Konsolos veya bu hususta görevlendirilmiş herhangi bir kişi.

Madde 13(2) şunları öngörmektedir :

"(2)   Yukarıdaki şekilde istenilen sadıkat sözü, ilgili olduğu yurttaşlığa kabul bel-
gesinin tarihinden üç aya kadar veya Bakanın hale göre müsaade edeceği
daha uzun bir süre zarfında verilir. Sadakat sözü ; söz konusu süre içinde
verilmediği takdirde belge herhangi bir surette geçerli olmaz ;

Ancak, sürenin uzatılmasına müsaade edildiğine dair belgenin üzerine
bir kayıt yapılmadıkça ve bu kayıt 12. madde altında yurttaşlığa kabul belgesini imzalamağa yetkilendirilen bir kişi tarafından imzalanmadıkça bu
fıkra altında sürenin uzatılmasına müsaade edildiği sayılmaz. "

* uygulanmayanları çiziniz.

PART II

Pledge of Allegiance to the Turkish Federated State of Cyprus.

I, ABDULLAH AYHAN, pledge allegiance to the Turkish Federated State of Cyprus and its laws.

(Signature)

ABDULLAH AYHAN

14 March 1980 Signed in my presence

(Signature) Judge or any other
authorized person.

Article 13 (2) of the law provides:

The above Pledge of Allegiance should be given within three months of the date of issuing this certificate. This deadline can be extended by order of the minister. In case the Pledge of Allegiance is not given within this period, this document is invalid.
For the extension of the deadline to be valid, there should be an attached document, according to article 12 of the Naturalization Law, which must be signed by an authorized individual.

Bibliography

BOOKS AND MONOGRAPHS

Adamson, David C. *The Kurdish War*. New York: Praeger, 1964.

Ahmad, Feroz. *The Turkish Experiment in Democracy, 1950-1975*. Boulder, Colorado: Westview Press, 1977.

Akça, Mehmet. *Kizil Makarios Çekil Kibristan* (Leave Cyprus, Red Makarios). Ankara: Nur Matbaasi, 1958.

Akyol, Izzet. *28 Auğustos 1955 Kibris Katliaminin iç Yüzü* (The Domestic Aspect of the Massacre of 28 August 1955 in Cyprus). Gönül Matbaacilik, 1955.

Alastos, Doros. *Cyprus: Past, Present and Future*. London: Committee for Cyprus Affairs, 1943.

Alasya, Halil Fikret. *Kibris Tarihi ve Kibris'ta Türk Eserleri* (Cyprus History and Turkish Monuments in Cyprus). Ankara: Türk Kültürünü Araştirma Enstitüsü, 1964.

————. *Kuzey Kibris Türk Cumhuriyeti Tarihi* (History of the Turkish Republic of Northern Cyprus). Ankara: Türk Kültürünü Araştirma Enstitüsü, Yayinlari, 1987.

Alasya, Halil Fikret, et al. *Kibris ve Türkler* (Cyprus and the Turks). Ankara: Türk Kültürünü Araştirma Enstitüsü, 1964.

Alexandris, Alexis. *The Greek Minority in Istanbul and Greek-Turkish Relations, 1918-1974*. Athens: Center for Asia Minor Studies, 1983.

Anadol, Cemal. *Türk Milliyetçilerinin Kitabi: Ne Amerika, Ne Rusya, Her Şeyin Üstünde Türkiye* (The Book of Turkish Nationalists: Neither America nor Russia, Turkey above Everything). Istanbul: Yaylacik Matbaasi, 1970.

Arberry, A. J., ed. *Religion in the Middle East*. 2 vols. Cambridge: Cambridge University Press, 1969.

Arfa, Hassan. *The Kurds: A Historical and Political Study*. London: Oxford University Press, 1966.

Armaoğlu, Fahir. *Kibris Meselesi 1954-1959: Türk Hükümeti ve Kamu Oyunun Davranişlari* (The Cyprus Question 1954-1959: The Turkish Government and Public Opinion). Ankara: Sevinç Matbaasi, 1963.

Armstrong, Harold Courtney. *Grey Wolf, Mustafa Kemal: An Intimate Study of a Dictator.* London: A. Barker, 1932; New York: Minton, Balch, 1933.

Ataöv, Türkkaya. *Turkish Foreign Policy, 1939-1945.* Ankara: Ankara Üniversitesi Basimevi, 1965.

Attalides, Michael. *Cyprus: Nationalism and International Politics.* New York: St. Martin's Press, 1979.

————, ed. *Cyprus Reviewed.* Nicosia: The Juris Cypri Association, 1977.

Ayoob, Mohammed. *The Politics of Islamic Reassertion.* New York: Saint Martin's Press, 1982.

Bahcheli, Tozun. *Greek-Turkish Relations since 1955.* Boulder, Colo.: Westview Press, 1990.

Bedevi, Vergi H. *Cyprus Has Never Been a Greek Island.* Nicosia: Cyprus Turkish Historical Association, 1963.

Berk, Bekir. *Patrikhane ve Kibris* (The Patriarchate and Cyprus). Istanbul: Siralar Matbaasi, 1962.

Berkes, Niazi. *The Development of Secularism in Turkey.* Montreal: McGill University Press, 1964.

————, ed. *Turkish Nationalism and Western Civilization: Selected Essays of Ziya Gökalp.* New York: Columbia University Press, 1959.

Bianci, Robert. *Interest Groups and Political Development in Turkey.* Princeton: Princeton University Press, 1984.

Bill, James and Carl Leiden. *Politics in the Middle East.* Boston: Little Brown & Company, 1984.

Birand, Mehmed Ali, *The Generals' Coup in Turkey: An Inside Story of 12 September 1980.* London: Brassey's Defence Publishers, 1987.

————. *Thirty Hot Days in Cyprus.* Istanbul: Milliyet Publications, 1976.

Blinkhorn, Martin and Thanos Veremis, eds. *Modern Greece: Nationalism and Nationality.* Athens: Sage-ELIAMEP, 1990.

Campbell, John C. *Defense of the Middle East.* 2d ed. New York: Praeger, 1960.

Clerides, Glafkos. *Cyprus: My Deposition,* vol. 1. Nicosia: Alithia Publishing, 1989.

Cobham, Claude Delaval. *Excerpta Cypria: Materials for a History of Cyprus.* Cambridge: The University Press, 1908.

Coufoudakis, Van. *Essays on the Cyprus Conflict.* New York: Pella Publishing Company, 1976.

Couloumbis, Theodore A. *The U.S., Greece and Turkey: The Troubled Triangle.* New York: Praeger, 1983.

Crawshaw, Nancy. *The Cyprus Revolt: An Account of the Struggle for Union with Greece.* London: George Allen, 1978.

Crouzet, François. *Le Conflit de Chypre: 1946-1959.* 2 vols. Bruxelles: Etablissements Emile Bruylant, 1973.

Cudsi, Alexander and Ali Hillal Dessouki, eds. *Islam and Power.* London: Croom Helm, 1981.

Cyprus is Turkish Party. *Enosis Denounced: Cyprus is Turkish.* Nicosia: Başkurt Press, n.d.

———. *Greek Atrocities against the Turks.* Nicosia: Bozkurt Press, 1956.

———. *Intercommunal Strife in Cyprus: Its Causes and Effect.* Nicosia: Halkin Sesi Press, 1958.

Davison, Roderic H. *Turkey.* Englewood Cliffs, N.J.: Prentice-Hall, 1968.

Demiray, Tahsin. *Tarihin Işiği Altinda Kibris ve 3 Dünya Harbinde Türk Stratejisi Bakimindan Önemi* (Cyprus in Historic Perspective and its Strategic Importance to Turkey in World War Three). Istanbul: Türkiye Basimevi, 1958.

Demokritos [pseud.]. *E Akeliki Egesia ke o Enoplos Agon: Marxistiki Kritiki* (AKEL's Leadership and the Armed Struggle: A Marxist Critique). Nicosia, 1959.

Denktash, Rauf R. *The Cyprus Triangle.* London: George Allen and Unwin, 1982.

Deveci, Hasan. *Cyprus: Yesterday, Today: What Next?* London: Cyprus Turkish Association, 1976.

Dodd, Clement H. *Politics and Government in Turkey.* Berkeley: University of California Press, 1969.

Donahue, John and John Esposito, eds. *Islam in Transition: Muslim Perspectives.* New York: Oxford University Press, 1982.

Eden, Anthony. *The Memoirs of Anthony Eden: Full Circle.* Cambridge: Riverside Press; London: Cassell; and Boston: Houghton Mifflin, 1960.

Edmonds, C. J. *Kurds, Turks, and Arabs.* London: Oxford University Press, 1957.

Ehrlich, Thomas. *International Crises and the Rule of Law: Cyprus, 1958-1967.* Oxford: Oxford University Press, 1974.

Engin Arin. *Atatürkçülük Savaşimizda Kibris Bariş Destanimiz* (Our Cyprus Peace Epic in our Fight for Atatürkism). Istanbul: Gün Matbaasi, 1975.

———. *The Voice of the Cypriot Turks; the Innermost Psychology of the Cyprus*

Problem. Istanbul: Atatürkist Cultural Publications, 1964.

Ertekün, Necati M. *The Cyprus Dispute and the Birth of the Turkish Republic of Northern Cyprus*. Lefkoşa (Nicosia): K. Rustem & Brother, 1984.

Esin, Emel. *Aspects of Turkish Civilization in Cyprus*. Ankara: Türk Kültürünü Araştirma Enstitüsü, 1965.

Esposito, John. *Voices of Resurgent Islam*. New York: Oxford University Press, 1983.

Feyzioğlu, Turhan. *Büyük Tehlike: Komünizm* (The Great Danger: Communism). Ankara: Ayyildiz Matbaasi, 1969.

Foley, Charles. *Legacy of Strife: Cyprus from Rebellion to Civil War*. Baltimore: Penguin, 1964.

Foley, Charles and W. I. Scobie. *The Struggle for Cyprus*. Stanford: Hoover Institution Press, 1975.

Foot, Hugh. *A Start in Freedom*. New York: Harper & Row, 1964.

Foot, Michael, and Mervyn Jones. *Guilty Men, 1957: Suez and Cyprus*. New York: Rinehart, 1957.

Frey, Frederick W. *The Turkish Political Elite*. Cambridge, Mass.: MIT Press, 1965.

Gallagher, Charles. *Contemporary Islam: The Straits of Secularism; Power, Politics and Piety in Republican Turkey*. New York: American Universities Field Staff, 1966.

Gellner, Ernest, and John Waterbury, eds. *Patrons and Clients in Mediterranean Societies*. London: Duckworth, 1977.

Georgallides, George. *A Political and Administrative History of Cyprus: 1918-1926*. Nicosia: Cyprus Research Center, 1979.

Gibbons, H. A. *The Foundations of the Ottoman Empire*. Oxford: Oxford University Press, 1916.

Greece and Terror. Ankara: The Cyprus Turkish Cultural Association, Head Office, 1985.

Grivas-Digenis, George. *Apomnemoneumata Agonos EOKA, 1955-1959* (Memoirs of the EOKA Struggle, 1955-1959). Athens, 1961.

————. *General Grivas-Digenis on Guerrilla Warfare*. New York: Frederick Praeger, 1962.

Grousset, René. *The Empire of the Steppes: A History of Central Asia*. New Brunswick, N.J.: Rutgers University Press, 1970.

Hackett, John. *A History of the Orthodox Church of Cyprus*. London: Methuen, 1901.

Harris, George S. *The Origins of Communism in Turkey*. Stanford: The Hoover Institution, 1967.

————. *Troubled Alliance: Turkish-American Relations in Historical Perspective, 1945-1971.* AEI Hoover Policy Studies, 1972.

————. *Turkey: Coping with Crisis.* Boulder, Colo.: Westview Press, 1985.

Hart, Parker T. *Two NATO Allies at the Threshold of War: Cyprus—A Firsthand Account of Crisis Management, 1965-1968.* Durham, N.C., and London: Duke University Press, 1990.

Helsinki Watch, *Paying the Price: Freedom of Expression in Turkey.* New York: International Freedom to Publish Committee of the Association of American Publishers, 1989.

Heyd, Uriel. *Foundations of Turkish Nationalism: The Life and Teachings of Ziya Gökalp.* London: Luzac, 1950.

————. *Revival of Islam in Turkey.* Jerusalem: Magnes Press, Hebrew University, 1968.

Hill, Sir George. *A History of Cyprus,* vol. 4. Cambridge University Press, 1952.

Hitchens, Christopher. *Hostage to History: Cyprus from Ottomans to Kissinger.* New York: The Noonday Press, 1989.

Hoskins, Halford L. *British Routes to India.* New York: Longman, 1928.

Hostler, Charles W. *Turkism and the Soviets: The Turks of the World and their Political Objectives.* New York: Praeger, 1957.

Hotham, David. *The Turks.* London: John Murray, 1972.

Howard, Harry N. *Turkey, the Straits, and U.S. Policy.* Baltimore: Johns Hopkins University Press, 1974.

Ibn Khaldun. *The Muqaddimah: An Introduction to History,* translated by Franz Rosenthal. Princeton: Princeton University Press, 1967.

Ierodiakonou, Leontios. *To Kypriako Problema* (The Cyprus Question). Athens: Papazisis, 1975.

Isaacs, Harold R. *Idols of the Tribe: Group Identity and Political Change.* New York: Harper Colophon Book, 1977.

Ismail, Sabahattin. *Kibris Sorunu* (The Cyprus Problem). Istanbul: K.K.T.C. Turizm ve Kültür Bakanliği Yayinlari, 1986.

Karpat, Kemal H., ed. *Political and Social Thought in the Contemporary Middle East.* New York: Frederick A. Praeger, 1968.

————, ed. *Turkey's Foreign Policy in Transition: 1950-1974.* Leiden: E. J. Brill, 1975.

————. *Turkey's Politics: The Transition to a Multi-Party System.* Princeton: Princeton University Press, 1959.

Karpat, Kemal H., et al. *Social Change and Politics in Turkey.* Leiden: E. J. Brill, 1973.

Kaymak, Faiz. *Kibris Türkleri Bu Duruma Nasil Düştü?* (How Did the Cypriot Turks Fall into this Condition?). Istanbul: Alpay Basimevi, 1968.

Kazancigil, Ali, and Ergun Özbudun, eds. *Atatürk: Founder of a Modern State*. Hamden, Conn.: Archon Books, 1981.

Kedourie, Elie. *Islam in the Modern World and Other Studies*. New York: Holt, Rinehart & Winston, 1981.

Kibris Türk Kültür Derneği. *Kibris'in Tarihi Gelişimi ve Kuzey Kibris Türk Cumhuriyeti* (Historical Developments in Cyprus and the Turkish Republic of Northern Cyprus). Lefkoşa (Nicosia), 1983.

Kibris'in iç yüzü. Kibris Türktür ve Türk Kalacaktir. Onu Ölünceye Kadar Müdafaa Etmeğe And Içtik (The Domestic Scene in Cyprus. Cyprus is Turkish and Shall Remain Turkish. We Give the Oath that We will Defend it until Death). Ankara: Güzel Istanbul Matbaasi, 1958.

Kinross, Lord. *The Ottoman Centuries: The Rise and Fall of the Turkish Empire*. New York: Morrow Quill Paperbacks, 1977.

————. *Atatürk: The Rebirth of a Nation*. London: Weidenfeld and Nicolson, 1964.

Koumoulides, John T. *Cyprus in Transition, 1960-1985*. London: Trigraph, 1986.

————, ed. *Greek Connections: Essays on Culture and Diplomacy*. Notre Dame: University of Notre Dame Press, 1987.

Kranidiotes, Giannos. *To Kypriako Problema: 1960-1974* (The Cyprus Problem: 1960-1974). Athens: Themelio, 1984.

Kürşad, Fikret, et al. *Kibris'ta Yunan Emperyalizmi: Megali Idea, Filika Eteria, Kilise* (Greek Imperialism in Cyprus: *Megali Idea*, The Society of Friends, The Church). Kutsun Yayinevi, June 1978.

Kyriakides, Stanley. *Constitutionalism and Crisis Government*. Philadelphia: University of Pennsylvania Press, 1968.

Kyrris, Costas. *History of Cyprus*. Nicosia: Nicocles Publishing, 1985.

————. *Peaceful Coexistence in Cyprus under British Rule (1878-1959) and after Independence*. Nicosia: Government of Cyprus Public Information Office, 1977.

Landau, Jacob M. *Pan-Turkism in Turkey: A Study of Irredentism*. Hamden, Conn.: Archon Books, 1981.

————. *Radical Politics in Modern Turkey*. Leiden: E. J. Brill, 1974.

Leder, Arnold. *Catalysts of Change: Marxist versus Muslim in a Turkish Community*. Austin: University of Texas Center for Middle Eastern Studies, 1976.

Lenczowski, George. *The Middle East in World Affairs*. Ithaca: Cornell

University Press, 1980.

Lewis, Bernard. *The Emergence of Modern Turkey*. London: Oxford University Press, 1969.

Lewis, Geoffrey. *Turkey*. London: Ernest Benn, 1965.

Luke, Harry. *Cyprus Under the Turks, 1571-1878*. London: Oxford University Press, 1921.

MacMillan, Harold. *Riding the Storm, 1956-1959*. London: MacMillan, 1969.

Mango, Andrew. *Turkey: A Delicately Poised Ally*. Washington Paper Series, No. 28. London: Sage Publications, 1975.

Manizade, Derviş. *Kibris: Dün, Bugün, Yarin* (Cyprus: Yesterday, Today, Tomorrow). Istanbul: Kibris Türk Kültür Derneği, Yaylacik Matbaasi, 1975.

Markides, Kyriacos C. *The Rise and Fall of the Cyprus Republic*. New Haven: Yale University Press, 1977.

Marriott, J. A. R. *The Eastern Question: An Historical Study in European Diplomacy*. 4th ed. Oxford: Oxford University Press, 1940.

Mayes, Stanley. *Cyprus and Makarios*. London: Putnam, 1960.

———. *Makarios: A Biography*. New York: St. Martin's Press, 1981.

McDonald, Robert. *The Problem of Cyprus*. Adelphi Paper No. 234. London: International Institute of Strategic Studies, Winter 1988/89.

McLaurin, R. D., ed. *The Political Role of Minority Groups in the Middle East*. New York: Praeger, 1979.

Military Balance: 1989-1990. London: International Institute of Strategic Studies, 1989.

Monroe, Elizabeth. *Britain's Moment in the Middle East, 1914-1956*. London: Chatto and Windus, 1963.

Mortimer, Edward. *Faith and Power: The Politics of Islam*. New York: Random House, 1983.

Naipul, V. S. *Among the Believers: An Islamic Journey*. New York: Alfred Knopf, 1981.

Özbudun, Ergun. *Social Change and Political Participation in Turkey*. Princeton: Princeton University Press, 1976

———. *The Role of the Military in Recent Turkish Politics*. Cambridge: Harvard Center for International Studies, 1966.

Özel, Mehmet. *Kara Cüppeli Kizil Papaz Makarios'a Açik Mektup* (Open Letter to Makarios, the Black-Robed Red Priest), 1958.

Pallis, A. A. *Greece's Anatolian Venture—And After*. London: Methuen, 1937.

Papadopoullos, Theodore. *Social and Historical Data on Population: 1570-1881*. Nicosia: Cyprus Research Center, 1965.

Papageorgiou, Speros, ed. *Archeion ton Paranomon Egraphon tou Kypriakou Agonos: 1955-1959* (Archive of Illegal Documents of the Cypriot Struggle: 1955-1959). 2nd ed. Nicosia: Epifaniou Publishers, 1984.

Patrick, Richard A. *Political Geography and the Cyprus Conflict: 1963-1971.* Department of Geography, Publication Series No. 4., University of Waterloo, 1976.

Piscatori, James, ed. *Islam in the Political Process.* Cambridge University Press, 1983.

Polyviou, Polyvios. *Cyprus: Conflict and Negotiation, 1960-1980.* London: Duckworth, 1980.

Psomiades, Harry J. *The Eastern Question: The Last Phase—A Study in Greek-Turkish Diplomacy.* Thessaloniki: Institute for Balkan Studies, 1968.

Purcell, H.D. *Cyprus.* New York: Frederick Praeger, 1969.

Rahman, Fazlur. *Islam.* New York: Anchor Books, 1968.

————. *Islam and Modernity: Transformation of an Intellectual Tradition.* Chicago: University of Chicago Press, 1983.

Rize, Ekrem. *Kibris Bir Numarali Türk Davasi* (Cyprus, the Number One Problem for Turkey). Istanbul: Türkiye Yayinevi, 1965.

Robinson, Richard. *The First Turkish Republic.* Cambridge: Harvard University Press, 1963.

Rustow, Dankward A. *Turkey: America's Forgotten Ally.* New York: Theo. Gans & Sons, 1968.

Saka, Mehmet. *Ege Denizi Alarinda Türk Haklari* (Turkish Rights over the Aegean Islands). Ankara: Yildiz Basimevi, 1955.

Salih, Halil Ibrahim. *Cyprus: An Analysis of Cypriot Political Discord.* New York: Theo. Gans & Sons, 1968.

————. *Cyprus: The Impact of Diverse Nationalism on a State.* University of Alabama Press, 1978.

Sarris, Neokles. *E Alle Pleura* (The Other Side). Athens, Gramme, 1977.

Sayilgan, Aclan. *Yakin Tehlike: Komünizm* (Close Danger: Communism). Ankara: Kardeş Matbaasi, 1963.

Schick, Irvin Cemil and Ertuğrul Ahmed Tonak, eds. *Turkey in Transition.* Oxford: Oxford University Press, 1987.

Servas, Ploutes. *Kypriako: Euthynes* (Cyprus: Responsibilities). Athens: Gramme, 1980.

Short, Martin and Anthony McDermott. *Destroying Ethnic Identity: The Kurds of Turkey.* New York: Helsinki Watch Report, March 1988.

————. *The Kurds.* London: Minority Rights Group, 1981.

Smith, Michael Llewelyn. *Ionian Vision: Greece in Asia Minor, 1919-1922.* London: Allen Lane, 1973.

Smith, Wilfred C. *Islam in Modern History.* Princeton: Princeton University Press, 1957.

Stephens, Robert. *Cyprus: A Place of Arms.* London: Pall Mall Press, 1968.

St. John-Jones, L. W. *The Population of Cyprus.* London: University of London, Institute of Commonwealth Studies, 1983.

Stoddard, Phillip, David Cuthell and Margaret Sullivan. *Change and the Muslim World.* Syracuse: Syracuse University Press, 1981.

Szyliowicz, Joseph. *A Political Analysis of Student Activism: The Turkish Case.* Beverly Hills: Sage Professional Paper in Comparative Politics, 1972.

Tamkoç, Metin. *The Turkish-Cypriot State: The Embodiment of the Right of Self-Determination.* London: K. Rustem, 1988.

———. *The Warrior Diplomats.* Salt Lake City: University of Utah Press, 1976.

Theocharides, I. P. *Names of Villages in the Occupied Area of Cyprus According to Ottoman Documents.* Nicosia: Kailas Press, 1980.

TMT Notlari (TMT Notes). Lefkoşa (Nicosia): Halkin Sesi, 1972.

Toynbee, Arnold J. *The Western Question in Greece and Turkey.* London: Constable, 1922.

Tsoucalas, Constantine. *The Greek Tragedy.* London: Penguin, 1969.

Turay, Sabahattin. *Kibris Türktür Türk Kalacactir* (Cyprus is Turkish and Turkish it Shall Remain). Aydin: Yeni Aydin Matbaasi, 1958.

Türk Kibris'a Dokunma. Kibris Türk Kalacaktir (Hands off Turkish Cyprus. Cyprus Shall Remain Turkish). Istanbul: Nurkök Matbaasi, 1955.

Türk Millî Talebe Federasyonu. *Kibris* (Cyprus). Ankara: 1964.

Türkeş, Alparslan. *Diş Meselelerimiz* (Our Foreign Problems). Istanbul: Ergenekon Yayinevi, 1974.

———. *Diş Politikamiz ve Kibris* (Our Foreign Policy and Cyprus). Istanbul: Kibris Türk Kültür Derneği, 1966.

———. *Dokuz Işik* (Nine Lights). Istanbul: Ergenekon Yayinevi, 1972.

———. *Temel Görüşler* (Basic Views). Istanbul: Dergâh Yayinevi, 1975.

Türkiye Millî Gençlik Teşkilâti (National Turkish Youth Organization). *Kibris Meselesi ve Türkiye Konferansi, 5 Mart 1954* (The Cyprus Problem and the Turkish Conference, 5 March 1954). Istanbul: Anıl Matbaası, 1954.

Tütsch, Hans. *From Ankara to Marrakesh: Turks and Arabs in a Changing World.* London: Allen and Unwin, 1964.

Váli, Ferenc A. *Bridge Across the Bosporus: The Foreign Policy of Turkey.* Baltimore: The Johns Hopkins Press, 1971.

Vasiliou, Nicos. *The Widening Economic Gap between Greek and Turkish*

Cypriots and Consequences for a Federal Solution. Nicosia, 1984.

Veremis, Thanos. *Greek Security: Issues and Politics*. Adelphi Paper No. 179. London: International Institute of Strategic Studies, 1982.

Volkan, Vamik. *Cyprus—War and Adaptation: A Psychoanalytic History of Two Ethnic Groups in Conflict*. Charlottesville: University of Virginia Press, 1979.

Volkan, Vamik and Norman Itzkowitz. *The Immortal Atatürk*. Chicago: The University of Chicago Press, 1984.

Voll, John O. *Islam: Continuity and Change in the Modern World*. Boulder, Colo.: Westview Press, 1982.

Watt, Montgomery. *Muhammad: Prophet and Statesman*. London: Oxford University Press, 1961.

Weber, Frank G. *The Evasive Neutral: Germany, Britain and the Quest for a Turkish Alliance in the Second World War*. Columbia, Missouri, and London: University of Missouri Press, 1979.

Weiker, Walter. *The Turkish Revolution, 1960-1961*. Washington, D.C.: The Brookings Institution, 1963.

Weisband, Edward. *Turkish Foreign Policy 1943-1945: Small State Diplomacy and Great Power Politics*. Princeton: Princeton University Press, 1973.

Worseley, Peter and Paschalis Kitromilides, eds. *Small States in the Modern World*. Nicosia: The New Cyprus Association, 1979.

Xydis, Stephen. *Cyprus: Reluctant Republic*. The Hague, Mouton, 1973.

Yalman, Ahmed Emin. *Turkey in the World War*. New Haven: Yale University Press, 1930.

———. *Turkey of Our Times*. Oklahoma: Oklahoma University Press, 1956.

Yücel, Celâlettin. *Diş Türkler* (The Outside Turks). Istanbul: Hun Yayinlari, 1976.

Yurdanur, Safa. *Kibris, Ecevit ve Ötekiler; Belgesel Inceleme* (Cyprus, Ecevit and the Others; A Documented Analysis). Istanbul: Şiroğlu Matbaasi, 1974.

ARTICLES

Ağaoğullari, Mehmed Ali. "The Ultranationalist Right " In *Turkey in Transition*, edited by Irvin Cemil Schick and Ertuğrul Ahmed Tonak, 177-219. Oxford: Oxford University Press, 1987.

Ahmad, Feroz. "Islamic Reassertion in Turkey." *Third World Quarterly* 10, no. 2 (April 1988): 750-769.

———. "The Islamic Assertion in Turkey: Pressures and State Response." *Arab Studies Quarterly* 4, no. 1-2 (Spring 1982): 94-100.

Akşin, Sina. "Turkish Nationalism Today." In *The Turkish Yearbook of*

International Relations, 1976, vol. 16, 118-132. Ankara: Institute of International Relations, Faculty of Political Science, University of Ankara, 1979.

Aktan, Resat. "Kibrisin Iktisadi Bünyesi ve Meseleri" (Problems of Economic Development in Cyprus). *Türk Kültürü* 16 (February 1964): 22-26.

Alasya, Halil Fikret. "Atatürk Kibris'ta" (Ataturk in Cyprus). *Türk Kültürü* 14 (December 1963): 5-6.

————. "Elenizm Hortluyor!" (The Specter of Hellenism!). *Türk Kültürü* 39 (January 1966): 287-288.

————. "Kibris Anayasasi ve Makarios" (The Constitution of Cyprus and Makarios). *Türk Kültürü* 7 (May 1963): 53-54.

————. "Kibris ve Atatürk Sevgisi" (Love for Cyprus and Atatürk). *Türk Kültürü* 13 (November 1963): 124-125.

————. "Kibris'i Tehdit Eden en Büyük Tehlike: Komünistlik" (The Biggest Danger Threatening Cyprus: Communism). *Türk Kültürü* 3 (January 1963): 56-58.

————. "Kibrist'a Türk Nüfusu ve Nüfusun Dağilişi" (Turkish-Cypriot Population and Population Distribution). *Türk Kültürü* 94 (August 1970): 663-669.

————. "Kibris'taki son Trajedi" (The Last Tragedy of Cyprus). *Türk Kültürü* 16 (February 1964): 6-9.

Alexandris, Alexis. "Imbros and Tenedos; A Study in Turkish Attitudes toward Two Ethnic Greek Island Communities since 1923." *Journal of the Hellenic Diaspora* 71 (1980): 5-31.

————. "To Meionotiko Zetema, 1954-1987" (The Minority Question, 1954-1987). In *Ellino-Tourkikes Scheseis: 1923-1987* (Greek-Turkish Relations: 1923-1987), edited by Alexis Alexandris, et al., 495-552. Athens: Gnosis Publishers, 1988.

Armaoğlu, Fahir. "Kibris'ta Türk Haklari" (Turkish Rights in Cyprus). *Türk Kültürü* 14 (December 1963): 7-11.

————. "Kibris ve Enosis" (Cyprus and *Enosis*). *Forum* 2, no. 1 (October 1954): 9-10.

Arnakis, George. "Turanism; An Aspect of Turkish Nationalism." *Balkan Studies* 1 (1960): 19-32.

Aslanapa, Oktay. "Kibris'ta Türk Eserleri" (Turkish Monuments in Cyprus). *Türk Kültürü* 16 (February 1964): 15-21.

Barkan, Ömer L. "Les Déportations comme Méthode de Peuplement et de Colonisation dans l'Empire Ottoman." *Revue de la Faculté des Sciences Economiques de l'Université d'Istanbul* 2 (1946-1950): 524-569.

Bayülken, Ümit Halük, "Türkiye'nin Diş Politikasi" (The Foreign Policy of

Turkey). *Dış Politika* 3 (March 1973): 3-19.

Beckingham, Charles F. "Islam and Turkish Nationalism in Cyprus." *Die Welt des Islam* 5 (1957): 65-83.

Bilge, Suat. "The Cyprus Conflict and Turkey." In *Turkey's Foreign Policy in Transition: 1950-1974*, edited by Kemal H. Karpat, 134-185. Leiden: E. J. Brill, 1975.

Crawshaw, Nancy. "Cyprus: A Failure of Western Diplomacy." In *Greek Connections: Essays on Culture and Diplomacy*, edited by John T. Koumoulides, 102-116. Notre Dame: University of Notre Dame Press, 1987.

Deliorman, Altan. "Bugünkü Mânâsi Ile 'Bozkurt'" (The Contemporary Meaning of the 'Bozkurt'). *Türk Kültürü* 5, no. 55 (May 1967): 470-475.

Denktash, Rauf R. "An Appeal to the Muslim World: Why A Northern State?" *The Muslim World League Journal* 2, no. 2, Mecca, Saudi Arabia (November/December 1983): 15-19.

———. "Cyprus Today." *Pakistan Horizon* 29, no. 1 (1976): 3-17.

———. "Turkish Federated State of *Kibris:* A Case for International Recogniton." *The Muslim World League Journal* 2, no. 2, Mecca, Saudi Arabia (November/December 1983): 20-21.

Ellis, Ellen. "Turkish Nationalism in the Postwar World." *Current History* 36 (February 1959): 86-91.

Ercümend, Kuran. "Türk Ordusu ve Milliyetçilik" (The Turkish Army and Nationalism). *Türk Kültürü* 47 (September 1966): 995-997.

Ertekün, Necati M. "A Tale of Two Peoples Inhabiting One Island." *Turkish Review Quarterly Digest* 21 (Autumn 1990): 45-68

Fox, Clifton. "Turkish Army's Role in Nation Building." *Military Review* 47 (April 1967): 68-74.

Geertz, Clifford. "The Integrative Revolution: Primordial Sentiments and Civil Politics in the New States." In *Old Societies and New States*, edited by Clifford Geertz, 105-157. New York: The Free Press, 1963.

Gonlübol, Mehmet. "A Short Appraisal of the Foreign Policy of the Turkish Republic: 1923-1973." In *The Turkish Yearbook of International Relations, 1974*, vol. 14, 1-19. Ankara: Institute of International Relations, Faculty of Political Science, University of Ankara, 1976.

Gruen, George. "Turkey's Relations with Israel and its Arab Neighbors." *Middle East Review* (Spring 1985): 33-43.

Harris, George S. "The Role of the Military in Turkish Politics." *Middle East Journal* 19 (Winter 1965): 54-66.

Helms, Christina Moss. "Turkey's Policy toward the Middle East: Strength through Neutrality." *Middle East Insight* (Fall 1988): 40-46.

Howaidi, Fahmi. "Cyprus: Arabia's Commentary." *Arabia: The Islamic World Review* 29 (January 1984): 14-15.

Inalcik, Halil. "Ottoman Methods of Conquest," *Studia Islamica* 2 (1954): 103-129.

Inan, Kâmran. "Cyprus, 1974 Crisis." *Diş Politika* 4 (June/July 1974): 66-70.

Kafesoğlu, Ibrahim. "Kibris Faciasi ve Tarih" (The Cyprus Tragedy and History). *Türk Kültürü* 16 (February 1964): 2-4.

Karpat, Kemal H. "The Military and Politics in Turkey, 1960-1964; a Socio-Cultural Analysis of a Revolution." *American Historical Review* 75 (October 1970): 1654-1683.

——. "The Turkish Left." *Journal of Contemporary History* 2 (April 1966): 169-186.

——. "War on Cyprus: The Tragedy of *Enosis*." In *Turkey's Foreign Policy in Transition: 1950-1974*, edited by Kemal H. Karpat, 186-205. Leiden: E. J. Brill, 1975.

Kazgan, Haytar. "Bati Bizi Anlar Mi?" (Does the West Understand Us?). *Türk Kültürü* 16 (February 1964): 12-14.

Khan, Saleem M. "Religion and Politics in Turkey." *Islam and the Modern Age* 2 (February 1971): 94-108.

Kitromilides, Paschalis M. "From Coexistence to Confrontation: The Dynamics of Ethnic Conflict in Cyprus." In *Cyprus Reviewed*, edited by Michael Attalides, 35-70. Nicosia: The Juris Cypri Association, 1977.

——. "Imagined Communities and the Origins of the National Question in the Balkans." In *Modern Greece: Nationalism and Nationality*, edited by Martin Blinkhorn and Thanos Veremis, 23-66. Athens: Sage-ELIAMEP, 1990.

Kitromilides, Paschalis M. and Theodore A. Couloumbis. "Ethnic Conflict in a Strategic Area: The Case of Cyprus." *The Greek Review of Social Research* 24 (1975): 270-291.

Köprülü, Orhan. "Fuat Köprülü: Ilim ve Siyaset" (Fuat Köprülü: Learning and Politics). *Türk Kültürü* 81 (July 1969): 628-631.

Landau, Jacob M. "The Fortunes and Misfortunes of Pan-Turkism." *Central Asian Survey* 7, no. 1 (1988): 1-5.

Leigh, Monroe. "The Cypriot Communities and International Law." *Turkish Review Quarterly Digest* 22 (Winter 1990): 47-60.

Lewis, Geoffrey. "Turkey: Islam in Politics; A Symposium." *Muslim World* 56 (October 1966): 235-239.

Margulies, R. and Yildiizoglu E. "The Political Uses of Islam in Turkey." *Middle East Report* 153 (July-August 1988): 12-18.

Orhonlu, Cengiz. "Bati Trakya Türkleri" (The Turks of Western Thrace). *Türk Kültürü* 17 (March 1964): 5-8.

———. "Bozcaada" (Tenedos). *Türk Kültürü* 83 (September 1969): 830-835.

———. "Gökçe Ada" (Imbros). *Türk Kültürü* 112 (February 1972): 15-21.

Örs, Dr. Yaman. "Certain Basic Misconceptions in the Field of History. Ancient Greeks, the West, and the Modern World." In *The Turkish Yearbook of International Relations, 1974*, vol. 14, 92-117. University of Ankara: Institute of International Relations, Faculty of Political Science, 1976.

Özoran, Beria Remzi. "Enosis Karşisinda Kibris Türkü" (The Cypriot Turk with Regard to *Enosis*). *Türk Kültürü* 31 (May 1965): 442-451.

———. "Enosis Oyunu" (The *Enosis* Game). *Türk Kültürü* 32 (June 1965): 512-520.

———. "Kibris Türklerinden Esirgenen Haklar" (Rights Denied to Cypriot Turks). *Türk Kültürü* 33 (July 1965): 574-576.

———. "Kibris Türkü ve Rum Tahrikleri" (The Cypriot Turks and Greek Provocations). *Türk Kültürü* 89 (March 1970): 332-341.

———. "Kibris Türk'üne Indirilen Yumruklar" (Blows Dealt against the Cypriot Turks). *Türk Kültürü* 57 (July 1967): 668-674.

———. "Mustafa Kemal, Ankara ve Kibris Türkü" (Mustafa Kemal, Ankara and the Cypriot Turk). *Türk Kültürü* 49 (November 1966): 79-89.

———. "Türkler ve Rum Orthodox Kiliseleri" (Turks and the Greek Orthodox Churches). *Türk Kültürü* 44 (June 1965): 698-703.

———. "Ziya Gökalp ve Kibris Türkleri" (Ziya Gökalp and the Cypriot Turks). *Türk Kültürü* 60 (October 1967): 897-902.

Özsu, Fatih M. "Kibris! O Yeşil Ada" (Cyprus! Oh Green Island) *Türk Kültürü* 123 (January 1973): 148-149.

Papadopoullos, Theodore. "Prosfate Exislamisme Agrotikou Plethysmou en Kypro" (Recent Islamization of the Rural Population in Cyprus). *Kypriakai Spoudai* 29 (1965): 27-48.

Pipes, Daniel. "Moscow's Next Worry: Ethnic Turks." *New York Times*, 13 February 1990.

Plümer, Aytuğ. "Unjust and Illegal Economic Warfare: The Case of Northern Cyprus." *Turkish Review Quarterly Digest* 22 (Winter 1990): 61-66.

Pollis, Adamantia. "Intergroup Conflict and British Colonial Policy." *Comparative Politics* 5 (July 1973): 575-599.

"Population: Getting More Crowded but Becoming Younger." In *Turkey in the 2000s*, 21-23. Istanbul: Nezi Demirkent, 1987.

Psomiades, Harry J. "The Cyprus Dispute." *Current History* (May 1965): 269–276, 305–306.

Reed, Howard. "Revival of Islam in Secular Turkey." *Middle East Journal* 8 (Summer 1954): 267–282.

Rustow, Dankward A. "The Army and the Founding of the Turkish Republic." *World Politics* 11, no. 4 (1959): 513–552.

Sherwood, Robert. "Turkish Islam on its Home Ground." *The Middle East* (January 1987): 26–29.

Siber, Şinasi. "Kibris Meselesi ve Rum Ortodoks Kilisesi" (The Cyprus Question and the Greek Orthodox Church). *Orkun* 1 (October 1962): 34–35.

Sondern, Frederick, Jr. "Istanbul's Night of Terror: An Eyewitness Account of One of the Most Destructive Riots of Our Times." *Reader's Digest* (May 1956): 185–192.

Tachau, Frank. "The Face of Turkish Nationalism as Reflected in the Cyprus Dispute." *Middle East Journal* 13 (Summer 1959): 262–272.

———. "The Search for National Identity among the Turks." *Die Welt des Islam* 8, no. 3 (1963): 165–176.

Tashan, Seyfi. "Contemporary Turkish Politics in the Middle East: Prospects and Constraints." *Middle East Review* (Spring 1985): 12–20.

Tevetoğlu Fethi. "Communism at Work in National Education." *Cultura Turcica* 2, no. 2 (1965): 141–152.

Thomas, Lewis. "Turkish Islam." *Muslim World* 44 (July/October 1954): 181–185.

Toprak, Binnaz. "The Religious Right." In *Turkey in Transition,* edited by Irvin Cemil Schick and Ertuğrul Ahmed Tonak, 218–235. Oxford: Oxford University Press, 1987.

Toroslu, M. "Bati Trakya Türkünün Çilesi" (The Suffering of the Turks of Western Thrace). *Türk Kültürü* 33 (July 1965): 565–572.

Türk Kültürunü Araştirma Enstitüsü. "Kibris Hâdiseleri Karşisinda" (In View of the Events in Cyprus). *Türk Kültürü* 16 (February 1964): 1.

"Turkish Federated State of *Kibris*: 8th Anniversary of Peace Operation." *The Muslim World League Journal* 4, Mecca, Saudi Arabia (February 1983): 61–63.

Ünal, Tahsin. "Bati Trakya Türkleri" (The Turks of Western Thrace). *Türk Kültürü* 76 (February 1969): 279–287.

"Unwanted Minority 'Dumped' in Cyprus." *The Guardian,* London, 13 October 1975.

Yalman, Ahmed Emin. "Letter to the Editor." *The Times,* London, 1

September 1955.

———. "The Struggle for Multiparty Government in Turkey." *Middle East Journal* 1 (January 1947): 46-58.

Yasin Özker. "Kibris Şehitlerine Ağit" (For the Martyrs of Cyprus). *Türk Kültürü* 16 (February 1964): 5-6.

———. "Kibris'tan Atatürk'e" (From Cyprus to Atatürk). *Türk Kültürü* 16 (February 1964): 10-11.

OFFICIAL DOCUMENTS

Great Britain. Foreign Office. "Conversation between Secretary of State and the Turkish Minister for Foreign Affairs on August 27, 1955." RG 1081/894. Confidential. 31 August 1955.

Republic of Cyprus. Government of Cyprus Public Information Office. *Colonization of Occupied Cyprus.* Nicosia, December 1979.

Turkey. Ministry of Foreign Affairs. Department of International Organizations. *Foreign Policy of Turkey at the United Nations,* vol. 3, *Cyprus Question,* edited and compiled by Ambassador Yüksel Söylemez. Ankara, 1983.

Turkey. Ministry of Foreign Affairs. *Turkey and Cyprus: A Survey of the Cyprus Question with Official Statements of the Turkish Viewpoint.* London: Embassy of Turkey, 1956.

———. "Request for Indictment Presented to Martial Law Tribunal No. 2." Document No. 1150-955/499. Istanbul, 9 February 1956. (Text of indictment included in a report by the U.S. Consul General in Istanbul: "American Consul General in Istanbul to Department of State." Telegram No. 563. Despatch No. 306. 20 February 1956.)

"Turkish Republic of Northern Cyprus." TRNC "Prime Ministry." "State" Planning Organization. Statistics and Research Department. *TRNC Statistical Yearbook, 1987.* Nicosia, December 1988.

United Nations. "Report of the UN Secretary-General on the UNFICYP." S/5764, Paragraph 113. New York, 16 June 1964.

———. "Report of the UN Secretary-General on the Operations of the UNFICYP." 12 December 1964. 19 UN SCOR Supplement. New York, October-December 1964.

———. "Report of the UN Secretary-General on the UNFICYP." S/6426, Paragraph 106. New York, 10 June 1965.

———. "Report of the UN Secretary-General on the United Nations Operations in Cyprus." S/21340. New York, 31 May 1990.

U.S. Congress. House. Committee on Foreign Affairs. Hearing before the Subcommittee on Europe and the Middle East. *Status of Negotiations on the Cyprus Dispute and Recent Developments in Cyprus.* 98th Cong., 1st sess., 2 November 1983. Washington, D.C.: U.S. Government Printing Office, 1983.

———. House. Committee on Foreign Affairs. Subcommittee on Europe and the Middle East. *U.S. Interests in the Eastern Mediterranean: Turkey, Greece, and Cyprus.* 98th Cong., 1st sess., 13 June 1983. Report prepared by Library of Congress, Congressional Research Service, Foreign Affairs and National Defense Division. Washington, D.C.: U.S. Government Printing Office, 1983.

———. Senate. A Staff Report to the Committee on Foreign Relations: *New Opportunities for U.S. Policy in the Eastern Mediterranean.* Washington, D.C.: Government Printing Office, April 1989.

U.S. Department of State. "American Consul General in Istanbul to Secretary of State." Control No. 2678. 6 September 1955.

———. "American Embassy in Ankara to Secretary of State." Despatch No. 344. Secret. 7 September 1955.

———. "American Consul General in Istanbul to Department of State." Despatch No. 159. 9 September 1955.

———. "American Consul General in Istanbul to Department of State. Subject: The Riots of September 6–7 in Istanbul." Despatch No. 116. 14 September 1955.

———. "American Consul General in Istanbul to Department of State." Despatch No. 138. Confidential. 29 September 1955.

———. "American Consulate in Izmir to Department of State. Subject: Aftermath of the Izmir Disturbances on September 6." Despatch No. 29. Confidential. 4 October 1955.

———. "American Embassy in Ankara to Department of State. Subject: Transmitting Copies of Embassy's Classified Briefing Paper on Turkey/Addendum: Anti-Greek Riots in Istanbul and Izmir." Despatch No. 153. Secret. 18 October 1955

———."American Embassy in Ankara to Department of State. Subject: The Istanbul–Izmir Disturbances of September 6, 1955." Despatch No. 228. Confidential. 1 December 1955.

———."American Consul General in Istanbul to Department of State." Telegram No. 563. Despatch No. 306. 20 February 1956.

———."American Consul General in Istanbul to Secretary of State." Despatch No. 633. 25 January 1957.

———."American Consul General in Istanbul to Department of State. Subject: Political Developments in Istanbul, May 1957." Despatch No. 384. 13 June 1957.

———. Bureau of Intelligence and Research. *Analysis of the Cyprus Agreements.* Intelligence Report 8047. (Reprinted in *Journal of the Hellenic Diaspora* 11, no. 4 (Winter 1984): 5-31.)

NEWSPAPERS AND PERIODICALS

TURKEY
Aydinlik (Istanbul)
Cumhuriyet (Istanbul)
Günaydin (Istanbul)
Güneş (Istanbul)
Hürriyet (Istanbul)
Milliyet (Istanbul)
Newspot (Ankara)
Sabah (Istanbul)
Tercüman (Istanbul)
Ulus (Ankara)
Vatan (Istanbul)
Yeni Sabah (Istanbul)
Zafer (Ankara)

TURKISH-OCCUPIED CYPRUS
Birlik
Halkin Sesi
Kibris
Kibris Postasi
Ortam
Soz
Yenidüzen

ENGLAND
Daily Mail
Daily Telegraph
Economist
Financial Times
Guardian
Observer
Sunday Times
The Times

FRANCE
International Herald Tribune (Paris)

UNITED STATES
Baltimore Sun (Baltimore)
Christian Science Monitor (Boston)
Newsweek (New York)
New York Times (New York)
New York Times Magazine (New York)
Reader's Digest (New York)
Wall Street Journal (New York)
Washington Post (Washington, D.C.)
Washington Times (Washington, D.C.)

MAPS

Kibris (Cyprus). In *Türk Kültürü* 94 (August 1970).

"Turkish Federated State of Cyprus." "Ministry of Tourism and Information." *Tourist Map of the "Turkish Federated State of Cyprus."* Nicosia, 1976.

Index

Adana, 32, 34, 36, 38, 84, 105, 194
Aegean islands: Pan-Turkish claims over, 78, 87, 156, 195
Aghas (landowners), 36
Agia Trias, 34
Agios Ambrosios, 179 fig. 6
Agios Chariton, 183
Agios Epiktitos, 181
Agios Georgios, 29
Agios Theodoros, 144, 183
Akça, Eftal, 135–136 table 7
AKEL (Communist Party of Cyprus), 55, 80, 103, 129; "class solidarity" with Turkish Cypriots, 79; Turkish perception that EOKA controlled by, 79
Akinci, Mustafa, 170
Akyüz, Yusuf Veli, 35, 45n. 16, 46n. 17
Alasya, Halil Fikret, 75; as prominent Pan-Turkish theoretician, 151–153; and *Türk Kültürü*, 152–153
Alexandretta, port, 64, 144
Alexandretta province. *See* Hatay
Altai Mountains, 60
Amic Valley, 36
Anatolian peasants settling in occupied Cyprus: secrecy surrounding colonization policy, 3–4, 6, 34; origins in Turkey, 32–34; traditional outlook of, 33; Islamic customs of, 33; practice of polygamy among, 33; Turkish government policy of transferring, 34, 39; recruitment of, 34–35; process of transferring, 35; government promises to, 35–36, 39; land given to as inducement for settlement, 35–36, 39; government pressure on, 36; forced relocation of populations in Turkey, 36, 39. *See*

also Settlers from Turkey in occupied Cyprus
Anglo-Turkish alliance: as means of pressuring Greece, 53; as precipitator of conflict between Greek and Turkish Cypriots, 53–54; during EOKA campaign, 53–54, 56–59; closeness of, 58; support of NATO for, 59; inability of Greek side to deal with, 59
Ankara News Agency, 86
Antakya, 86
Antalya, 32, 41, 84, 86, 194
Antalyans in Cyprus, 41
Anti-Greek riots in Turkey (6 September 1955): 72n. 46, 79, 85, 90; number killed and injured in, 95; role of bombing of Atatürk's birthplace in Thessaloniki, 110, 112; role of Turkish press in inciting, 111; role of *Kibris Türktür* in organizing, 111–118; role of Menderes government in, 97, 112; role of students in, 112; role of labor unions in, 114; role of army units in, 115; role of religious fanaticism in, 116; Armenian and Jewish property attacked during, 117; *lumpenproletariat* and socio-economic discontent in, 117; advanced planning of, 114, 118; effects on Greek minority, 95–96, 118; passive reaction of Greek government to, 96–97, 119, 158; impact on Cyprus issue, 97, 158; reaction of U.S. to, 118–119; trial and acquittal of *Kibris Türktür* leaders, 119–120; U.S. diplomatic reports on, 109, 114–115, 117–118
Anti-Greek sentiment in Turkey,